D1346552

WITHDRAWN

LIVERPOOL JMU LIBRARY

3 1111 01391 4492

Postfeminist Gothic

Postfeminist Gothic

Critical Interventions in Contemporary Culture

Edited by

Benjamin A. Brabon

and

Stéphanie Genz

Selection, editorial matter and introduction © Benjamin A. Brabon and
Stéphanie Genz 2007; Chapters © contributors 2007

All rights reserved. No reproduction, copy or transmission of this
publication may be made without written permission.

No paragraph of this publication may be reproduced, copied or transmitted
save with written permission or in accordance with the provisions of the
Copyright, Designs and Patents Act 1988, or under the terms of any licence
permitting limited copying issued by the Copyright Licensing Agency, 90
Tottenham Court Road, London W1T 4LP.

Any person who does any unauthorized act in relation to this publication
may be liable to criminal prosecution and civil claims for damages.

The authors have asserted their rights to be identified
as the authors of this work in accordance with the Copyright,
Designs and Patents Act 1988.

First published in 2007 by
PALGRAVE MACMILLAN
Houndmills, Basingstoke, Hampshire RG21 6XS and
175 Fifth Avenue, New York, N.Y. 10010
Companies and representatives throughout the world.

PALGRAVE MACMILLAN is the global academic imprint of the Palgrave
Macmillan division of St. Martin's Press, LLC and of Palgrave Macmillan Ltd.
Macmillan® is a registered trademark in the United States, United Kingdom
and other countries. Palgrave is a registered trademark in the European
Union and other countries.

ISBN-13: 978–0–230–00542–6 hardback
ISBN-10: 0–230–00542–X hardback

This book is printed on paper suitable for recycling and made from fully
managed and sustained forest sources.

A catalogue record for this book is available from the British Library.

A catalog record for this book is available from the Library of Congress.

10 9 8 7 6 5 4 3 2
16 15 14 13 12 11 10 09 08 07

Printed and bound in Great Britain by
Antony Rowe Ltd, Chippenham and Eastbourne

Contents

Acknowledgement

Postfeminist Gothic: Critical Interventions in Contemporary Culture developed out of our work on a special issue of the Manchester University Press journal *Gothic Studies* on "Postfeminist Gothic." We would like to thank William Hughes for his advice on both projects.

Notes on Contributors

Lucie Armitt is Professor in English at the University of Salford. Her principal publications include *Fantasy Fiction* (2005), *Contemporary Women's Fiction and the Fantastic* (2000), *Readers' Guide to George Eliot* (2000), *Theorising the Fantastic* (1996) and *Where No Man Has Gone Before: Women and Science Fiction* (1991). She is currently working on a book on twentieth-century Gothic for the University of Wales Press.

Fred Botting is Director of the Institute for Cultural Research, Lancaster University, where he teaches Media, Cultural and Film Studies. He has written widely on the Gothic and cultural theory and has co-authored and edited *The Tarantinian Ethics* (2001), *Bataille* (2001) and *The Bataille Reader* (1997).

Benjamin A. Brabon lectures on the Culture, Media and Society Programme at Napier University, Edinburgh. His primary area of research is Gothic fiction from the late eighteenth and nineteenth centuries. In addition to authoring a number of articles on the Gothic, he has co-edited a special issue of *Gothic Studies* on "Postfeminist Gothic" and he is currently working on two books entitled *Gothic Criticism: A Reader* and *Darkness and Distance: Gothic Cartography and the Mapping of Great Britain*.

Linda Dryden is Reader in Literature and Culture at Napier University, Edinburgh. She is the author of *Joseph Conrad and the Imperial Romance* (2000) and *The Modern Gothic and Literary Doubles* (2003). Dr Dryden has written numerous articles on Conrad and includes among her research and publishing interests Stevenson, Wells, and popular culture. She is on the committee of the Joseph Conrad Society (UK) and is co-editor of the *Journal of Stevenson Studies*. Dr Dryden has recently completed the manuscript for *Stevenson and Conrad: Writers of Land and Sea*, co-edited with Stephen Arata and Eric Massie.

Stéphanie Genz is Lecturer in Literature and Culture at Napier University, Edinburgh. She received her Ph.D. from the University of Stirling, Scotland. Her research interests include gender theory and contemporary British and American literature and film. She is the co-editor of a special issue of *Gothic Studies* on "Postfeminist Gothic" and the author of a number of articles on postfeminism in *Feminist Theory* and *The Journal of*

Popular Culture. She is currently working on a book-length study on postfeminism, *Postfeminism: Texts, Contexts, Theories*.

Judith Halberstam is Professor of English at the University of Southern California. Her research interests include critical theory, film and popular culture, queer theory and nineteenth-century British literature. She is the author of *Skin Shows: Gothic Horror and the Technology of Monsters* (1995), *Female Masculinity* (1998) and *The Transgender Moment: Gender Flexibility and the Postmodern Condition* (2004).

Donna Heiland is the author of *Gothic and Gender: An Introduction* (2004). She has also published essays on a variety of topics, grounding her scholarship in the study of eighteenth-century British literature and over time becoming particularly interested in how eighteenth-century texts and concerns inform contemporary writing. Formerly Associate Professor of English at Vassar College, she is now Vice President of the Teagle Foundation.

Diane Long Hoeveler is Professor of English and Coordinator of Women's Studies at Marquette University, Milwaukee, Wisconsin. She is the author of *Romantic Androgyny: The Women Within* (1990) and *Gothic Feminism* (1998); co-author of *Charlotte Brontë* (1997); and co-editor of the MLA's *Approaches to Teaching Jane Eyre* (1993) and *Approaches to Teaching Gothic Fiction* (2003). In addition, she has co-edited *Comparative Romanticisms* (1998), *Women of Color* (2001), *The Historical Dictionary of Feminism* (1996, 2004), *Romanticism: Comparative Discourses* (2006), and *Interrogating Orientalism* (2006). Her new book is *Genre Riffs: Literary Adaptations in a Hyperbolic Key*.

Claire Knowles received her Ph.D. from the University of Melbourne, where she taught Gothic fictions for many years. Her Ph.D. examined female poetic tradition in the late eighteenth and early nineteenth centuries, and she has an article on the little-known nineteenth-century poet Susan Evance appearing in the *Keats–Shelley Journal* in 2006. She is currently an Associate Lecturer in the School of English, Journalism and European Languages at the University of Tasmania.

Rhonda V. Wilcox, Ph.D., is Professor of English at Gordon College in Barnesville, Georgia. She is the editor of *Studies in Popular Culture* and a founding editor of *Critical Studies in Television*. She is the author of *Why Buffy Matters: The Art of Buffy the Vampire Slayer* (2005), the co-editor of *Fighting the Forces: What's at Stake in Buffy the Vampire Slayer* (2002), the co-editor of *Slayage: The Online International Journal of Buffy Studies* (a peer-reviewed quarterly now in its sixth year), and the author of many articles and book chapters on good television.

Anne Williams is Professor of English at the University of Georgia. She has published *Prophetic Strain: The Greater Lyric in the Eighteenth Century* and *Art of Darkness: A Poetics of Gothic*, both with the University of Chicago Press. She has edited *Three Vampire Tales* for Houghton Mifflin's New Riverside Series and is co-editing *Shakespearean Gothic* with Christy Desmet, forthcoming from the University of Wales Press. She has held fellowships from the NEH, the ACLS, the Rockefeller Foundation and the National Humanities Center, and is completing a book-length manuscript, *"Monstrous Pleasures": Horace Walpole's Gothic Operas*.

Gina Wisker is Head of the Centre for Learning and Teaching and teaches English at the University of Brighton. Gina's research interests include postcolonial women's writing and popular genres, particularly Gothic and horror. Her publications include *Postcolonial and African American Women's Writing* (2000), beginners guides to Angela Carter, Virginia Wolf, Toni Morrison and Sylvia Plath (2000–3), *Horror Fiction* (2005), *The Postgraduate Research Handbook* (2001), *The Good Supervisor* (2005) and numerous essays on Gothic and horror in *Gothic Studies*, *Femspec* and *Diagesis*, among others. Gina edits the new horror e-journal *Dissections*.

Introduction:
Postfeminist Gothic

Benjamin A. Brabon and Stéphanie Genz

This collection of essays addresses and examines the intersection of two much-debated and controversial concepts: postfeminism and Gothic. The resulting category of "postfeminist Gothic"[1] demarcates a new space for critical enquiry that re-invigorates previous debates on the Gothic, in particular the notion of the Female Gothic and its relation to second-wave feminism, as well as shedding light on the contemporary postfeminist conundrum. That this will not be a straightforward companionship or symbiosis is made explicit by the evasiveness and multiplicity of meaning exhibited by both terms: the Gothic has always resisted a monological definition and exceeded the laws of genre and categorical thinking, being as Fred Botting notes "an inscription neither of darkness nor of light, a delineation neither of reason and morality nor of superstition and corruption, neither good nor evil, but both at the same time" (9), and prefixing it with the equally polysemic "postfeminist" seems to complicate matters even further. Rather than putting forward a definite and singular signification of Gothic, postfeminism and by extension postfeminist Gothic, the following essays uncover and raise a new set of questions involved in this critical positioning: What does it mean to "post" feminism? How does the adjective "postfeminist" modify Gothic (and its various associations and subheadings) and what does the notion of "postfeminist Gothic" imply? As the variety of essays and topics in this collection attest, the answers to these questions are multiple and diverse, ranging from wholehearted dismissals and rejections of the possibility of "postfeminist Gothic" to scepticism and an optimistic embracing of the category. This collection is premised upon an interrogation and exploration of these terms, providing a site of exchange and debate, dialogue and conflict. It is not asking so much what postfeminist Gothic *is*; rather, it is asking about the future of Gothic and its connections with (post)feminism.

1

Post-ing feminism

The postfeminist phenomenon has confounded and split contemporary critics with its contradictory significations, definitional ambiguity and pluralistic outlook. Commentators have claimed the term for various and even oppositional understandings and appropriations, ranging from backlash to Girl Power to poststructuralist feminism.[2] The point of contention that separates these different interpretations of postfeminism arises in part from the semantic confusion around the prefix and an argument as to how a "post-ing" of feminism can be read and explained. As Misha Kavka observes, the question that has haunted – or enlivened, depending on your point of view – the debate on and use of "postfeminism" can be summarized as "how can we make sense of the 'post' in 'postfeminism' " (31). Although the very structure of the term "postfeminism" seems to invoke a narrative of progression insisting on a time "after" feminism, the directionality and meaning of the prefix are far from settled and stable. The "post" prefix can be employed to point to a complete rupture, for as Amelia Jones declares, "what is post but the signification of a kind of termination – a temporal designation of whatever it prefaces as ended, done with, obsolete" (8). Diametrically opposed is the idea that the prefix denotes a genealogy that entails revision or strong family resemblance. In this case, the "post" signifies reliance and continuity, an approach that has been favoured by advocates of another "post" derivative, postmodernism. More problematically, "post" can also occupy an uneasy middle ground, signalling a contradictory dependence on and independence from the term that follows it. This is the viewpoint taken by Linda Hutcheon, who detects a paradox at the heart of the "post" whereby "it marks neither a simple and radical break from [the term that follows] nor a straightforward continuity with it; it is both and neither" (17).[3]

Adding to this interpretive struggle is the fact that the root of postfeminism, feminism itself, is also characterized by polyphony and multiplicity that undermine the possibility of a universally agreed agenda and definition. Indeed, as Geraldine Harris emphasizes, feminism has never had "a single, clearly defined, common ideology" or been constituted around "a political party or a central organization or leaders or an agreed policy or manifesto, or even been based upon an agreed principle of collective action" (9). Instead, feminism can at best be said to have working definitions that are always relative to particular contexts, specific issues and personal practices. From this perspective, the attempt to establish and settle *the* meaning of postfeminism looks more and more futile and even misguided as each articulation of the term is by itself a definitional act that (re)constructs the meaning of feminism and its own relation to it. There is no *original* or *authentic* postfeminism that holds the key to its definition. Nor is there a secure and unified origin from which this genuine postfeminism could be fashioned. Rather than pre-empting any interpretation of postfeminism, we adopt an understanding of it as a network of possible relationships that allows for a variety of permutations and readings, from antifeminist retro-sexism to anti-essentialist poststructuralist feminism. Our examination is undoubtedly informed by a postmodern awareness of the relativization of the metanarratives of Western history and enlightened modernity, Lyotard's loss of *grand narratives*. As is evidenced by the breadth and diversity of the essays in this collection, postfeminism is not a fixed conceptual category but an open and changeable problematic that signifies in conflicting ways. Our underlying aim in selecting the essays and putting together this collection has not been to secure the meaning of postfeminism, to establish it, if you like, as a locus of truth, but rather to provide a space for debate where postfeminism remains open to interrogation.

In order to unravel this definitional plurality, the interconnections of "post" and "feminism," prefix and root, have to be explored. Jane Kalbfleisch's discussion of the feminism–postfeminism coupling is particularly useful in this respect as she analyses a number of rhetorical positions that underlie different articulations of postfeminism. Kalbfleisch describes how a "rhetoric of opposition" has effected a polarization of feminism and postfeminism whereby division is given presence through the assumption that feminism and postfeminism are fully distinguishable and distinct. In this sense, "postfeminist" denotes a non-feminist stance and can be read as a term of negation that tries to move beyond the era of feminism and its theoretical and cultural practices. This rupture can be interpreted positively as liberation from old and constraining conditions and as an affirmation of new developments, or it can be read as a deplorable regression and a loss of traditional values and certainties. The rhetoric of opposition thus takes the form of both anti- and pro-postfeminism, either rejecting the term as an opportunistic move on the part of patriarchy or embracing it and thereby superseding earlier feminist movements.

On the pro-postfeminist side of the debate, one finds a generation of young women who appear to speak from somewhere outside and above feminism. In this instance, the term "postfeminism" is used to suggest that the project of feminism has ended, either because it has been completed or because it has failed and is no longer valid. The most prominent advocates of this standpoint, Naomi Wolf, Katie Roiphe, Natasha Walter and Rene Denfeld, support an individualistic and liberal agenda that relies on a mantra of choice and looks upon feminism as a "birthright" that no longer needs to be enforced politically (Denfeld 2).[4] Contrastingly, the anti-postfeminist proponents preserve a myth of feminist linear progress by locating postfeminism with a sexist patriarchy and media as the latest version of "the same old thing." The media Trojan horse is seen to have co-opted and appropriated the idea of female equality while harbouring antifeminist weaponry and gutting the underlying principles of the feminist movement. This negative reading of postfeminism inserts a hyphen between "post" and "feminism," implying that feminism has been sabotaged by its new, trendy prefix to the extent that, as Tania Modleski notes, "texts … in proclaiming … the advent of postfeminism, are actually engaged in negating the critiques and undermining the goals of feminism, in effect, delivering us back into a prefeminist world" (3).[5]

Rather than situating feminism and postfeminism antithetically, the second rhetorical position that Kalbfleisch identifies, "the rhetoric of inclusion," relies on a polarization of a different kind to eradicate the overlap between feminism and postfeminism. In this case, postfeminism is pitted against some "Other" (for example, postmodernism and poststructuralism) in a move that allows for the presumed commonalities among feminists and postfeminists while effectively erasing their potential differences (258).[6] The critical tension within the (post)feminism coupling is defused in this way as the two terms are conflated into one and incorporated into another discursive scheme. Academic circles in particular have adopted this theoretical approach, discussing postfeminism as "a pluralistic epistemology dedicated to disrupting universalising patterns of thought" (Gamble 50). The absorption of postfeminism into what could broadly be conceived as a project of postmodernist cultural critique runs the risk of repressing its importance in other domains, specifically its place in the public debate on feminism and the modern woman. In our understanding, postfeminism exists both as a descriptive popular category and as an academic theoretical tendency and, even within these situated contexts, it does not necessarily aim for coherence.[7]

Instead of containing postfeminism within a series of well-defined boxes (academia and media, Girl Power and backlash, popular feminism and poststructuralist anti-essentialism), we maintain that it is more productive and critically challenging to look upon it as a resolutely dialogic and paradoxical stance, literally a point of interrogation. Postfeminism highlights an engagement with and "post-ing" of feminism, but what this prefixing accomplishes, how it defines feminism and what its outcomes are remain issues of frequently impassioned discussions. Patricia Mann offers a useful description by identifying postfeminism as a "frontier discourse" that "bring[s] us to the edge of what we know, and encourages us to go beyond" (208). This collection provides a survey of the debates surrounding postfeminism and resists the critical shortcut to a unitary definition that fixes postfeminism's directionality as either feminist or non-feminist, academic or popular, subversive or contained, neo-conservative or radically revolutionary. Adopting Kalbfleisch's terminology, we have sought to read postfeminism through the lens of a "rhetoric of anxiety" that foregrounds "conflict, contradiction and ambiguity" and allows "our differences to function as 'forces of change' " (259).

Gothic/feminism

At the risk of stating the obvious, it is important to point out that an examination of a new critical category termed "postfeminist Gothic" cannot avoid addressing the relationships between and intersections of Gothic and feminism. To narrow down this field further, what is particularly relevant in the context of a discussion of postfeminist Gothic is the link between second-wave feminism, which commonly refers to the emergence of the women's liberation movement in the late 1960s, and the notion of the Female Gothic first coined by Ellen Moers in her influential study of women's literature *Literary Women* (1976). Moers's brief definition of the term has often been noted for its deceptive simplicity; it is "easily defined" as "the work that women writers have done in the literary mode that, since the eighteenth century, we have called the Gothic" (90). Building her case partly around a reading of *Frankenstein* as a "birth myth" that reveals "the motif of revulsion against newborn life, and the drama of guilt, dread, and flight surrounding birth and its consequences" (93), Moers identifies the Female Gothic as the mode par excellence that female writers have employed to give voice to women's deep-rooted fears about their own powerlessness and imprisonment within patriarchy. Following Moers's lead, critics have drawn on the Female Gothic to describe a familiar set of narratives that revolve around an innocent and blameless heroine threatened by a powerful male figure and confined to a labyrinthine interior space.[8] Most famously exemplified by Ann Radcliffe's romances, the Female Gothic plot is traditionally resolved by explaining and rationalizing supernatural elements and affirming a happy ending that reintegrates the female protagonist into a wider community through marriage, symbolizing her "wedding to culture" (Williams 103).[9]

Although these traits of the Female Gothic remain fairly constant, there has been much debate on how they should be interpreted and whether they should be understood as transgressive or conservative. Ellen Moers's original formulation of the Female Gothic has also come under attack for its blind spots regarding race and sexual orientation and its essentializing tendencies to equate the writer's biological sex with the text's gendered nature.[10] In fact, Moers's conception of the category is very much a product of its time, emerging from the rise of feminist consciousness and feminist literary criticism in the late 1960s and 1970s. Moers herself acknowledges the importance of this historical context, noting in the preface to *Literary Women* that "the dramatically unfolding, living literary history" of "the new wave of feminism, called women's liberation" taught her to concentrate on "the history of women to understand the history of literature" while also pulling her "out of the stacks" and making the writing of the book "much more of an open-air activity" (xiii). Other critics have confirmed this link between feminist history and the Female Gothic, explaining that the latter resulted from "the change in consciousness that came out of the women's liberation movement of the late 1960s" and as such can be understood as "an expression of the 'second wave' of American feminist literary criticism, which focused on uncovering the lost tradition of women's literature" (Showalter 127; Fitzgerald 9). Reflecting the excitement and urgency of the early days of the women's liberation movement, the initial responses to the Female Gothic tended to emphasize its subversive elements and interpret it as a protest against patriarchal society and a confrontation with mothering/femininity.[11]

The problems that this connection with the second wave engendered came to the fore in the 1990s when, partly as a result of the introduction of poststructuralist theories into feminist analyses, the Female Gothic came to be seen as a critical category that was "unsatisfyingly simple" in its assumptions about "the intrinsic femaleness of Gothic fiction" and its acceptance of "gender as the bedrock of explanation" (Williams 11; Clery 203; Miles 134).[12] As Robert Miles suggests in his introduction to the 1994 special issue of *Women's Writing*, the Female Gothic has "hardened into a literary category" that has led early feminist criticism into an "impasse" (131, 132). It appears that the Female Gothic has become trapped in its own Gothic history, with voices growing louder and asking whether the category has "anything left to offer" (Fitzgerald 8). This scepticism has been extended to second-wave feminist criticism and its tendency to focus on and reproduce women's subordinate social position and victim status. Diane Long Hoeveler makes this point in her aptly entitled

Gothic Feminism (1998), arguing that feminist criticism has encouraged a celebration of passivity by representing women as victims who, paradoxically, use their victimization as a means of gaining empowerment. "Discussions of the female gothic, like analyses of 'feminism,' " she writes, "have, unfortunately, uncritically participated in the very fantasies that the genres have created for their unwary readers" (3). Hoeveler makes a direct link between the Female Gothic and the contemporary antifeminist stance of "victim feminism," explaining that both rely on an ideology of "female power through pretended and staged weakness," the so-called Gothic feminism (7).[13] In this sense, the Female Gothic is complicit in the development of "victim feminism" and what Hoeveler terms "professional femininity," whereby women adopt a masquerade of docility and "wise passiveness" to achieve their aims and triumph over "a male-created system of oppression and corruption, the 'patriarchy' " (3, 7, 9).

This firmly establishes a nexus between the Female Gothic, second-wave feminism and theories of female victimization as well as a view of a corrupt and ubiquitous patriarchy that seeks to dominate and suppress women. However, as Judith Butler reminds us, it is important to resist such universalizing standpoints as in the effort to "identify the enemy as singular in form," we are applying "a reverse-discourse that uncritically mimics the strategy of the oppressor instead of offering a different set of terms" (13). Although we do not wish to deny Ellen Moers's rightful place in the history of Gothic and feminist criticism and we also acknowledge, as Andrew Smith and Diana Wallace note in their introduction to a special issue of *Gothic Studies* (2004), that "the term 'Female Gothic' is still a flexible and recognisable term" (6), we are also convinced that Gothic and feminist categories now demand a self-criticism with respect to their own totalizing gestures and assumptions. We need to re-examine the relationship between Gothic and feminism in a way that does not take "the shortcut to a categorical or fictive universality of the structure of domination" or an essentializing positioning of women as innocent victims (Butler 4). A glance at the variety of essays and topics in this collection gives credibility to the notion that "we are no longer in a second wave of feminism" (Gillis and Munford 2) and, by extension, that we might also have crossed a psychological barrier and reached a new critical space beyond the Female Gothic (and its ghosts of essentialism and universalism). We advance the notion of "postfeminist Gothic" to mark this point in Gothic and feminist criticism that asks us to remain self-critical and alert about the complex issues surrounding the processes of power in contemporary culture.

We agree with Helene Meyers that "the Gothic ... becomes a site to negotiate between the scripts of 'male vice and female virtue' " (often used as an apt description of the literary Gothic) and the "'gender skepticism' associated with much poststructuralist criticism" (xii). Yet, unlike Meyers, we adopt the framework of postfeminism to interpret this moment in Gothic and feminist criticism. In *Femicidal Fears* (2001), Meyers defines postfeminism in terms of a backlash and "the conservative, retrogressive politics of Reagan and Thatcher" (15). In Meyers's account, postfeminism effects a "flight from femaleness" in its denial of the Gothic world and women's victim status therein and, as a result, it threatens to become "anti-Gothic Gothic" (144, 118). Contrastingly, we do not seek so much to uncover the Gothic potential of postfeminism (which undoubtedly is part of the postfeminist spectrum of meaning); rather, we want to explore how Gothic changes when prefixed by the modifier "postfeminist." By entitling our collection *Postfeminist Gothic*, we endeavour to open up both terms to a variety of interpretations and significations, instead of narrowing down their respective paradoxes and ambiguities. As Anne Williams points out in *Art of Darkness* (1995), "most – perhaps all – Gothic conventions express some anxiety about 'meaning' " (67). What the following essays demonstrate is that postfeminism is engaged in a similar struggle and that "postfeminist Gothic" is a contentious new category and critical realm that revitalizes Gothic and feminist criticism and invites new perspectives beyond the theories of the second wave and the Female Gothic.

Postfeminist Gothic

"Gender ... is the law of the Gothic genre," Robert Miles notes in his introduction to *Women's Writing*, but he also maintains that it "is not the key to the Gothic genre (still less the reverse)"; rather, the task is "to unlock these shapes" (134). As the essays in this collection attest, gender and the relationships between the two sexes remain important issues that postfeminist Gothic engages with. Questions of femininity and masculinity are taken up by a number of contributors who debate their relevance and meaning for a postfeminist Gothic world. What the essays accomplish though is not just a description of "the contours" of gender but a probing further and a questioning of those very constructions (Miles 134).

Lucie Armitt sets up the postfeminist Gothic frame in her opening essay on contemporary women's writing. Focusing on three female-authored and woman-centred novels, her analysis revolves around the question of how women's story is articulated within postfeminist Gothic and how the violence and Gothicism that second-wave feminism exposed in women's lives under patriarchy are represented in this context. Armitt revisits Freudian notions of the uncanny, melancholia and narcissism in her reading of haunted families, male psychopaths, circular journeys and narrative culs-de-sac.

The violence inherent in heterosexual relationships is also taken up by Judith Halberstam's essay, which concentrates on Ronnie Yu's 1998 neo-splatter film *Bride of Chucky*. Halberstam discusses the representation of embodiment in horror as a form of gender flexibility and she analyses how the neo-splatter film deploys queer and transgender theories of the body to portray queerness as the antidote to the "horror of heteronormativity." Highlighting the queer potential of social relations, Chucky and his doll bride Tiffany deliver "searing critiques" of domesticity, monogamy and couplehood, only to be engulfed in the end by the violence of the heterosexual matrix. For Halberstam, the underlying question is "whether bodies that splatter produce gender stability or whether they dismantle the very conventions upon which that stability depends."

In the following essay, Rhonda V. Wilcox addresses the complexities of gender construction, narrative structure and character patterns in her analysis of *Witchblade* (2001–2). Wilcox situates the series in a postfeminist Gothic context by discussing the main female protagonist, Sara Pezzini, as a feminist heroine who also provides postfeminist pleasures, in particular in her relationship with the multiple male characters who can be recognized as variations and reconstructions of the Gothic hero–villain. Wilcox underlines the series' narrative experimentation as a source of postfeminist pleasure, and she also draws attention to the complications associated with postfeminism and its conflicting meanings.

Benjamin A. Brabon further investigates the position of the postfeminist Gothic man in his examination of hegemonic masculinity in *Falling Down* (1992) and *Fight Club* (1999). Centring his discussion on the figure of the "spectral phallus," Brabon argues that the previously assumed common sense of "what it means to be a man" has given way to fragmentary and incoherent expressions that attest to a contemporary crisis of masculinity. He argues that the postfeminist man now occupies the position of the traditional Gothic heroine as his masculinity is feminized and no longer signifies phallic and aggressive violence but instead is characterized by anxiety, dissatisfaction and inefficacy.

Stéphanie Genz then turns her attention to postfeminist femininity in her analysis of contemporary tales of transformation that remake the Gothic monster, historically marginalized and positioned as excessive and other, into a highly attractive and feminine Cinderella figure. She explores the paradoxical aspects of female embodiment illustrated by the postfeminist Gothic *femme* who adopts the disciplinary practices of femininity to achieve agency and autonomy. Postfeminist Gothic femininity is engaged in a contradictory process of resignification that simultaneously opens up the construction of feminine meanings and creates a haunted realm of feminine disempowerment. With specific reference to Fay Weldon's *The Life and Loves of a She Devil* (1983), Genz discusses the transformative pattern from old/monstrous outsider to monstrously feminine Cinderella who inhabits an ambiguous borderland between patriarchal object and feminist subject.

Anne Williams examines a similar metamorphosis in her analysis of *The Stepford Wives*, Ira Levin's 1973 novel that was adapted to the screen in 1975 and then remade in 2004 in an expensive Hollywood production. Williams investigates how the 1970s novel and horror film, both particularly Gothic in their emphasis on female bodies that are transformed into house-keeping robots designed to embody a nostalgic, overtly Victorian notion of femininity, have mutated into a camp comedy that rewrites the Gothic conventions of the earlier versions and shifts its focus from patriarchy's constraints to women's own agency. Whereas the *Stepford Wives* novel and first film were firmly rooted in the ideas of second-wave feminism, the 2004 version exhibits a comic optimism that offers insights into the changing faces of Gothic and feminism and the possible meanings of postfeminism.

In her essay on the nexus of the *Candyman* films (based on Clive Barker's 1985 short story *The Forbidden*), Diane Long Hoeveler connects the issues of gender and race in her examination of the figure of the postfeminist female Gothic detective. She analyses the sadism inherent in the representation of black men and white women who, in their pursuit of the meaning and identity of the monstrous black male body, turn the latter into the castrated object of the films' – and their – visual desire. The *Candyman* films (1992, 1995) thus invert the white liberal ideology of Barker's original story and instead highlight the undead history of racism and miscegenation in America, as the white woman seizes the power of the black man and installs herself in the position of both victim and victimizer.

The colonial past is also interrogated by Gina Wisker in her discussion of the postcolonial/postfeminist Gothic of Canadian/Trinidadian/Jamaican writer Nalo Hopkinson. Focusing on Hopkinson's short story "A Habit of Waste," which describes a black woman swapping her body for a white cosmeticized female ideal, Wisker explores how postcolonial/postfeminist Gothic women writers engage in a critique of oppressive versions of history and self and the resulting internalized self-damage and negative self-image.

By rejecting the established roles offered to her by patriarchy and colonialism, the postfeminist/postcolonial Gothic heroine exposes and undercuts disempowering myths of the Other and re-scripts her life and body shape.

Oppression based on race is also the focus of Donna Heiland's essay, which considers the Gothic history of slavery in what is now Canada through reference to George Elliott Clarke's verse drama *Beatrice Chancy* (1999). Recounting the often-discussed life of Beatrice Cenci (most notably told in Percy Shelley's *The Cenci*), Clarke's drama reinforces and criticizes Gothic conventions, in particular through its engagement with the aesthetic of the sublime. Heiland analyses how sublimity and slavery are not represented in abstract terms but are made concrete and grounded in pain. The sublime exposed as pain thus becomes a catalyst for change, pointing a way through the horrors to a changed vision and a future of continued, liberationist struggle.

Claire Knowles's essay addresses another convention of the literary Gothic in her examination of the discourse of sensibility and its relevance for a postfeminist age. Arguing for a "coexistence of temporalities," Knowles uses Gothic fiction to trace the connections between eighteenth-century and twenty-first-century representations of feminine empowerment. She describes how the postmodern/postfeminist television series *Buffy the Vampire Slayer* (1997–2003) enters into a dialogue with earlier Gothic fictions, in particular through its portrayal of Buffy as a modernized version of the Radcliffean heroine of sensibility.

Not sensibility but monstrosity is the subject of Linda Dryden's essay, which analyses the development of the Gothic *femme fatale* in the science fiction context of *Star Trek: First Contact* (1996). Focusing on the figure of the Borg Queen as a power-crazed and sexy cyborg, she argues that the postfeminist female Gothic monster is the reincarnation of an earlier female type in Gothic fiction, the terrible and beautiful *femme fatale* vividly depicted in H. Rider Haggard's *She* (1887). For Dryden, this retrograde attempt to re-appropriate a Gothic paradigm confirms the uncertain position of postfeminism and its prefeminist attitudes to female sexuality.

The final essay in the collection brings together a number of issues and ideas as it engages with the "knot" of Gothic, postmodernity and postfeminism in its analysis of the Gothic heroine's "lines of flight." Drawing on the theoretical insights of Deleuze and Guattari, Fred Botting examines the possibility of an "awomanly" space, a new mode of becoming that brings forth unpredictable and troubling monstrous forms. Centring his discussion on the *Alien* series, Botting traces diverse lines of flight and fright that complicate and compound traditional patterns and gendered assumptions. In this movement, various versions of the "post" are exposed: postmodernity, post-human, postfeminist, post-Gothic.

Postfeminist Gothic engages with these very "postings" and foregrounds the contradictions, ambiguities and multiplicities involved in these critical positionings. We hope that the following essays encourage new lines of interpretation to open up that continue to broaden and challenge the meanings of "postfeminist Gothic."

Notes

1. We also examine the term "postfeminist Gothic" in our introduction to a special issue of *Gothic Studies* 9.1 (2007). This collection is a development of that work.
2. For example, see Susan Faludi's *Backlash: The Undeclared War against Women* (1992), Naomi Wolf's *Fire with Fire: The New Female Power and How It Will Change the 21st Century* (1993) and Ann Brooks's *Postfeminisms: Feminism, Cultural Theory and Cultural Forms* (1997) for more on these different versions of postfeminism.
3. For more on the "programmatic indeterminacy" and "motivational ambiguity" of the prefix "post," see Rotislav Kocourek's "The Prefix Post- in Contemporary English Terminology: Morphology, Meaning, and Productivity of Derivations" (1996).
4. See Naomi Wolf's *Fire with Fire* (1993), Katie Roiphe's *The Morning After: Sex, Fear and Feminism* (1993), Natasha Walter's *The New Feminism* (1998) and Rene Denfeld's *The New Victorians: A Young Woman's Challenge to the Old Feminist Order* (1995) for more on their individual positions.
5. The most influential example of this view of postfeminism through reference to a rhetoric of relapse is that of Susan Faludi, who in *Backlash* (1992) portrays postfeminism as a devastating reaction against the ground gained by second-wave feminism. Simultaneously "sophisticated and banal, deceptively 'progressive' and proudly backward," the postfeminist backlash masks itself as an ironic, pseudo-intellectual critique of feminism that seeks "to retract the handful of small and hard-won victories that the feminist movement did manage to win for women" (12).
6. See, for example, Ann Brooks's *Postfeminisms* (1997), which defines postfeminism as "the intersection of feminism with a number of other anti-foundationalist movements including postmodernism, post-structuralism and post-coloniaism" (1).
7. We argue against the dichotomization of different postfeminist versions that has been upheld in academic and media circles alike. Most critical analyses discuss postfeminism as a bifurcated term that consists of two distinct and competing strands, one defined as mainstream feminism and the other as postmodern feminism. In an attempt to impose a hierarchical structure, reviews of media postfeminism are almost invariably accompanied by an obligatory footnote on progressive academic postfeminism (see, for example, Ann Brooks's introduction in *Postfeminisms* [1997]). We contend that this distinction signals an unwillingness to engage with postfeminism's plurality, while also risking recreating the artificial separation between the academic

ivory tower and popular culture that has hampered critical analysis. For more on this, see Stéphanie Genz's. "Third Way/ve: The Politics of Postfeminism" (2006).

8. As Robert Miles summarizes the plot's broad contours: "a heroine caught between a pastoral haven and a threatening castle, sometimes in flight from a sinister patriarchal figure, sometimes in search of an absent mother, and, often, both together (that is to say, we encounter variations on Ann Radcliffe's *A Sicilian Romance)*" (131).

9. This distinguishes the Female Gothic from the Male Gothic (typified by M. G. Lewis's *The Monk*), which posits the supernatural as a reality and has a tragic plot that sees the male protagonist being punished for his transgression of social taboos. See Anne Williams's *Art of Darkness: A Poetics of Gothic* (1995) for more on the distinction between Male and Female Gothic.

10. For more on these critiques of the Female Gothic, see Lauren Fitzgerald's "Female Gothic and the Institutionalization of Gothic Studies" in the special issue of *Gothic Studies* 6.1 (2004) on the Female Gothic.

11. Also see Claire Kahane's "The Gothic Mirror" (1985) for a reading of the Female Gothic as an engagement with the problems of femininity, represented in terms of the relationship between a daughter and the spectral presence of her mother.

12. Similar objections have been levelled at second-wave feminism by anti-foundationalist critics who highlight the limitations of identity politics and the false unity of master narratives. For more on the debates surrounding the intersections of feminism and postmodernism/poststructuralism, see Nancy Fraser and Linda Nicholson's "Social Criticism without Philosophy: An Encounter between Feminism and Postmodernism" (1990).

13. For more on "victim feminism" see Naomi Wolf's *Fire with Fire* (1993). As Wolf emphasizes, "much feminist discourse is unrelievedly grim; waking up to feminism includes a certain pride in being able to stare unflinchingly at the 'horror, the horror' of it all. Horrifying the world of sexism truly is, but this sometimes monolithic focus on the dire ... leads straight to burnout" (213). Rene Denfeld's *The New Victorians* (1995) offers another account of this "gothic feminism" by discussing feminism as the "New Victorianism" that promotes a "victim mythology" and recreates "the very same morally pure yet helplessly martyred role that women suffered from a century ago" (10). "The woman," she writes, is "revered on the pedestal, charged with keeping society's moral order yet politically powerless – and perpetually martyred" (16–17).

Works cited

Botting, Fred. *Gothic*. London: Routledge, 1996.
Brabon, Benjamin A., and Stéphanie Genz, eds. *Postfeminist Gothic*. Spec. issue of *Gothic Studies* 9.1 (2007).
Brooks, Ann. *Postfeminisms: Feminism, Cultural Theory and Cultural Forms*. London: Routledge, 1997.
Butler, Judith. *Gender Trouble: Feminism and the Subversion of Identity*. London: Routledge, 1990.
Clery, E. J. "Ann Radcliffe and D. A. F. de Sade: Thoughts on Heroinism." *Female Gothic Writing*. Ed. Robert Miles. Spec. issue of *Women's Writing* 1.2 (1994): 203–14.

Denfeld, Rene. *The New Victorians: A Young Woman's Challenge to the Old Feminist Order*. New York: Warner Books, 1995.

Faludi, Susan. *Backlash: The Undeclared War against Women*. London: Vintage, 1992.

Fitzgerald, Lauren. "Female Gothic and the Institutionalization of Gothic Studies." *Female Gothic*. Ed. Andrew Smith and Diana Wallace. Spec. issue of *Gothic Studies* 6.1 (2004): 6–18.

Fraser, Nancy, and Linda J. Nicholson. "Social Criticism without Philosophy: An Encounter between Feminism and Postmodernism." *Feminism/Postmodernism*. Ed. Linda J. Nicholson. London: Routledge, 1990. 19–38.

Gamble, Sarah. "Postfeminism." *The Routledge Companion to Feminism and Postfeminism*. Ed. Sarah Gamble. London: Routledge, 2001. 43–54.

Genz, Stéphanie. "Third Way/ve: The Politics of Postfeminism." *Feminist Theory* 7.3 (2006).

Gillis, Stacy, and Rebecca Munford. "Harvesting Our Strengths: Third Wave Feminism and Women's Studies." *Journal of International Women's Studies* 4.2 (2003): 1–6.

Harris, Geraldine. *Staging Femininities: Performance and Performativity*. Manchester: Manchester UP, 1999.

Hoeveler, Diane Long. *Gothic Feminism: The Professionalization of Gender from Charlotte Smith to the Brontës*. Liverpool: Liverpool UP, 1998.

Hutcheon, Linda. *A Poetics of Postmodernism: History, Theory, Fiction*. London: Routledge, 1988.

Jones, Amelia. " 'Post-Feminism' – A Remasculinization of Culture." *M/E/A/N/I/N/G An Anthology of Artists' Writing, Theory and Criticism* 7 (1990): 7–23.

Kahane, Claire. "The Gothic Mirror." *The (M)other Tongue: Essays in Feminist Psychoanalytic Interpretation*. Ed. Shirley Nelson Garner, Claire Kahane and Madelon Sprengnether. Ithaca, NY: Cornell UP, 1985. 334–51.

Kalbfleisch, Jane. "When Feminism Met Postfeminism: The Rhetoric of a Relationship." *Generations: Academic Feminists in Dialogue*. Ed. D. Looser and A. E. Kaplan. Minneapolis: U of Minnesota P, 1997. 250–66.

Kavka, Misha. "Feminism, Ethics, and History, or What Is the 'Post' in Postfeminism." *Tulsa Studies in Women's Literature* 21.1 (2002): 29–44.

Kocourek, Rotislav. "The Prefix Post- in Contemporary English Terminology: Morphology, Meaning, and Productivity of Derivations." *Terminology: International Journal of Theoretical and Applied Issues in Specialized Communication* 3.1 (1996): 85–110.

Mann, Patricia S. *Micro-Politics: Agency in a Postfeminist Era*. Minneapolis: U of Minnesota P, 1994.

Meyers, Helene. *Femicidal Fears: Narratives of the Female Gothic Experience*. Albany, NY: State U of New York P, 2001.

Miles, Robert. Introduction. *Female Gothic Writing*. Ed. Robert Miles. Spec. issue of *Women's Writing* 1.2 (1994): 131–42.

Modleski, Tania. *Feminism without Women: Culture and Criticism in a "Postfeminist" Age*. London: Routledge, 1991.

Moers, Ellen. *Literary Women*. 1976. London: The Women's Press, 1978.

Roiphe, Katie. *The Morning After: Sex, Fear and Feminism on Campus*. Boston: Little, Brown, 1993.

Showalter, Elaine. *Sisters' Choice: Tradition and Change in American Women's Writing.* Oxford: Clarendon Press, 1991.

Smith, Andrew, and Diana Wallace. "The Female Gothic: Then and Now." *Female Gothic.* Ed. Andrew Smith and Diana Wallace. Spec. issue of *Gothic Studies* 6.1 (2004): 1–7.

Walter, Natasha. *The New Feminism.* London: Virago, 1999.

Williams, Anne. *Art of Darkness: A Poetics of Gothic.* Chicago: U of Chicago P, 1995.

Wolf, Naomi. *Fire with Fire: The New Female Power and How It Will Change the 21st Century.* New York: Random House, 1993.

1

Dark Departures: Contemporary Women's Writing after the Gothic

Lucie Armitt

The Gothic was always a family affair, and the family it courted perpetually in decay. Traditionally, that decay was haematological, either literally, as in vampire narratives, where, according to Nina Auerbach, one finds the "unabashed blood-awareness only animals enjoy" becoming transformed, in the face of the late twentieth-century AIDS epidemic, into "a blight," or metaphorically, in the Gothic's traditional preoccupation with aristocratic (ig)nobility and misdemeanours (96, 175). The key female role, therefore, became that of "new blood," an unsuspecting ingénue quivering with dread *and* excitement, usually propelled into (mis)adventure through the premature death of her mother – not infrequently caused by childbirth, branding the young woman victim and murderer in one.

Though "larger than life," such plots strike a chord of realism in the woman reader, for second-wave feminism told us that Gothicism was inherent in women's lives under patriarchy, especially in relation to literature and the environment. Hence, Nicole Ward Jouve's compulsively gripping study of the Yorkshire Ripper, *"The Street Cleaner"* (1986), situated the police investigation of, and public outcry over, the thirteen murders and seven maimings of women in northern England between 1975 and 1981 within an environment in which "prostitutes were used as unwilling live bait," and women everywhere were haunted by imagined threats built into their own homes and gardens: "my particular fear focused on having to get coal from the shed after sundown" (9, 17). Gillian Rose's study of women's relationship to the built environment, though more optimistic than Ward Jouve's, cautioned us to "be vigilant about the consequences of different kinds of spatiality, and to keep dreaming of a space and a subject which we cannot yet imagine" (354).

In this essay the primary question is to what extent the violence Ward Jouve identified as being "at work in the nooks and crannies of the landscapes" during the second wave still manifests itself in postfeminist Gothic (18). As Sarah Gamble observes, questions about the validity of postfeminism tend to oscillate around precisely such issues of "victimisation, autonomy and responsibility," for its advocates are "critical of any definition of women as victims who are unable to control their own lives" (43–4). However, controlling one's life is only part of the struggle: the three novels on which this essay is based, *After You'd Gone* (2000) by Maggie O'Farrell, *Fingersmith* (2002) by Sarah Waters and *Case Histories* (2004) by Kate Atkinson, certainly share a woman-centred perspective, but that perspective is trained on untimely death. All three are retrospectively narrated (hence "post-" or "late-"ness providing their narrative rationale) and each concerns itself with living with a maternal prehistory. Thus we are articulating women's "story" from within a presiding framework of feminist fore-mothering – one which shapes postfeminism, not least in framing the discourse in relation to which it is "post." And what of the Gothic – is that now playing dead?

Certainly there are clarion calls for the death of the Gothic, not through any lack of love for it – on the contrary, *everything*, apparently, can now be Gothic – but (and in striking parallel to the place of feminism in a postfeminist age) because of its apparent cultural redundancy. As Freud said as early as 1919, "All supposedly educated people have ceased to believe officially that the dead can become visible as spirits" ("The Uncanny" 365). Without superstition, one has only briefly to question what fuels the Gothic before recognizing the horrors that ordinary and extraordinary contemporary life can still provide – within and beyond the context of gender.

Roger Luckhurst, in his own critique of the tendency to brand everything Gothic, focuses especially on what he calls "the notable revival over the past twenty years of a newly Gothicized apprehension of London" (527–8). The connection between London and the Gothic is not new, of course. Charles Dickens's *Oliver Twist* (1838), the Victorian novel with which Waters's *Fingersmith* (set in 1862) most closely engages, introduces London in tones of disillusionment:

> A dirtier or more wretched place [Oliver] had never seen ... the only stock in trade appeared to be heaps of children ... crawling in and out at the [shop] doors, or screaming from the inside ... drunken men and women ... positively wallowing in filth; and from several of the doorways, great ill-looking fellows were cautiously emerging, bound, to all appearance, on no very well-disposed or harmless errands. (57)

Such a view of the Victorian capital melds seamlessly with Waters's contemporary description of architectural landmarks such as St Paul's Cathedral, standing "dark and humped above the tips of broken roofs," or her description of the River Thames, which her character Sue perceives "flows like poison ... is littered with broken matter ... [and] froths like sour milk" (370–1). Neither are such descriptions unfamiliar to us as historical images; they come ready packaged in our mind's eye, conveyed into our living-rooms via classic movies such as Rouben Mamoulian's *Doctor Jekyll and Mr Hyde* (1931). However, to those of us living in the "real" world of the early twenty-first century, that vision of London had been consigned to history, left behind with Jack the Ripper (as opposed to the Yorkshire Ripper, who was never the Capital's problem) and child chimney-sweeps: that is, until 7 July 2005.

I first read O'Farrell's *After You'd Gone* on a train to London on the morning of 7 July, arriving at Kings Cross/St Pancras station shortly after the first tube bombing. Coincidentally, Farrell's novel is about a woman living in the wake of her lover's death in a London bomb-blast: "That day, news of the bombing just seemed to seep through London like an urban form of osmosis. Even before newspapers could rush out stories on the explosion, rumours were spreading from person to person" (282). As fiction met fact, I immediately recalled the role Freud attributes to the omnipotence of thoughts in our experiencing of the uncanny owing, as he puts it, to "the distinction between imagination and reality [being] effaced, as when something that we have hitherto regarded as imaginary appears before us in reality" ("The Uncanny" 367).

After You'd Gone: The narrative (as) cul-de-sac

Freud's reading of the uncanny also has its metropolitan moments. Take, for instance, his confessional recounting of an unwilling perpetual return to a "red light district":

> Nothing but painted women were to be seen at the windows ... and I hastened to leave the narrow street at the next turning. But after having wandered about for a time without inquiring my way, I suddenly found myself back in the same street, where my presence was now beginning to excite attention. I hurried away once more, only to arrive by another *détour* at the same place yet a third time. Now, however, a feeling overcame me which I can only describe as uncanny, and I was glad enough to find myself back at the piazza I had left a short while before, without any further voyages of discovery. ("The Uncanny" 359)

However, accompanying the uncanniness of such returns, culs-de-sac (or "dead ends") can also signal the presiding pattern of melancholia.

As its title suggests, *After You'd Gone* is a novel about chance, journeys and "lateness." The key scene takes place at a railway terminus, with Alice making an impromptu visit to see her sisters, travelling by train from London to Edinburgh. Though we are aware there is something "strange" about the visit, the fact that it happens at the start of the book, coupled with the convolutions of narrative chronology subsequently employed, makes it impossible to realize now what the reader only later learns, namely that Alice has emerged from a pit of grief to take this journey, John having been killed some weeks previously. Both sisters and Alice's niece await her arrival eagerly and solicitously on the platform, treating her like a fragile and brittle ornament. Visiting the ladies' toilet on arrival, Alice has some form of vision as she dries her hands: "she saw something so odd and unexpected and sickening that it was as if she'd glanced in the mirror to discover that her face was not the one she thought she had" (6). Though precisely what she has seen is left unclear at this stage, the immediate result is that she gets straight back on the train, leaving the bewildered and distressed family members on the platform, and returns to London.

On some level we can identify, in this pattern, a clear comparison with the dynamics Freud identifies with the melancholic, namely a "turning away from any activity ... not connected with thoughts of [the loved one]" ("Mourning" 252). Furthermore, as Alice travels back on the train, this sense of "turning away" continues as "She avoid[s] the eye of the reflection whizzing along beside her in another, reversed, tilted ghost carriage that skimmed over the fields as they hurtled towards London" (7). In fact, it is in this form of the mirrored surface that the cul-de-sac manifests itself most absolutely – as image propelled into the middle distance, only to be flung back at the viewer. Only later do we learn that what we took to be a "turning away" is in fact a face-to-face encounter. Standing in the ladies', Alice notices:

> The front of the dryer has a small, square mirror stuck to it ... You allow the depth of your eye's focus to zone in ... for a second, maybe two, then you allow it to relax into the tiny mirror's distance ... you are suddenly convinced you've seen, flitting from one side of the miniscule square to the other, your mother ...
>
> ... Behind you ... is a full-length one-way mirror ... Right next to it, leaning against what they thought was just a full-length mirror, are your mother and a man ...

You could press your fingers against the glass at the point where your mother's temple is resting. Or where his shoulder is leaning. (284–5)

So, the one-way mirror allows access for the onlooker, whilst blocking access for the viewed. This dynamic returns elsewhere, as the distressed Alice peers into her own hallway mirror. Contemplating that "It must have an image of [John] locked away somewhere in its depths," she "allows herself to imagine that he is standing just behind it, his face pressed up close to the surface, watching her passing beneath him, missing him, grieving for him, and no matter how hard he bangs on the glass, he cannot make her hear him" (293). The similarity between this willed proximity and the previously unwanted proximity of the image of her mother and lover on the other side of the mirror is very clear. Alice longs for John to haunt her, but the only phantom in her house is that of her mother. Here, we return to Ward Jouve's words in *"The Street Cleaner"*: "When you are fascinated, you just can't help looking at the very thing you want to avoid ... Even when you close your eyes ... it still materializes within you" (17). Now that Alice's mother's image fills her head, there is no reflective space left for John.

It is intriguing that Alice's sense of entrapment within glass derives from her mother, for in both professional and personal terms Alice's mother, Ann, consciously positions herself within a "glass ceiling." Training as a botanist, sitting in a university lab drenched in sunlight entering through multiple windows, Ann slices open her hand with a scalpel, an act described largely as self-willed choice rather than accident. The man who saves her (a fellow student) in effect removes her need to prove her worth on the professional ladder, offering instead marriage – along with its trappings. So Ann chooses the dead-end path, becoming a shadow-self ghosting the life she should have had, inhabiting the space outside the window to which her own daughter will not pay attention on the train home from Edinburgh.

However, Ann's path is, in turn, revealed to be an inheritance from her own mother, Elspeth, whose parents abandoned her at the age of seven on a beach, choosing "the higher path" of missionary work over parenthood. As Elspeth turns, she finds in their stead "the upright figure of a housemistress for St Cuthbert's School for Girls, who took her by the elbow and led her up the beach and on to a train for Edinburgh and boarding-school. She didn't see them or North Berwick again for seven years" (47). Note, here, that seven (conventionally a lucky number) takes on a double resonance. First, it is also the number of years of bad luck one is reputed to have on shattering a mirror and, second, it results here in seven years' bad luck being doubled (her age plus the number of years she will be parted from her parents). That this is the originary act instilling the cul-de-sac patterning into Alice's maternal bloodline is revealed by the route her grandmother takes: to Edinburgh and by train – a single journey Alice will later repeat (though by return) in being drawn to and then repulsed by the revelation of her mother's double life. This reiteration of the power of contagion in relation to bloodlines returns us to the Gothic and, via doubling, the uncanny. In Atkinson's novel *Case Histories*, which tells a plot of multiple deaths, doubling and reflection once again hold the key to family secrets.

Case Histories: **Death by numbers**

Case Histories details four separate deaths, which take place over twenty-four years and which are gradually revealed to be connected, albeit circuitously. This, then, is another novel about melancholia and haunted families and one that has additional similarities to *"The Street Cleaner."* Like the Yorkshire Ripper, who was "a family man, happily married or so it seemed, with a good job, a mortgage on a nice house in a nice area ... a courteous manner, a soft voice," the pivotal "monster" of Atkinson's text is Victor, a Cambridge don of middling ability who marries a nurse and fathers four daughters (10). Where Victor deviates from the Yorkshire Ripper, however, is that he murders by proxy. Hence, in sexually abusing his first daughter, Sylvia, he violates her mind and body to the extent that she becomes incapable of interacting with her environment and, in a further ironic echo of Peter Sutcliffe, the Yorkshire Ripper, hears voices that lead her to murder her three-year-old sister, Olivia, believing she is doing so in the name of "salvation":

> Sylvia thought that she was going to be the sacrifice, martyred because God had chosen her. But it turned out that it was Olivia ... Olivia was sacred now. Pure and holy ... and safe ... She would never have to ... choke on Daddy's stinky thing in her mouth, never feel his huge hands on her body making her impure and unholy. (407)

Looking down at the little corpse, Sylvia recognizes that only Victor can act as accomplice, because "He would know what to do" (407). Read implicitly, this suggests Victor will have to help or fall prey to blackmail. Read literally, however, her thoughts brand Victor a serial offender, and although we never read of any murders Victor commits at first hand, we do read that when Sylvia "gave up her place at Girton, where she was due to start a maths degree, to enter the convent it seemed as if Victor might actually kill her" – and, of course, we certainly learn he is responsible for his own wife's death (111).

Similar to Elspeth's doubled spell of seven years' bad luck in *After You'd Gone*, in *Case Histories* Victor's profession of mathematician ensures numbers have a central importance here. When Victor marries Rosemary, she is eighteen, precisely half his age, and a virgin. When they return from honeymoon she is in "a state of shock" and perceives Victor to be "already beg[inning] to drain her" (25, 26). Victor refuses to wear condoms, perceiving them as a threat to his masculinity, and it is when he impregnates Rosemary for a fifth time, with a child who will develop alongside an undiscovered tumour (the mirror image of her own mother's death from stomach cancer), that he causes another doubling, this time in death, with both mother and baby dying shortly after the birth. One of the more ironic observations made of Victor, an expert in "probability and risk" (here by his second daughter, Amelia), derives from her erroneous belief that this "man who studied risk for a living had never taken one in his life" (102).

Victor's very name is sufficient to endow him with Gothic monster status and, as in *Frankenstein*, *After You'd Gone*, and indeed Sutcliffe's own story, his monstrosity is the culmination of a family narrative. Victor loses his own mother to an asylum at the age of four, where she dies six years later of TB. Like Sutcliffe, Victor is not "a great physical specimen" and compensates for the fact by physically destroying women (24). Systematically, the family starts to unravel. Sylvia's retreat into the convent replaces her blood sisters with other nuns and, as the ripple effect spreads out across the family, those left behind become haunted by the dark departures of both Sylvia and Olivia, a haunting that appears first as melancholia and then as narcissism: "There was a ghost lived in this house, Amelia thought, but it wasn't Olivia, it was her own self. The Amelia she would have been – should have been if her family hadn't imploded" (119).

It is hard, here, to sympathize too closely with Amelia, a comparatively unsympathetic character who turns away from sex as if in affinity with Sylvia. What the reader dislikes most about her is the self-centredness of her martyrdom. However, Freud reminds us that "people never willingly abandon a libidinal position," inviting a more empathetic reading of the connections between melancholia and narcissism. Where, under narcissism, he argues that the (usually) female "sufferer" withdraws attraction from another object-choice in order to internalize it *as* attraction, the melancholic withdraws attraction in order to internalize it as self-loathing. Equally, self-loathing can become a weapon used against those who love the sufferer: "The woman who loudly pities her husband for being tied to such an incapable wife as herself is really accusing her *husband* of being incapable" ("Mourning" 253, 257; emphasis in original).

Might this kind of inverse logic explain the relationships of another father in Atkinson's novel, Theo? A widower, Theo has two daughters, one dead, one living. Unlike Amelia, Theo is a broadly positive character, a "good" father, and yet we learn first the unreliability of his self-image. When he is walking home after having been diagnosed "morbidly obese" by his doctor, we discover "He had thought of himself as cheerfully overweight, a rotund Santa Claus kind of figure" (41). The second thing we learn is that his relationship with his two daughters is predetermined by the early death of his wife, with the consequence that he holds uneven affection for the two girls. Both daughters physically resemble their mother, but only Jennifer shares her mother's solemnity; Laura is "carefree" (43). Jennifer's greater identification with the mother is the reason, ironically, why Theo "didn't love her as much as he loved Laura" (43).

Ravelled up in this story of maternal death, then, is a complex explanation of Theo's skewed psyche. Though his self-image is initially falsely positive (at that point in the novel Laura is still alive), gradually it is transformed into guilt at outliving Laura and loving Jennifer inadequately. This uneven affection also returns us to his wife. Almost as an aside, Theo reveals that having two young daughters prevented him from having "time even to mourn his poor wife" (42). In that phrase "poor wife" we hear an echo of Freud's case of the "incapable wife." Where Theo claims to pity his wife, he really pities himself. Furthermore, in the act of sympathizing with her, he actually constructs a narrative in which his libidinal withdrawal is not only confirmed, but also backdated: "Valerie and Theo had been fond of each other rather than passionate, and Theo didn't know if the marriage would have lasted if she'd lived" (42). How far, in this context, can we accept at face value his unequal protestations of affection for his daughters? Bearing in mind that the convolutions of the narrative structure reveal Laura to be dead even as Theo is telling us she is alive, and considering we never actually encounter Jennifer in the narrative, is it not as likely that Theo retells the story of his love for Laura after her death as he does the story of his love for his wife after hers?

Such double narratives and contradictions characterize Theo's relationship to Laura elsewhere, too. In his obsession with solving the case of her death (which itself appears to overwrite the lack of "retribution" [his word] he should have inflicted on the hospital after his wife's death), he starts to behave in the manner of the psychopath he hates, hoarding images of Laura's corpse in

> [a]n upstairs bedroom that looked like a police incident room – photographs and maps pinned to the wall, flowcharts and whiteboards, timetables of events ... And a good number of those things Theo shouldn't have been in possession of ... Ghastly pictures of his daughter's body which Theo handled with a kind of professional detachment. (150)

As Ward Jouve again recognizes, "it's no good saying '[the killer] was mad.' That explains nothing. He could have been mad and compulsively collecting butterflies, or had celestial visions, or believed he was Puss-in-Boots" (33). Theo's compulsive collection of memorabilia might augment other evidence that Laura's death is a symptom rather than the cause of Theo's narcissism. After all, such is Theo's self-regard that despite casting doubt on his love for others, he never casts doubt on their love for him – hence his rationale for not committing suicide after Laura's death: "then Jennifer would know ... that he loved Laura more than her" (128). *Case Histories*, for all its preoccupation with death, is post-Gothic rather than Gothic. What, though, happens if we invoke the uncanny in our consideration of the relationship between mourning, melancholia and narcissism? This may explain the distinction one might draw, in political terms, between novels such as *After You'd Gone* or *Case Histories*, on the one hand, and Sarah Waters's *Fingersmith*.

Fingersmith: Third-wave Gothic

Waters's novel is as preoccupied with death and doubling as O'Farrell's and Atkinson's, but here the result is a diversion into criminality. Sue and Maud, the two central protagonists, have both lost mothers in dubious circumstances and, unbeknown to them (or, for much of the novel, the reader), were swapped at birth. Brought up in different classes in surrogate families constructed around moral or social deviance (Maud's "uncle" is a collector of pornography who brings Maud up to act as amanuensis on his books; Sue's "mother" is a baby farmer, her "father" a fence for stolen goods), the women develop a strangely detached understanding of grief. Sue, believing herself to be the daughter of a hanged murderess, observes:

> how could I be sorry, for someone I never knew? I supposed it was a
> pity my mother had ended up hanged; but, since she *was* hanged,
> I was glad it was for something game, like murdering a miser over a
> plate, and not for something very wicked, like throttling a child. (12)

Maud's detachment is more self-willed and openly vicious in character:

> I sit and gaze at the [grave]stone, that I have kept so neat and free
> from blemish. I should like to smash it with a hammer. I wish – as
> I have wished many times – that my mother were alive, so that
> I might kill her again. I say to Sue: "Do you know, how it was she
> died? It was my birth that did it!" – and it is an effort, to keep the note
> of triumph from my voice. (277)

If melancholia is a trap sprung by endless returns to the site of trauma,
then *Fingersmith's* narrative traces out a melancholic pattern clearly as
evocative of the cul-de-sac as *After You'd Gone*. Maud has been told that
her mother died in a madhouse and led to believe her own fate will be
similar. Given the inevitability of an endlessly reiterated pattern, "escape"
can only be effected by the intrusion of a stranger, this being the villain of
the piece, Richard Rivers (known in the text as "Gentleman").

Gentleman is the character who stands in for the psychopath in this
text, and, though he tries to compare himself to Robin Hood, Sue com-
pares him openly to the Devil (30, 146). Furthermore, in the fears the
young Sue has of Bill Sikes coming to the door, which we read about
shortly before the first arrival of Gentleman, the implicit comparison
between the two characters is fixed in the reader's mind. However,
where Dickens's Sikes uses physical violence, Gentleman uses psychological violence (albeit backed up by the hint of physical force). When
he first outlines to the assembled "family" his corrupt intentions for Sue,
the plot is structured according to a circular pattern. He will take Sue to
Briar to act as lady's maid to Maud; he will woo Maud by offering her
painting lessons and then he will persuade her to elope with him. Once
the marriage is consummated he will be eligible to inherit Maud's fortune, at which point he will abandon her in a madhouse run by an
acquaintance of his and return Sue to Lant Street, three thousand pounds
the richer. Sue accepts the role only (aside from the money, of course)
because a return journey is built into the plan. However, unbeknown to

Sue (and the reader for much of the book), this is not Gentleman's plan at all, but Mrs Sucksby's, who is using Gentleman to retrieve Maud. Sue is the price to be paid, not the ticket-holder, and in fact it is Sue who is abandoned in the madhouse. Nevertheless, it seems that all roads lead to Lant Street, and using an accomplice of her own, Sue succeeds in escaping and returns. Afraid to enter in case she meets Gentleman, Sue first takes a room in a house opposite and keeps watch. As she peers through the pane, she sees Mrs Sucksby at her own window, talking to somebody who is gradually revealed to be Maud. Sue's traumatic response is strikingly similar to that of O'Farrell's Alice on spying her mother in the two-way mirror: "I turned from the glass ... 'Tell me who I am!' " (475–6).

In response to perceived treachery, Sue also mirrors Maud's previously articulated desire for murder: "She [Maud] has made Mrs Sucksby love her, as she made – Oh! I'll kill her, tonight!" (476). In a novel about melancholia, breaking the cycle of endless recurrence might well involve death, for "true" mourning can then replace "false" melancholia. In fact, death does come, though not via the anticipated route. Despite operating through similarly circular journeys to *After You'd Gone* and *Case Histories, Fingersmith* is also a narrative of genuine transformations. Sue tells us, at the start of the novel, that "Everything that came into our kitchen looking like one sort of thing, was made to leave it again looking quite another" (10). The kitchen being the space where transformations take place appears to take us away from the Gothic and towards family saga, playing on the womanly domestic ideal of Victorian marriage and motherhood, whereby raw materials are miraculously transformed into culinary delights. However, the Gothic returns once we realize that very little cooking takes place here. Instead, though undoubtedly a feminized space in the sense that Mrs Sucksby really does rule the roost (if not the roast), it both mimics and subverts the warming and homely connotations of the hearth: "We did not feel the cold much at Lant Street, for besides our ordinary kitchen fire there was Mr Ibbs's locksmith's brazier" (14). It is therefore entirely appropriate for Gentleman to meet his death here, knifed like a spitted pig at Maud's hand: "The dark blood turned suddenly crimson. Gentleman's waistcoat and trousers were soaked with it, and Mrs Sucksby's taffeta gown was red and running" (503).

Such bloody excess is encountered earlier in the text in two passages that have already connected Maud with slaughter. The first is her imagined "memory" of her own birth:

> I imagine a table, slick with blood. The blood is my mother's ... There is so much of it ... the women have set down china bowls; and so the

silences between my mother's cries are filled – *drip drop! drip drop!* ... The table has straps upon it ... [one] keeps apart her legs, so that I might emerge from between them. When I am born, the straps remain ... they put me upon her bosom and my mouth finds her breast ... There is only, still, that falling blood. (179–80)

The second is a scene from "ordinary" life at Briar. Throughout Maud's time with her uncle she is forced to wear gloves around the house. Her uncle is supposedly protecting the pages of his precious books, but in insisting that she also wears the gloves at table, he inflicts upon Maud a barbaric form of dining that turns a routine domestic ritual into a noxious bloodbath:

[My uncle] has my knife taken away, and I must eat with my fingers. The dishes he prefers being all bloody meats, and hearts, and calves' feet, my kid-skin gloves grow crimson – as if reverting to the sub-stance they were made from. My appetite leaves me. I care most for the wine. I am served it in a crystal glass engraved with an M ... [It is] to keep me mindful, not of my name, but of that of my mother; which was Marianne. (196)

What both scenes reveal is that Maud lives with a continual sense of having her mother's blood on her hands. Here we recall Auerbach's words, for rather than the "unabashed blood-awareness only animals enjoy," what confronts Maud when she looks at her plate is a realization that her uncle's appetite is actively to consume the innocence of youth: hence he *becomes* the animal. Striking out at Gentleman therefore consti-tutes more murder by proxy, but now it is the victim, not the perpetrator, who is substituted. Leaving Briar for the final time, Maud stands over her uncle's sleeping form and lifts his razor from the dressing-stand. Confounding our expectations with the words "But this is not that kind of story. Not yet," she takes the razor to his books, not his throat (290). However, in that final phrase "Not yet," we locate the overture to Gentleman's murder – as if his stabbing, when it comes, also signifies the final defeat of her uncle (no wonder he refuses her the use of a table-knife!).

Certainly the stabbing heralds a double death. Though Maud kills Gentleman, both she and Sue fall silent as Mrs Sucksby stands accused of the crime, and, as Sue watches Mrs Sucksby hang from the same window at which Mrs Sucksby viewed the hanging of the woman Sue had thought was her mother (but now knows to have been Maud's), the repetition is this time illusory. With the cutting of the thread that has woven these young women into one plot, they leave Lant Street separately, to be reunited only later and on their own terms. But how transformatory is the ending of *Fingersmith*? Though Sue inherits half of Briar, social elevation is not her goal. Instead, discovering Maud has decided to put her "training" to use and earn her living through writing pornography, Sue takes on the role of her amanuensis, requiring her to learn to read. Though, on the face of it, progress, a firm connection has already been established in *Fingersmith* between young women's literacy and exploitation – so much so that Maud formerly envied Sue her illiteracy.

In terms of melancholic culs-de-sac, then, the future for both women looks grim – until we recall that when Maud first left Briar, she anticipated the possibility of returning to it changed, but only in death: "I think of the ghost I shall make: a neat, monotonous ghost, walking for ever on soft-soled feet, through a broken house, to the pattern of ancient carpets" (287–8). Despite Sue's hard-edged exterior, superstitious dread is her weakness: though criminals hold no fear for her ("I was family" [86]), the same cannot be said for ghosts. Mistaking Maud's gown, hanging on the wardrobe door, for an apparition, Sue notes that "My heart leapt so hard into my mouth, I seemed to taste it" (87). When Terry Castle speaks of the cultural trope of *The Apparitional Lesbian*, she employs the ghostly metaphor to speak of both the invisibility of lesbian culture and its potency. For one cannot banish something one cannot see – instead it will rise unbidden and beyond control: Sue must learn to embrace ghosts if she is to have a new future.

It is therefore in the realm of the Gothic that *Fingersmith* stands apart from *After You'd Gone* or *Case Histories*. Where their female protagonists inherit the status of victim through the distaff bloodline, although Sue and Maud begin as victims, the spilling of Gentleman's blood marks the end of all that. This returns us to the issue of "victimisation, autonomy and responsibility" raised by postfeminism. Waters's novels persistently refuse to reclaim women "for good," neither saving them nor solving their problems; instead they enable women to become properly defined *as* women. And it is testimony to the ongoing allure of the Gothic that, in *Fingersmith*, such definition becomes clearest after dark: "It was like kissing the darkness. As if the darkness had life, had a shape, had taste ... It was like I was calling the heat and shape of her out of the darkness" (141–2). However, Waters's tribute to the past and to women's ongoing search for self-definition remains rooted in a feminism that environmentally situates its women within the evils of patriarchy (it can be no coincidence that Gentleman is a name applicable to many, rather than one). In this respect she is neither "late," nor "post," though she certainly comes "after" the second wave. Certainly, none of these three novels could exist without feminism, but where Atkinson and O'Farrell could be called "postfeminist," Waters is clearly "third wave" in her outlook: she actively belongs to a feminist tradition of writing and hence affirms her place in what Gamble calls the "history of feminist struggle" (44). The future, then, lies in paying homage to the past – something at which the Gothic always excels!

Works cited

Atkinson, Kate. *Case Histories*. 2004. London: Black Swan, 2005.

Auerbach, Nina. *Our Vampires, Ourselves*. Chicago: U of Chicago P, 1995.

Castle, Terry. *The Apparitional Lesbian: Female Homosexuality and Modern Culture*. New York: Columbia UP, 1993.

Dickens, Charles. *Oliver Twist*. 1838. London: Dent, 1907.

Freud, Sigmund. "The 'Uncanny.'" *Art and Literature*. Ed. Albert Dickson. London: Penguin, 1990. 335–76. Vol.14 of *The Penguin Freud Library*. Ed. Angela Richards and Albert Dickson. 15 vols.

——. "Mourning and Melancholia." *On Metapsychology: The Theory of Psychoanalysis*. Ed. Angela Richards. London: Penguin, 1991. 245–68. Vol.11 of *The Penguin Freud Library*. Ed. Angela Richards and Albert Dickson. 15 vols.

Gamble, Sarah. "Postfeminism." *The Routledge Companion to Feminism and Postfeminism*. Ed. Sarah Gamble. London: Routledge, 2001. 43–54.

Luckhurst, Roger. "The Contemporary London Gothic and the Limits of the 'Spectral Turn.'" *Textual Practice* 16.3 (2002): 527–46.

O'Farrell, Maggie. *After You'd Gone*. 2000. London: Review, 2001.

Rose, Gillian. "Making Space for the Female Subject of Feminism." *Mapping the Subject*. Ed. S. Pile and M. Keith. London: Routledge, 1995. 354. Rpt. in *Key Thinkers on Space and Place*. Ed. Phil Hubbard *et al.* London: Sage, 2004. 233.

Ward Jouve, Nicole. *"The Street Cleaner": The Yorkshire Ripper on Trial*. London: Marion Boyars, 1986.

Waters, Sarah. *Fingersmith*. 2002. London: Virago, 2003.

2
Neo-Splatter: *Bride of Chucky* and the Horror of Heteronormativity

Judith Halberstam

In a scene at the end of Ronnie Yu's 1998 neo-splatter film *Bride of Chucky* that is reminiscent of a whole decade of glorious, scream-filled horror films, various characters face off across a freshly dug grave and begin a fight to the bitter end, or at least a fight to one of the many bitter ends that the various monsters will meet in the next ten minutes. In the splatter films of the late 1970s and 1980s, this final confrontation would have featured a loose-limbed girl in tattered clothing and her horrifying tormentor bathed in the blood of his victims and high on the carnage he has wreaked. Against all odds, the "Final Girl" would prove herself to be a wily adversary and, by hook or by crook, she would slay the monster and deliver herself and her community from evil (see Clover, *Men, Women and Chainsaws*). In the conclusion to Yu's masterpiece, the stand-off features two evenly matched couples: Chucky and his doll bride Tiffany and the human teenage pair, Jesse and Jade. As it turns out, it is the human bride and groom who prove to be far more bloodthirsty, homicidal and violent than their diminutive adversaries. Chucky, a serial killer whose soul has migrated from his human body to the body of a "Good Guy" doll, is shot dead (again) by Jesse, his human counterpart, and although his bloodthirsty spate of murders seems like reason enough for his death penalty, we are still left to wonder whether he might have been the good guy after all. He and his foul-mouthed bride have delivered searing critiques of romance, domesticity, love and couplehood throughout their ghastly Bonnie and Clyde run, and their relationship is a testament to the horror of heteronormativity.

In this essay, I track the evolution of three features of the splatter film within the neo-splatter genre and I want to track these features through a reading of *Bride of Chucky*. The larger purpose of this essay is to comment on the representation of embodiment in horror as a form of gender flexibility. In my earlier work on slasher films, *Skin Shows*, I read Stretch from *Texas Chainsaw Massacre 2* as representative of the emergence in horror of new gender regimes and new modes of spectatorship. Here, I want to argue that the neo-splatter film builds upon very specific queer and transgender theories of the body and self-consciously depicts queerness not as the monster that threatens community but as the antidote to the horror of heteronormativity or marriage, domesticity, monogamy and family. The three transformations from splatter to neo-splatter that I will track are, first, the emergence of the couple as a replacement for the asexual, androgynous and patently queer final girl. The second transformation is of gay and transsexual characters in neo-splatter from monster to normative sidekicks. Formerly, the homosexual or transsexual (as in *Psycho* or *Dressed to Kill*) would occupy the place of the monster and would have to die or succumb to the law; more recently, gays have been represented as nerds who die quickly, and the transsexual has been eliminated as an explicit character altogether. But, as we will see, queerness in neo-splatter is not eliminated completely; rather it is realized separate from the body of the queer as a set of non-normative relations. Third, I want to revisit Judith Butler's book *Bodies That Matter* to see what the relationship might be between her description of the violence of the heterosexual matrix and the representation of the violent disarticulation of all foundational identities in neo-splatter. In other words, this essay asks whether bodies that splatter produce gender stability or whether they dismantle the very conventions upon which that stability depends.

In my earlier work on horror film, I used Butler's theories of gender disorder alongside Carol Clover's brilliant formulation of the Final Girl to explore the queer potential of low-budget horror. For Clover, the Final Girl is a site of "shared masculinity" for the male viewer, a conduit for forbidden male masochistic fantasies, and she provides evidence of elastic modes of spectatorial identification. In my work, the Final Girl, with her androgynous look and name, her survival skills, her ability to wield chainsaws and her distance from heterosexual romance, becomes a potent symbol of queer adolescent rebellion and female masculinity. What happens to queer gender in neo-splatter if the genre no longer depends upon the Final Girl?

When I named my chapter on *Texas Chainsaw Massacre 2* in *Skin Shows* "Bodies That Splatter," I was obviously borrowing Judith Butler's title for her foundational set of essays on "the discursive limits of sex." For Butler, materiality is the site where a certain drama of sexual difference plays itself out and, in the process, reveals and reinvests in a sedimented history of sexual hierarchy and sexual erasures. According to Butler, maleness and masculinity, and femaleness and femininity, are bound to one another, not through the body, but through the way in which bodies are made intelligible. The masculinity of the male is secured through an understanding of his body as impenetrable and as capable of penetrating. Femininity, then, becomes that which can be and must be penetrated but which cannot penetrate in return. Butler argues that these gendered positions are located within a gridlike structure of signification, "the heterosexual matrix," and rival possibilities for the organization of sexuality (particularly the phallicization of the lesbian and the feminization of the gay man) are prohibited through the mechanisms of shame and disgust (52). Butler summarizes: "the very formulation of matter takes place in the service of an organization and denial of sexual difference, so that we are confronted with an economy of sexual difference as that which defines, instrumentalizes, and allocates matter in its own service" (52).

Bodies that matter, then, are not simply those bodies that count, those bodies that are legible within a normative framework; "bodies that matter," as a term, asks for a thorough and critical evaluation of the way in which legibility operates in the first place. Butler links the process of legitimation very clearly to violence, and she suggests that prohibited sexual arrangements, systems and subject positions are brutally suppressed within any and all truth-regimes. By reworking Butler's brilliant phrase from *Bodies That Matter* into "bodies that splatter," we commit ourselves to tracking the path of the storm and accounting for the bodies that register the violence of their own exclusion. Not all bodies that splatter are female, but all do become feminine (penetrable) in the process of splattering; not all bodies that remain whole are male, but those female bodies that withstand the assault tend to signify as masculine (impenetrable). And those female bodies that refuse to splatter and that penetrate male bodies with knives and spikes and stakes represent the phallicized lesbian who, for Butler, has been rendered unthinkable by feminist and phallogocentric discourses alike.

Chucky's bride is no Final Girl, and indeed her body does splatter in gory detail several times during the film. Her human form is fried to death when Chucky pushes the TV into her bathtub as she sobs to a rerun of *The Bride of Frankenstein*; her doll form is rudely penetrated with cold steel by Chucky in one of his many parting blows ("Get off my knife," he growls as she grunts out one last line of endearment); and her dead form is reanimated momentarily, *Alien* style, when, in the film's final scenes, she gives bloody birth to Chucky Jr. Complete with black fingernails, Jennifer Tilly's Betty Boop voice and a mean plastic grimace on her doll face, Chucky's bride is a classic slasher film victim. She is the one who believes her man can change, who sticks by him despite his violence and abuse and who dies trying to save his latest victims from his rage. She is the phallic mother at the start of the film, the subjugated wife later on and, finally, she is all body, all matter, just a womb for a new monster, another sequel: *Seed of Chucky*! *Bride of Chucky*, in fact, omits the Final Girl character altogether and couches its critique of heterosexuality less in terms of the bodies that do not matter within heteronormativity and more as a call for new forms of family, new modes of relationality and a release, finally, from the archaic and suffocating sexual hierarchies of heteronuclearity.

Bride of Chucky is overtly feminist in a way that the Final Girl splatter films could not be; Tiffany, one of horror film's finest castrating bitches, delivers powerful feminist speeches in defence of equal rights in marriage, and she ultimately kills her mate rather than allow him to humiliate her further. But, although it mounts a scathing attack on the institution of marriage and the resulting forms of domesticity and family that marriage engenders, *Bride of Chucky*, like many neo-splatter films, no longer casts the masculine Final Girl as an alternative form of womanhood – independent, physically strong, emotionally autonomous and implicitly queer. Instead, what serves as the putative alternative to the bad marriages between older people in *Bride of Chucky*, as in many of the neo-splatter films (including *Scream* and *I Know What You Did Last Summer*), is the rather slim possibility that better marriages will emerge in the next generation. But, as the endless line of sequels in neo-splatter implies, the next generation usually just represents new and more bloody ways for couples to dismember each other. The true alternative raised by neo-splatter, and by *Bride of Chucky* in particular, lies in the queer social relations and counterpublics that the films imagine and call into being.

Bride of Chucky is the fourth film in the *Child's Play* series. The first film in the series, from 1988, *Child's Play* (directed by Tom Holland), introduced horror audiences to the fantastic narrative of a serial killer, Charles Ray Lee, who knows just enough voodoo to transubstantiate his soul from his dying body to the body of the only other creature within reach: Chucky, the Good Guy doll. After bringing down the toy store with his satanic magic, Chucky is salvaged by a homeless man who then sells Chucky to a struggling housewife for her son's birthday. Once he has been invited into the home, and indeed introduced in a strangely homoerotic/paedophilic scene into little Andy's bed, Chucky begins to wreak destruction by killing the babysitter with a hammer to her face. Andy's relationship to Chucky is reminiscent of the rapport between the little boy and his imaginary friend in *The Shining* and, as in *The Shining*, the relationship is a sanctuary for the boy from an impending Oedipal crisis. Only Andy can hear his friend talk, and only Andy knows that evil is afoot. Andy's mom is a single parent, but she begins a romance with the police officer who comes to investigate the babysitter's death. The police officer then completes the Oedipal triangle for Andy, who is now torn between the law of the father and a patently narcissistic and homo-erotic relationship to his little friend/phallus. The patently Oedipal rendering of horror in this instance shows the nuclear family to be in danger from the unrestrained impulses of the id, located always in the pre-adolescent homoerotic boy, and it demands that Andy transfer his identification from Chucky, the bad guy, to the police officer, the good guy, while renouncing his mother as an object of desire but simultaneously guarding against the homosexual potential of this renunciation. The dismantling of Chucky at the end of the film clearly represents a castration threat directed at Andy, and he now knows that his survival depends upon giving up on his child's play.

The predictability of the first three *Child's Play* films has everything to do with their textbook adherence to psychoanalytic narratives of gender development. It is only when a girl doll enters the picture that we can finally glimpse something outside the eternal cycle of animation, frenzy, transgression, discipline and punishment supporting domestic order and gender stability. The director of *Bride of Chucky*, Ronnie Yu, is best known for his work on Hong Kong action films and, in particular, for his classic *The Bride with White Hair*. By taking on this new bride film and moving from action to horror, from special stunts to special effects, Ronnie Yu was able to fuse two rather distinct genres and bring a new narrative complexity to the *Child's Play* series in the process. Apart from reprising *The Bride with White Hair* and its particular interest in gender ambiguity, Yu's film pays homage to the classic Hammer films, and *The Bride of Frankenstein* in particular, but the update brings with it some new insights about marriage, weddings and coupledom. Yu plays with the Oedipal framework and refuses to allow Tiffany's range to be limited to mother/bride. Yu also allows for the queerness of the narrative of doll sex and romance to surface, and so although we are denied the queerness of the Final Girl, the entire notion of transubstantiation is linked in perverse and oblique ways to postmodern understandings of queer and specifically transgender embodiment.

Bride of Chucky begins with a scene of castration and then switches into what we can call reverse castration. As in other films in the series, the film begins with some odd shots that bring us down to eye level with the doll. Shot from below and at an angle, the opening sequence shows a police officer on a stormy night entering a US law building and searching the evidence depository. The camera pans over hockey masks and other serial-killer-type disguises, until it arrives at a locker filled with paraphernalia from unsolved crimes. He grabs a garbage bag and heads out into the rain to deliver its contents to an unnamed female who speaks to him over the car phone reminding him not to look in the bag because "curiosity killed the cat." The officer arrives at the designated meeting place to deliver his ungodly package, but he cannot resist opening the bag. As he looks inside, the camera switches to the reverse shot and looks back at the officer from the garbage bag's depths; at this moment, as the viewer is sutured to the discarded doll, a hand pulls back the officer's head and slashes his throat. The camera now shifts back to ground level and follows the killer's steps around the police car. Jennifer Tilly, as the human version of Tiffany, dressed in a black patent leather dress, high heels and fishnet stockings, pauses to file her nails with the murder weapon and then grabs her precious cargo from the patrol car. The warehouse now looks oddly like a church, and as Tiffany pulls a piece of Chucky's broken head out of the garbage bag, the light shines on the happy couple, inviting us to see them as a bride and groom, embarking upon their bloody honeymoon.

But first the bridegroom must be reassembled. The opening credits roll over this remarkable scene of reverse castration by which Tiffany rebuilds her plastic man. The camera roams around Tiffany's trailer to a heavy-metal soundtrack, and we see newspaper clippings about former incarnations of Chucky. Tiffany digs through a large chest of old dolls and scavenges for body parts for her beloved, a doll arm here, an ear there. Next she takes a large darning needle and begins to sew Chucky back together, leaving huge stitched scars and gaps where Chucky's insides are spilling out. She uses a staple gun to make more subtle adjustments, and the camera gives us garish close-ups of the needle and the staples penetrating Chucky's plastic flesh. The limb that is missing from Chucky's butchered body is his arm, and Tiffany expertly digs out an arm from her doll chest and in a paradigmatic moment of reverse castration she skewers it into place. The next shot shifts to Chucky's point of view as if the phallic retrieval has restored some semblance of subjectivity and, as we watch through the cavity of one of his eye sockets, Tiffany opens her mouth to reveal a plastic eyeball. She pulls the eyeball from her mouth and pushes it towards the camera/viewer and into place. With his eyes intact, Chucky can assume the male gaze and Tiffany takes up a seductive pose as the object to be looked at. The reverse shot from below appraises the reassembled Chucky and the angle makes him look larger than life; the restored arm juts out suggestively and his macabre grin assures us that "Chucky's back."

What are we to make of this Frankensteinian scene of monstrous birth? And what is the purpose of the reverse castration and the spectacle of phallic restoration. I argue that this is a profoundly queer scene of embodiment in which Chucky becomes much more than the mother's little man, and in which Tiffany's power is located far beyond the power of giving birth. This opening is the powerful mirror to the final scene of the film, in which Tiffany does literally give birth to Chucky Jr and his birth does actually kill her. This unnatural birth does not kill Tiffany; instead it invests her with incredible erotic powers and it establishes Chucky and Tiffany as a sort of demonic butch–femme couple. Chucky, I suggest, is an incarnation here of what Judith Butler, in *Bodies That Matter*, calls "the lesbian phallus." In a traditional Freudian rendering of this scene Chucky might be rendered as Tiffany's phallus, just as the baby becomes the mother's phallus in the classic psychoanalytic understanding of femininity. However, as Butler points out, the Freudian and the Lacanian readings of the phallus misunderstand profoundly the relationship between penis and phallus, and although both theorists propose the transferability of the phallus, and both deny that the phallus stands for any particular body part, neither theorist is willing to allow that the phallus may be attached to a non-male body.

Butler exploits this blind spot of both Freudian and Lacanian psychoanalysis, the persistent and contradictory essentialism by which the phallus is supposed to symbolize the power dynamics of the social order but is also simplistically blurred with anatomical maleness, and she takes the whole concept of the phallus to its logical extreme by associating it most forcefully with its transferability, its plasticity and its displacement from the penis. Butler writes: "The viability of the lesbian phallus depends upon this displacement. Or, to put it more accurately, the displaceability of the phallus, its capacity to symbolize in relation to other body parts or other body-like thing, opens the way for the lesbian phallus, an otherwise contradictory formulation" (84).

Chucky represents the lesbian phallus, a dildo-like sex toy, in a number of different ways. First, his phallic capacity is constantly de-linked in the film from his penis. Even though he claims to be anatomically correct in the climactic doll sex scene, he also insists over and over that "size doesn't matter" and that his plasticity is his real advantage over fleshly versions of manhood. When he and Tiffany are making love in the honeymoon suites in Niagara, she stops him and asks whether they should use a rubber; he answers indignantly, "Honey, I'm all rubber!"

Second, in the initial reverse castration scene, Chucky's masculinity is located not in his penis but in his arm; this is the body part that represents the completion of his reassembly, and this is the body part that the camera locates as the source of his phallic power. Later in the film when Chucky prepares to kill Warren, the evil stepfather and Chief of Police, Tiffany says: "Sometimes I think you were born with a knife in your hand." If, as Carol Clover suggests, the knife in horror films represents the phallus and is just another tool of penetration, the power of Chucky's arm is linked neatly within a slasher system to the power of the phallus. Finally, Butler suggests that the displacement away from the penis that the phallus demands allows for other bodylike things to symbolize the phallus. Chucky is precisely a bodylike thing: neither man nor beast, masculine but not exactly male, childlike but not a boy, he represents the play of the bodily signifier and, as Tiffany quickly attests, an alternative site of erotogenic pleasure.

Chucky is the lesbian phallus because he represents an alternative masculinity to Tiffany, and she chooses his masculinity over fake alternatives, such as her tattooed and pierced boyfriend Damien, and rejects him only when Chucky mistakes his contingent and relational phallic power for the natural order of things. In the film's denouement, Tiffany turns on Chucky precisely because his misogyny, spurred on by Jesse's taunting, allows him to forget his plasticity. At this moment of crisis, Tiffany also becomes too human and she taunts him angrily: "Plastic is no substitute for a nice hunk of wood!" As their plastic identities resolve rapidly into a familiar pattern of male narcissism and female castration, they leave the erotic potential of their plastic union behind and begin the slow dance of death and marriage. But before the marriage that begins the unravelling of this perverse, unnatural and powerful alliance, Chucky and Tiffany, along with the human couple Jesse and Jade, set out on a road trip looking for love, romance, a wedding and a honeymoon. As they journey together, the two couples leave a trail of dead bodies in their wake, but they also hold at bay the horror of heteronormativity that threatens to engulf and empower the queer potential of their desires, their alliances, their bonds and their futures.

Bride of Chucky combines the genres of horror, action, road movie and romance all in one. The road trip part of the film begins when Chucky decides that he and Tiffany must travel to New Jersey to find the corpse of Chucky's former self Charles Lee Ray. The corpse was buried along with an amulet that will allow Chucky and Tiffany to transfer into human bodies. Tiffany arranges for her neighbour, the hunky Jesse, to transport the dolls in return for cash. Jesse has been trying unsuccessfully to date the Chief of Police's stepdaughter, Jade, but has been thwarted by the corrupt policeman and his cronies. Jesse and Jade become fugitives when they decide to run away together and get married on the way to delivering the dolls to New Jersey. Jesse asks Jade to marry him as Tiffany and Chucky stand witness in the car: Tiffany is moved by the romance of it all, but Chucky responds caustically: "I give them six months, three if she gains weight!" As the star-crossed lovers make their way to Niagara, honeymoon capital of the nation, Chucky surreptitiously kills the various people who stand in their way: he dispenses with the evil stepfather with a nail gun, blows up a corrupt police officer as he sits in his car, and then he and Tiffany create a bloodbath at the honeymoon suites. The trail of carnage causes Jade and Jesse to turn on each other as each suspects the other of being the killer. Only their friend, the very gay and very nice boy David, knows what they are up to and counsels them along the way.

In a book about the queer potential of weddings, *The Wedding Complex*, Elizabeth Freeman describes the wedding in opposition to the marriage as a site of possibility. She says: "the wedding holds promises that marriage breaks" (42). For Freeman, the wedding produces and imagines social and cultural relations and kinship forms even as the heterosexual marriage erases these other modes of desire. In a sense, the wedding, as a ritual, as a communal form, as an act that conjures up eccentric forms of belonging, keeps the marriage at bay and postpones the seemingly inevitable fall into order and convention. In readings of seminal American texts that situate the wedding as a disruption to Oedipal narratives of becoming and belonging, Freeman examines the fantasies the wedding sets in motion; whereas sometimes these are fantasies of national belonging, at other moments the wedding facilitates the fantasies of minority forms of kinship and queer desire. Freeman writes: "The power of the wedding lies in its ability to make worlds through doing aesthetic work on affiliation, attachment, and belonging, and in the way it preserves exactly what it claims to renounce: cultural possibilities for organizing social life beyond either the marital or mass imaginary" (44). The social identity of the bride, Freeman argues, is particularly suggestive for women who want to re-craft femininity. Linking bridal identity to drag, Freeman explains that bridehood ornaments the contemporary female body, and she shows that bride drag, like other forms of drag, might be seen as a gesture towards "lost kinship systems, imagined or real bygone patterns of exchange, dwelling, promising and so on" (37). If Chucky's drag has to do with his plasticity and his performance as the lesbian phallus, Tiffany's drag has everything to do with her status as bride.

There are four couples in *Bride of Chucky*, three honeymoons and two weddings. Each couple is located within a different stage of heteromarriage: Jesse and Jade represent the premarital and adolescent stage of rebellious sexuality; a conniving couple who rob Jesse and Jade at the honeymoon suites occupy the stage of just-married couple who have already descended into the horror of heteronormativity; an older couple, retirees, represent the bleak future of the marriage dyad and they end up dead when Chucky re-appropriates their trailer. Chucky and Tiffany represent temporal disorder: they are premarital in the sense that they occupy the role of children; they are the Gothic future of the heteronormative couple in that they have returned from the dead to haunt new generations; and they represent the present-tense potential of the wedding given that Tiffany is always and never a bride, always and never married. There are several lone males in the film: the stepfather, his police officer crony, Damion (Tiffany's suitor), and David, the gay boy. All die: Warren is brutally stabbed, the police officer is incinerated and David is run over by a truck. The film slyly gives credence to the conservative rationale for marriage – namely, that married men live longer – but it also represents the lone male as vulnerable to violence without the protection of a phallic female. Ultimately, however, by positing the couple as the form that survives, *Bride of Chucky* reminds us of the violence that marriage does to other forms of being and belonging.

One particularly violent scene is worthy of close attention because the violence for once is directed against the couple form and because the act of murdering the couple serves as foreplay for the consummation of Chucky and Tiffany's plastic love and forms the backdrop to their own wedding. Chucky and Tiffany, Jade and Jesse have stopped for the night at the honeymoon suites in Niagara. Jesse and Jade have reluctantly had a wedding service, and they are sunk in the miserable aftermath known as marriage. As they check into their room, another honeymoon couple bursts in on them, pretending to have mistaken Jesse and Jade's room for their own. In the ensuing confusion, the con artist couple snatch Jesse's wallet and Tiffany's engagement ring; after having their proposal that the two couples enjoy a swinger evening together rejected, they leave the newlyweds miserable and broke. The con artists return to their own room, count up the loot and prepare to celebrate, honeymoon style, in their waterbed with a mirrored ceiling. As the couple begin to have sex, the camera glances across the bed to show Tiffany standing in the unusual position of the female voyeur. Classic heteromasculine pornography, whose conventions are often utilized in the slasher film, usually offers up sexually suggestive images of two women for a male gaze. Here the formula is reversed and heterosex is offered up to the queer gaze. Tiffany shifts out of voyeur mode when she locks eyes in the ceiling mirror with the other woman: the woman begins to scream; her husband mistakes her fear for pleasure but turns finally to follow her gaze and sees the horrific spectacle of Tiffany with a champagne bottle in hand. Tiffany throws the bottle up at the mirror and the shards of glass rain down upon the copulating couple, turning their love nest into a blood bath and transforming the fluids of sexual exchange from semen to blood and water.

Needless to say, this is a complex and overdetermined scene of sex and violence. Tiffany, as female voyeur, combines desire and violence in precisely the way that so many monsters in other slasher films, from *Peeping Tom* to *Halloween*, have done. And, like Mark from *Peeping Tom*, she fixates on the image itself as the meeting place of sex and violence. By shattering the glass image of the con couple rather than attacking the flesh itself, Tiffany locates the representational space as prior to rather than proceeding from the real. Her act of violence occurs, in other words, in the realms of the symbolic and the imaginary, and the real violence that follows from that prior enactment is merely the effect of some much more profound rupture. The lesbian potential actualized in the moment when Tiffany and the honeymooning bride lock eyes cannot be realized in the honeymoon suite; it must be played out between Tiffany and Chucky in the plastic sex that follows. Significantly, as the two dolls (mirror images of the mirror images we have just seen, copies of copies) lie romantically entwined in front of a blazing fire, Chucky goes to retrieve the wedding ring from the severed finger of the honeymoon bride and, after struggling to dislodge it from the formerly human finger, he slides it, blood and all, onto the thumb of his bride. He does not ask Tiffany to marry him, at this point; instead, down on bended knee, he says: "Tiffany, will you be my bride?" Making Tiffany the bride rather than the wife, leaves both Chucky and Tiffany firmly in the realm of the wedding and offers a potent critique of the realm of marriage. "Why are you crying?" he asks Tiffany. "I always cry at weddings," she responds.

After the wedding, the honeymoon ends all too quickly as Chucky and Tiffany take Jesse and Jade with them to New Jersey in the hopes of switching bodies. Along the way, the potential of the lesbian phallus, bridal drag, reverse castration and the wedding complex disintegrate into the horror of heteronormativity. As in most slasher films, sex is the beginning of the end and, sure enough, Chucky and Tiffany's tryst in the honeymoon suites loses its queer potential all too quickly as they begin to contemplate shifting their relationship to human bodies. As Chucky explains to Jesse, he and Tiffany consider their doll bodies to be *rentals* while they look for real homes to buy. Transubstantiation raises the distinct possibility of transgenderism and, even though Ronnie Yu situated transgenderism as a flesh-and-blood subject position in *The Bride with White Hair*, in *Bride of Chucky* the possibility is avoided altogether. In other words, gender-appropriate switching (boy to boy, girl to girl) is the only configuration that the film considers, and the potential homoerotic reading of the occupation of one body by another is avoided by heterocentrist exchanges between Chucky and Tiffany about the desirability (rather than habitability) of their human opposites. Desire and identification are kept firmly in place within the heterosexual matrix, and the last part of the film pits the two couples against each other.

The web of queer relations that has animated the film's fantasy of belonging and being is quickly narrowed down to marital couplehood and, as if to register the expulsion of other modalities of embodiment or desire, the gay character David arrives on the scene only to be spectacularly crushed by a speeding big rig truck. Just before he dies, David finds Warren's body in Jesse and Jade's van and he imagines that Jesse and Jade are, after all, the accused honeymoon killers. His horror at finding Warren's body causes him to leap out of the van and into the path of the truck. David is right in some sense: Jesse and Jade, Chucky and Tiffany are all honeymoon killers; their couplehood has literally killed the other, illegitimate forms of relationship that surround them. For their trouble, the two couples end up in a Sartrean form of hell, stuck in a Winebago together cruising towards New Jersey.

Slasher film has always been a site for alternative configurations of embodiment, belonging, family, desire and identification. The new slasher films, steeped as they are in irony and self-consciousness, seem to have taken a complex and innovative low-budget cinema and turned it into multimillion-dollar mass entertainment. But the genre is expansive, and the critique of family and normativity that, as Robin Wood's work showed in the 1980s, formed and still forms the heart of the horror project lives on in some surprising places. *Bride of Chucky* recognizes the potential of the narrative of plastic embodiment that the earlier *Child's Play* films set in motion and it marries horror and violence not to doll subjectivities but to their project of becoming human. Becoming human in this film is explicitly linked to becoming heterosexual, becoming coupled, becoming adult and becoming reproductive. As the trailer carrying the dolls and the humans travels ever closer to its macabre destination, the grave of Charles Ray Lee, the two couples become more and more alike and more and more horrifying. Tiffany bakes cookies for her man while Jade and Jesse try to goad Tiffany and Chucky into a domestic dispute. When Tiffany finally turns her feminist rage on Chucky, spurred on by Jade, she gets shoved into the oven by Jade for her trouble and fries to a crisp while Jesse overpowers Chucky. This ends Tiffany's attempt at feminist bonding and she now limps after Chucky and towards her final end. When Chucky Jr bursts forth from her pulverized doll body in the film's last moments, we see the price she has paid for trading in her plastic affections for fleshly desires: the scene of reverse castration that promised so much at the film's start now returns to haunt Tiffany as she is slain by woman's oldest enemy: not a madman with a chainsaw but the violent, bloody and horrific effects of heteronormativity.

Works cited

Butler, Judith. *Bodies That Matter: On the Discursive Limits of Sex.* New York: Routledge, 1993.

Clover, Carol. *Men, Women and Chainsaws: Gender in the Modern Horror Film.* Princeton, NJ: Princeton UP, 1993.

Freeman, Elizabeth. *The Wedding Complex: Forms of Belonging in Modern American Culture.* Durham, NC: Duke UP, 2002.

Halberstam, Judith. *Skin Shows: Gothic Horror and the Technology of Monsters.* Durham, NC: Duke UP, 1995.

3
Bite-Size Pieces: Disassembling the Gothic Villain in *Witchblade*

Rhonda V. Wilcox

Witchblade begins in the Gothic. The two-season TNT television series, which ran for twenty-three episodes and twenty-four hours during 2001 and 2002, was based on the Top Cow Productions comic book, and despite various differences between the productions in the two media, the Gothic elements are something they have in common. The Witchblade itself is a supernatural weapon that can be worn only by a chosen woman warrior; it takes various forms, sometimes appearing as a bracelet, sometimes as a metal gauntlet with a protruding blade. It once belonged to Joan of Arc, but now has attached itself to Sara Pezzini, a New York City homicide detective. The two-hour pilot episode, directed by series producer Ralph Hemecker, visually unites the Witchblade itself with Gothic imagery. Shots of stone gargoyles are intercut with images of the Witchblade gauntlet, presented in such close-up that it may be difficult for some to recognize the object. The overlapping, curving metal plates of the silver-grey gauntlet echo the curving shapes of the Gothic stone building in which the Witchblade is housed, a museum apparently placed in a former church. And these images are intercut with obscured views of a person – someone whose gender is not at first apparent – but who turns out to be Detective Sara Pezzini. So, from the beginning, through the camera work and editing, Sara Pezzini is identified with the Witchblade, which is identified very overtly with the Gothic through the Gothic buildings. And, of course, it is a traditional position for the woman in the Gothic to be identified with a dark, fearful, womblike space. But this is just the beginning.

Sara Pezzini is on some levels a second-wave feminist hero, contesting the traditional female place in the Gothic, but the show also allows for certain pleasures that might be termed postfeminist. Lisa Yaszek has recently written a short history and definition of the term; as she says,

" 'postfeminism' seems to be used in even more complex and contradictory ways than 'feminism' itself" (1). One interpretation – widely contested, for example by Yaszek, but often accepted in the popular press – is
the idea that we can now operate freely because of "the completion of the
feminist project" (7). The idea that feminism has finished its work is, if
you'll pardon me, silly – in all the senses of that word, including the
ancient notion of innocence, naïveté.[1] For myself, I prefer to use the term
to indicate that we now operate after *some* of the work of second-wave
feminism has succeeded – after feminism has started, not after it has
ended. I address later the choice to use "third-wave feminism" or "postfeminism," but for now I use them interchangeably.[2] Judith Butler has
declared that "laughter in the face of serious categories is indispensable
for feminism" (x); her comment was made in the context of gender construction, but I would choose to apply it more generally. Laughter and
play of mind are important shields. The excessiveness of certain elements
of *Witchblade* (a notably Gothic quality) also leads to the ludic, a kind of
playfulness that I think of as one of the more positive elements of some
postfeminisms. One should be careful not to overgeneralize; many
second-wave feminists (and I would like to think I come close to qualifying)
have a sense of humour. But "according to many third wavers, second
wave feminism is repressive and restrictive," and some even think that
"second wave feminists hate sex and perpetuate Victorian sexual ideals"
(Dicker and Piepmeier 14, 15). As Dicker and Piepmeier assert, the idea of
the puritanical second-wavers versus the sexually relaxed third-wavers is
itself a way of creating a narrative about women that is meant to divide
(15–16). Granted, the narrative oversimplifies the truth; nonetheless a
more playful sexual attitude may be one of the benefits of, one of the
products post, the work of the second-wavers.[3]

Thus an element of *Witchblade* that can be considered postfeminist is
its combination of a physically and emotionally strong female protagonist with the fantasy pleasure available through the harem of male characters surrounding that protagonist – most of whom constitute various
versions or aspects of the Gothic hero–villain. Further, the series complicates the fantasy by interrupting it at the conclusion of the first
season: Sara's magic undoes the entire narrative, sending it back in time
to the series' beginning, a strategy that can be seen as dangerous on
many levels – perhaps dangerous in a good way in terms of its social
message; dangerous in a more problematic way in terms of its aesthetics.

The Gothic itself has long been seen as dangerous in both good and
bad ways, both social and aesthetic. As Dani Cavallaro points out, in the
eighteenth and nineteenth centuries, "it was common to associate

Gothicity with tastelessness" (9), and many still make that association. Cavallaro argues that this disparagement was corollary to seeing Gothic as a female-produced and female-consumed type of writing, though others have pointed out that it is difficult to know how many men were reading Gothic novels (10). Fred Botting notes that the term "Gothic" was "used derogatively about art, architecture, and writing that failed to conform to the standards of neoclassical taste," and that " 'Gothic' signified the lack of reason, morality, and beauty of feudal beliefs, customs, and works" (3). And David Punter claims that even today, authors of the Gothic "and indeed its critics [are] pilloried by the cultural police" (xii). I confess that when I pulled out my videotapes of the original pilot episode, I found written on the label in my handwriting the words *"Witchblade* – HAH!" – as if to make sure that anyone who happened to be looking through my television library would know that I of course recognized this "tastelessness," as Cavallaro terms it. When I was reviewing the series in order to write this essay, I kept thinking of the term "overwrought" – because, for example, of the use of slow-motion fight scenes, sometimes operatically emotional musical scoring, and sometimes embarrassingly elevated language. (Characters in the twenty-first century just really shouldn't say "Behold!" to anyone, at least not if it is meant seriously.) When my husband watched an episode with me, he asked, "Don't you think this is kind of overwrought?" It really is. But I say here, as I said to him then: Agreed, it's overwrought, but at least it's wrought in the first place. One has merely to consider some of the characters' surnames – Vicky Poe, Bruno Dante, Elizabeth Brontë: all named after thematically relevant authors – to see that. And I hope to show that it is wrought more thoroughly as we proceed.

So, *Witchblade* does follow the pattern and suffer the dangers of traditional Gothic aesthetic. It also, perhaps less obviously, follows in the path of the Gothic socially. Some critics argue that the Gothic is transgressive socially: it forces us to recognize the Other, which we have turned into a monster, or which can assume the attractive face of a dangerously seductive man, a Gothic hero–villain; with the heroine often endangered in the mysterious castle, it allows us to recognize the entrapment of women – something truly frightening in the eighteenth and nineteenth centuries, and not completely different today. Gilbert and Gubar, in *The Madwoman in the Attic*, note that "heroines who characteristically inhabit mysteriously intricate or uncomfortably stifling houses are often seen as captured, fettered, trapped, even buried alive" (83); the text highlights the social problem. But others argue that the Gothic always re-inscribes traditional values in the end, always makes clear that this is escapism. One might parallel the ambivalence in the Gothic with the ambivalence in the term "postfeminism." As Tania Modleski notes, often works of popular culture express "legitimate grievances" while "neutralizing these grievances" (41). Helen Stoddart comments more specifically on this Gothic pattern: "Though the hero-villain may temporarily function as a vehicle for fantasies of unregulated desire and ambition or for sympathizing with the socially persecuted, the undeniable nature of his 'otherness' ... always ultimately provides a means of distancing and disavowing his actions as unfeasible or illegitimate" (114). But what do we say of a narrative that at first kills all of the Gothic hero–villains, then re-boots the entire story, bringing them to life again when the protagonist's magic sends everything back to the beginning?

Perhaps first we should examine more carefully the original presentation. Sara Pezzini can herself be seen as representing a certain kind of feminism; she competes in a man's world on men's terms. She is in many ways the extreme opposite of the traditional Gothic heroine. In the pilot's wordless introductory sequence, we see a hand shutting off an alarm clock; we see arms pulling jeans up over men's underwear – not boxers, but briefs; we see a helmeted figure riding a motorcycle through the streets. The sequence begins with the sound of a single rock guitar. Only when the character pulls off the motorcycle helmet outside the 11th Police Precinct do we see long hair tumble down – and the face of a woman. We might have guessed, if we had paid close attention to the music playing as she rides: "She Moves in Mysterious Ways." Promotionals for the series called her "New York's toughest cop." Marc Silvestri, an executive producer for the pilot, says that her world has "the flavor of *NYPD Blue* with elements of the fantastic" (Allstetter 27). And in a promo consisting of a brief interview with Yancy Butler, the actor who plays Sara Pezzini, Butler says, "I definitely give Buffy a run for her money"; she points out that the character is "vulnerable," too.[4] Sara Pezzini, or "Pez" as she is sometimes called, is the daughter of a police officer who died when she was fifteen (though we later learn that – appropriately for a Gothic heroine – she was adopted). Her rarely seen mentor, Captain Joe Siri, was her father's partner. And later in the series, we learn that both these men were killed by the White Bulls, a secret society (Gothically enough), a group patriarchal in the grossest sense – a society Sara fights to expose with the help of good-guy male friends. She fights and shoots with the best of them; she even boxes against a man in a charity match – and wins. She is called a good detective even by Captain Bruno Dante, a character who dislikes her and has a fully patriarchal attitude towards women.

She has clearly trained herself to succeed in masculine patterns of behaviour, and as a result is more than once called "bitch" at work. The series directly acknowledges sexism in the workplace, and the strength required to stand against it.

When Sara first encounters the Witchblade, she has chased a suspect into a Gothic building, the museum that houses it. We are shown paintings of Joan of Arc wearing the gauntlet and blade and, as the series proceeds, we learn that other women – only women – have worn it throughout history: the Irish Chtain, Cleopatra (to judge by the visuals), the anti-Nazi spy Elizabeth Brontë. So the Witchblade is matrilineal, though Sara is fostered by males (she almost never speaks of her mother but we often see images of the child Sara with her father). The gauntlet has a red stone on one knuckle, which also appears in the bracelet form. On the gauntlet, the metal closes over the red stone like an eyelid – an eyelid that opens when Sara initially approaches it. We in the audience gaze at her from the point of view of the stone. But this is not a typical Mulveyan gaze: we look into her as she looks into it, or us; the look is held for several moments, as we inhabit the matrilineal object of power while it chooses, or recognizes, Sara; and she seems to be recognizing something in her turn. Shortly after this, in the battle with her suspect, the Witchblade comes crashing out of its display case and miraculously lands on Sara's arm. Now the woman warrior has a blade. If Sara can be seen as colonizing male territory, it is of course appropriate that her weapon is a phallic one; the blade is extendable and retractable, no less.

But Sara is not just a masculinized woman, a male female. One might note, for instance, that the various forms of the Witchblade – bracelet, gauntlet – can be seen as suggesting access to both the female and the male. Furthermore, the basics of Sara's characterization may suggest one tradition of feminism, but the series as a whole allows her to play with pleasures that some types of feminist would not see as appropriate. This is, as noted earlier, an element of the series that might be called postfeminist or third-wave feminist. And although Sara herself may be seen in some ways as an anti-Gothic heroine, she is nonetheless surrounded by men who are descended from the Gothic – for the most part, variations on the Gothic hero–villain. As many will remember, the Gothic hero–villain is in a number of ways a variation on the Byronic hero; he is a powerful, attractive figure who tends to transgress the bounds of society. The principal men surrounding Sara Pezzini are Kenneth Irons, Ian Nottingham, Danny Wu, Conchobar, Gabriel Bowman and Jake McCarty.

Kenneth Irons is a billionaire powerbroker fascinated by the Witchblade and its history. He fits into the category of what Fred Botting terms "malevolent aristocrats" (3). In Avril Horner's terms, this Gothic character is the "scheming, wicked older man who wishes to seduce or kill her for his own ends" (116). Though he is the head of a modern conglomerate, he is usually presented before a giant fireplace in a cavernous room, evoking the past; and indeed, both his vast home and his company headquarters serve as the modern Gothic castle into which Sara is often drawn. Irons's character at first seems ambiguous and potentially sympathetic. He offers to teach Sara about the Witchblade, which he, with his great wealth, has researched for many long years. He offers to be her protector, to take her to see the world with him – clearly implying a sexual invitation as well. That Sara spurns him fits not only the pattern of the modern independent woman, but also the pattern of the virtuous Gothic heroine. But that this handsome, wealthy, powerful man wants her is part of the fantasy – possibly for Sara; probably for the posited audience member.

Irons's servant, his highly trained bodyguard Ian Nottingham, displays other elements of the Gothic hero–villain. He is physically dark and certainly mysterious; he appears and disappears in wraithlike fashion, implying physical control; he swirls his cape-like coat as well as any vampire; and his long, dark hair often obscures his shadowed face. Helen Stoddart (112), in her discussion of the hero–villain, describes him as having a dark, piercing gaze and being gloomy and unpredictable – all characteristics that describe Nottingham. The actor who played the part, Eric Etebari, received enough Internet fan attention that his role was expanded for the second season. "Who's the pirate?" asks one woman character on first seeing Ian ("Static"). Sara repeatedly supernaturally "sees" both Ian and herself in armour. "Crazy psycho Galahad" is another phrase used for him ("Thanatopis"), alluding to the knight of extreme sexual purity: Nottingham seems devoted to Sara to the exclusion of all others, an exemplar of a curious kind of courtly love. Cavallaro also comments on the tendency of the Gothic to describe "the collapse of degenerate fathers and illegitimate sons": it is reported that Nottingham is Irons's illegitimate son, and it certainly seems that Irons raised him; Nottingham calls him "Father," and the degenerate Irons does collapse, after being kept relatively youthful for an unnaturally long time by a potion brewed from a wielder of the Witchblade (Irons is actually ninety-six). Nottingham, however, like Sara, is an adopted child. Fascinated by the warrior woman, he finally transgresses his father's restrictions and tells her that he loves her – though she seriously doubts whether she can trust him, and in fact turns her blade on him. Her problem is not solved when he asserts that she could not "use the blade against [her] own flesh and blood" ("Thanatopis"). Like Heathcliff (not to mention Byron) before him, Nottingham carries the dangerous scent of incest. In fact, we learn by the end of the first season that he was "created from" (presumably cloned from) the "preserved stem cells" of Sara's grandmother, the spy Elizabeth Brontë; he is, essentially, Sara's uncle. His devotion to her is such that, near the end of season one, he sacrifices his life to delay her pursuers; in that incarnation, Ian Nottingham fulfils unattainable passion through sacrifice. But, as he seems to have done before, Irons has his scientists bring Ian back in a new, colder, slightly less hairy version that shows the darker side of the attraction: New Ian licks the side of Sara's face, both of them now aware of his incestuous intentions. He will shortly end up dead, in appropriate Gothic fashion – dangerous desire evoked and repudiated.

Danny Wu, Sara's beloved friend and partner, fits in the Gothic pattern as well. Cavallaro writes about Orientalism and the Other in the Gothic (115), as well as about the characteristic of "racial alterity" (163). Danny Wu is emotionally closest to Sara Pezzini, but physically he is the farthest: he is killed in the pilot and spends the rest of the first season as a ghost. It is perhaps not surprising that she is kept most distant from the racially "Other" character, and it is also worth noting that he is married as well (another mark of sexual distance from Sara). The writers seem to recognize the dangers of the pattern Danny Wu follows, and they attempt to prevent the character's presentation from degenerating into stereotype by the use of humour. "So enlighten me, oh wise Asian master," Sara wryly says to her ghost-friend on one of the many occasions when a fellow cop finds her apparently talking to herself ("Parallax"). In another episode ("Apprehension"), Danny tells her, "You are turning into something you are not," and Sara asks, "What is that, the I Ching?" "No," Danny answers, "Radio Head." (The actor, Will Yun Lee, makes the most of such moments.) In the Periculum, the initiation to see whether Sara is worthy to wield the Witchblade, her spiritual guide Danny is the only one who can stay with her – and, in fact, as she nears death, they can physically feel each other. In this episode, he wears formal robes, accentuating his Orientalism and his work as guide to the other world, in which she is tested. One of the most interesting things about the second season is that Danny is brought back to flesh and blood and human failings. But for season one, he gets to be one more fantasy male focusing exclusively on Sara. She is the only one who can see him, and he seems to exist only for her.

Alongside her Asian companion, Sara is given an Irish lover as a kind of ethnic Other. (She declares herself to be half Irish.) The singer/ songwriter Conchobar, also known as John Patrick Doherty, is drawn to

Sara because of their connection in a past life: as the Irish warrior woman Chtain, she loved him in the past. Conchobar (who named himself after the legendary hero) is shadowed by the dark side of the Gothic because, when Sara first meets him, he is one of her suspects for a particularly Gothic murder involving the sacrifice by stone sword of young women in candlelit caves. He is, of course, wrongly accused; he will, of course, die tragically, though the series has the grace not to kill him at the end of the first episode in which he appears. But if the fantasy is to be surrounded by a set of fascinating males, and if most of the posited viewers would not consciously, comfortably indulge in a fantasy of polygamy, then the man with whom Sara has a satisfying physical, sexual relationship must die.[5]

The character Gabriel Bowman is an Internet version of the medieval scholar. He is the enterprising owner of Talismaniac.com, a company which traffics in ancient artefacts over the Web. His own business place/home is as dark and mysterious as any Gothic space, and filled not only with historically interesting items but also with objects of magical power. Step into Talismaniac, and you will see skulls; you also see the drum kit last played by Keith Moon before his death. Furthermore, Gabriel Bowman seems to have a touch of the fey about him: he is the only person other than Sara who ever (for a moment) sees the ghost of Danny Wu. Gabriel represents a disapproved desire in that he is clearly much younger than Sara. And it is worth noting that one of the pleasures of the series is that Yancy Butler's Sara is no teenager; she looks to be in her thirties – in contrast with the much younger drawn figure in the comic books. Gabriel usually presents himself as a friend, but occasionally breaches the polite surface with a suggestion of sexual possibility, with remarks such as "You were thinking you could trust the handsome, dashing Gabriel" ("Thanatopis") or "Admit it – you think pale, erudite guys are kinda sexy" ("Static"). And kudos to any series that uses the word "erudite" in prime-time sex talk. But Gabriel, too, will end up dead, untouched by Sara sexually, at the end of season one.

The last of Sara's harem is her rookie partner, a replacement for Danny Wu: Jake McCarty. Jake fits in perfectly as a fantasy figure, but I must admit that he has nothing of the Gothic about him: he is, quite literally, a California surfer, blond and hard-bodied. The audience, and Sara, gun at the ready during a mistrustful narrative point, watch him through frosted glass as he showers and emerges to hastily cloak himself in only a strategically placed plastic bowl emptied of its candy. Jake was a well-known surfing champion who retired to train for law enforcement. Though he himself does not mention his surfing past, Sara and the audience soon learn of it. He is presented as a neophyte in Sara's dark world – New York City Gothic – though he is not as innocent as he seems: he is in fact an undercover FBI agent. Like Sara, he is trying to unmask the secret male society responsible for her father's death, and *he* ends up no less dead.

Witchblade, then, allows for the enjoyment of a strong, brave, moral female protagonist while simultaneously invoking a set of fantasy relationships grounded in the Gothic past. The very multiplicity of the Gothic hero–villain variants, all focusing on Sara Pezzini, establishes that this is a fantasy – a fantasy of desire as well as a fantasy of power. Audience consciousness centred in the female protagonist is allowed the imaginary pleasure of access to wealth, physical power, youth, intelligence, physical beauty and more, incarnated in the men who desire her. The rejection or death of these characters in traditional Gothic plot patterns means that the Gothic heroine's choice re-inscribes accepted middle-class values and refuses to transgress. These are dangerous men and should not be available to her. Every one of the males mentioned above is killed before or during the last episode of season one. In a sense this can be seen as realistic: the forces aligned against Sara Pezzini are such that it would be virtually impossible for her and her allies to prevail.

But the series makes an interesting choice, and it is grounded in months of narrative. In the "Periculum" episode, in which Sara is tested, wrapped in emphatically snakelike extensions of the blade, we learn that the Witchblade "is a branch ripped from the tree of the knowledge of good and evil." Thus the series cites the central story in which woman is condemned for having led to our expulsion from Paradise, to our mortality – and, indeed, all those around Sara end up dead by the last episode of the season, "Transcendence." Last to die is Kenneth Irons: having literally stabbed Sara in the back, he then vampirically pleads for a taste of her blood, which will keep him alive. Once more, the Satan of the story offers her worldly knowledge: "I will tell you everything," he whispers, the camera close on his mouth; "I will find out for myself," she spits back, bloody-lipped. This Eve wants knowledge, too, but on her own terms. With a painting of the martyr Joan in the background, Sara raises her blade in the same stance. At the beginning of each episode of *Witchblade*, a giant image of the pockmarked moon is seen behind the title letters; often, early in an episode, the sun is shown, close enough for us to see the solar flares. The images seem always to suggest that there is a larger, longer story than the incidents in any given episode. Now, at the season's end, Sara raises her blade, with lightning running out of it to the clouds above, the world beyond; and, having earned the power, she undoes the story in which she has been caught; she rejects, if

I may put it so, the patriarchal narrative. Time runs backwards, to return to the first day of the story, the day she first encounters the Witchblade. This fantasy, this temporal revision, might even be said to parallel the narrative experimentation that Lisa Yaszek notes as one element of post-feminism (or third-wave feminism) to be found in both science fiction and ChickLit – though the *Witchblade* writers are mainly men.[6]

On some level this is a very satisfying conclusion: Ian, Jake, Gabriel – all Sara's men are still alive, even Danny Wu, since he died on the day after she found the blade. Sara has been able to protect them all, and now they are available again for her to enjoy. But of course the problem is that an action such as hers tends to make it difficult for viewers to suspend disbelief; there is a distinctly soapy odour of the infamous scene in the *Dallas* series when the supposedly dead Bobby appears in the shower, and an entire season is revealed to have been the dream (or nightmare) of his wife Pam. The *Witchblade* writers try to attenuate the aesthetic blast: they have one recurring character (Lazar – cf. Lazarus) note that this will be the only occasion when Sara can make time run backwards (though it is not explained why) and that she will remember little. And there are various benefits to using this particular reset button: as noted before, Danny gets to stop being the wise Asian ghost and gets to be a real boy; Gabriel Bowman and Sara experience interesting déjà vu. Perhaps, too, the choice to reverse time allows the series to make all the more obvious and heavy-handed the death and rejection of all Sara's men as originally played. The emphasis of the sheer numbers, starkly displaying the pattern, may thus work to resist the re-inscription of traditional values that occurs when we silently sink the taboo men, like Irish Jack in the movie *Titanic*. Whether or not this postmodern self-consciousness of structure exists in the minds of the writers or only in the minds of certain audience members is unclear. This is not, after all, *Buffy the Vampire Slayer*, written by an avowed feminist (Joss Whedon) in collaboration with many excellent female writers (including Jane Espenson) – though certainly it seems likely that the more overtly feminist elements of the protagonist's character were intended by Ralph Hemecker and at least some of the other series' creators. But however it was constructed, this complexity is in the text.

It must be acknowledged that the text is flawed, indeed, overwrought – as is so much of the Gothic. But it should also be acknowledged that *Witchblade* is carefully wrought. Although it is not great art, it is nonetheless fertile fantasy and, at least in some ways, an intriguing attempt to resist the unceasing pressures of the world, fictional and real. At the end of the pilot, we see the billionaire Irons in his hall of paintings of the past wielders of the Witchblade, most prominently Joan of Arc, who bears Sara's face. In voiceover we *hear* Sara say, "There is no finale – no single, final image," while we *see* Irons gaze at a comic book cartoon image of Sara with the Witchblade. This is all he sees. But the audience sees more. Many of us in the audience know that this series was born from a comic book presentation. The conclusion of the first season – with the juxtaposition of television and comic book media, and the juxtaposition of two narratives in one time frame – is another way of showing that there is no single, final image. As Judith Halberstam says, in the Gothic text, "meaning itself runs riot" (2). This is not a simple presentation.

The elements of the Gothic to be found here, as in most Gothic texts, show division of meaning, and the text's attitude towards feminism is similarly complex. And, in fact, the Gothic and the postfeminist are both elementally ambivalent. Transgression or containment? Third-wave feminist Patricia Pender argues that "this binary formulation is itself part of the bogey" (43). Many third-wavers recognize this paradox. As for the term "postfeminist," it can indeed carry the danger of prefeminist attitudes – as can the Gothic itself. Once a word has been let loose, it seems unlikely that it can be swallowed again. We can argue that "postfeminism" is a bad word (Bad Word!) – but that is rarely, so far as I can recall, a successful strategy. Or, as I might have put it some months before beginning this essay, the Gothic *Witchblade* (hah!) is in some ways postfeminist (hah!). For my own usage, I do intend to prefer "third-wave feminism" to "postfeminism," because I hope thus to be less likely to convey the wrong idea of my views. But given the apparent persistence of the latter term, perhaps instead of simply condemning, we can keep trying to point out the complications in the meaning of "postfeminism" and claim some of the meanings for ourselves – just as we claim aspects of the Gothic. *Witchblade* is one example of part of the postfeminist Gothic territory we might claim.

Notes

1. Dicker and Piepmeier provide a useful survey of indicators of current inequalities between males and females (3–7) and cite political writer Susan Estrich's 2000 observation that "at the rate we're going, it will be another 270 years before women achieve parity as top managers in corporations and 500 years before we achieve equality in Congress" (4). I thank Patricia Pender for her recommendation of this and other useful sources, and Lisa Yaszek for her helpful feedback as well.
2. Put very roughly, first-wave feminists were the ones trying to get women the vote; second-wave feminists were those in the twentieth century who realized

that just getting the vote was not enough. (There are, of course, many feminisms.) The terms "third-wave feminist" and "postfeminist" are (again, roughly) chronologically alike in that they come after second-wave feminism. I resist the pressure to box in the usages of these terms, and I certainly do not claim to be able to give a full-fledged definition in this essay, much less this end-note. From my perspective, the proponents of third-wave feminism and post-feminism have much in common – in part, a more relaxed attitude because they do inherit benefits from earlier feminists. Those who claim the name "third-wave feminist" are more likely to be concerned that the refusal to iden-tify with the term "feminist" indicates a failure to understand the widespread social attitudes underlying many problems women face, not to mention the men involved in the same problematic system. (See, for example, Baumgardner and Richards.) This is a concern I share. As for the term "postfeminist," it can be interpreted in drastically different ways. For example, postfeminism can be taken to imply that feminism is dead (see Yaszek's complaints), or postfemi-nism can mean that feminism is crossed with postmodernism and all the para-dox and multiplicity of vision that implies. (Of course, some who call themselves third-wave feminists focus on paradox, too; see Pender.) For the lat-ter view, see Brabon and Genz, who of course connect this aspect of postfemi-nism with the Gothic, and see the later comments in my essay. I hope the essay will convey some of the nuances of the terms.

3. Consciousness-raising about the sexual double standard must of course be placed in the context of many other factors, from birth control pills to AIDS.

4. *Buffy the Vampire Slayer*, which ran from 1997 to 2003, was by the beginning of *Witchblade* well established in the popular consciousness as a show centring on an unusually strong female protagonist who also had access to supernatural power. Of course, Buffy is "vulnerable," too; see Wilcox, especially chapter 7.

5. Cf. the American Monomyth pattern described by Jewett and Shelton Lawrence: a woman beloved by the cowboy/gunfighter will likely end up dead. Thus, although Conchobar's death marks a sexual delimiter for the protagonist, it is a delimiter shared traditionally by males in American popular texts.

6. Of the twenty-four hours of script, only two are written by women.

Works cited

Allstetter, Rob. "Watching Witchblade." Comic strip. *Witchblade* 1.42 (Sep. 2000): 26–9.

"Apprehension." *Witchblade*. Dir. Robert Lee. Writ. Richard C. Okie. TNT. Broadcast 7 August 2001.

Baumgardner, Jennifer, and Amy Richards. *Manifesta: Young Women, Feminism, and the Future*. New York: Farrar, Straus, & Giroux, 2000.

Botting, Fred. "In Gothic Darkly: Heterotopia, History, Culture." *A Companion to the Gothic*. Ed. David Punter. Oxford: Blackwell, 2000. 3–14.

Brabon, Benjamin, and Stéphanie Genz. "Postfeminist Gothic." Introduction. *Gothic Studies* 9.1 (May 2007), forthcoming.

Butler, Judith. *Gender Trouble: Feminism and the Subversion of Identity*. New York: Routledge, 1990.

Cavallaro, Dani. *The Gothic Vision: Three Centuries of Horror, Terror, and Fear.* London: Continuum, 2002.

Dicker, Rory, and Alison Piepmeier. Introduction. *Catching a Wave: Reclaiming Feminism for the 21st Century.* Boston: Northeastern UP, 2003.

Gilbert, Sandra M., and Susan Gubar. *The Madwoman in the Attic: The Woman Writer and the Nineteenth-Century Imagination.* New Haven, CT: Yale UP, 1979.

Halberstam, Judith. *Skin Shows: Gothic Horror and the Technology of Monsters.* Durham, NC: Duke UP, 1995.

Horner, Avril. "Transgression." *The Handbook to Gothic Literature.* Ed. Marie Mulvey-Roberts. New York: New York UP, 1998. 286–7.

Jewett, Robert, and John Shelton Lawrence. *The American Monomyth.* Garden City, NY: Anchor/Doubleday, 1977.

Modleski, Tania. *Feminism without Women: Culture and Criticism in a "Postfeminist" Age.* New York: Routledge, 1991.

Mulvey-Roberts, Marie, ed. *The Handbook to Gothic Literature.* New York: New York UP, 1998.

"Parallax." *Witchblade.* Dir. and Writ. Ralph Hemecker. TNT. Broadcast 12 June 2001.

Pender, Patricia. " 'I'm Buffy and You're ... History': The Postmodern Politics of *Buffy the Vampire Slayer.*" *Fighting the Forces: What's at Stake in* Buffy the Vampire Slayer. Ed. Rhonda V. Wilcox and David Lavery. Lanham: Rowman & Littlefield, 2002. 35–44.

"Periculum." *Witchblade.* Dir. Neill Fearnley. Writ. Roderick Taylor, Bruce A. Taylor. TNT. Broadcast 24 July 2001.

Punter, David, ed. Introduction. *A Companion to the Gothic.* Oxford: Blackwell, 2000.

"Sacrifice." *Witchblade.* Dir. David S. Jackson. Writ. Richard C. Okie. TNT. Broadcast 3 July 2001.

"Static." *Witchblade.* Dir. Neill Fearnley. Writ. Richard C. Okie. TNT. Broadcast 24 June 2002.

Stoddart, Helen. "Hero-Villain." *The Handbook to Gothic Literature.* Ed. Marie Mulvey-Roberts. New York: New York UP, 1998. 111–15.

"Thanatopis." *Witchblade.* Dir. James Whitmore Jr. Writ. Richard C. Okie. TNT. Broadcast 31 July 2001.

"Transcendence." *Witchblade.* Dir. David S. Jackson. Writ. Ralph Hemecker. TNT. Broadcast 21 August 2001.

Wilcox, Rhonda. *Why Buffy Matters: The Art of* Buffy the Vampire Slayer. London: I. B. Tauris, 2005.

Witchblade. Movie pilot. Dir. Ralph Hemecker. Writ. J. D. Zeik. TNT, 2001.

Yaszek, Lisa. "I'll Be a Postfeminist in a Postpatriarchy, or, Can We Really Imagine Life after Feminism?" 29 Jan. 2005: 1–9. *Electronic Book Review.* 12 Dec. 2005 <www.electronicbookreview.com>.

4
The Spectral Phallus: Re-Membering the Postfeminist Man

Benjamin A. Brabon

Gender, according to Judith Butler, "is the repeated stylization of the body, a set of repeated acts within a highly rigid regulatory frame that congeal over time to produce the appearance of substance, of a natural sort of being" (*Gender Trouble* 33). During the second half of the twentieth century, this "rigid regulatory frame" was transformed and destabilized from within its own bounds as white heterosexual man's position of authority was contested. Although the concept of "hegemonic masculinity" has historically been seen as the stronghold of gender, ritualistically reproducing itself as the bastion of heteronormativity, it has come increasingly under attack, becoming a "historically mobile relation" (Connell 77). In other words, what it means to "be a man" has given way to fragmentary, incoherent and contradictory expressions that attest to a contemporary crisis in masculinity. Shedding its perceived seamlessness and impermeability, masculinity, as Coward notes, is "no longer a position from which to judge others but a puzzling condition in its own right" (94).

The emasculation of men, due in part to what Faludi identifies as the development of "ornamental culture," has left them devoid of any "meaningful social purpose" (*Stiffed* 35, 598).[1] Unsurprisingly, men in some quarters were quick to target what they saw as the defining factor in the unsettling of their position and to attribute the blame to one of the most important social forces that changed the status quo of twentieth-century society: feminism. Overexposed to "strong and angry women," these men complained that they had been pushed from their patriarchal pedestal into taking up "a female view" and turning into "stereotypical sissies" and "yoghurt eaters" (Faludi, *Backlash* 339–41).

Soon conglomerating into a recognizable "men's movement," "the New Age masculinist community," they believed that they had been forced into a dialogue with their own masculinity and as a result now had to confront the possibility that they had "awakened their feminine principle only to be consumed by it. They had gone 'soft' " (341). The response to this supposed softness, spearheaded by Robert Bly – the "New, New Man" – in the 1980s and early 1990s, saw the Iron John movement claim the hearts, heads and dollars of many mainstream Americans. Although, according to Bly, it was not a counterattack on the women's movement, merely an attempt to reawaken men to "the deep masculine," feminists located Bly's "wild-man" retreats as part of an ongoing backlash against feminism orchestrated by the New Right.[2]

In this essay, I intend to problematize these "backlash" scenarios through a consideration of the gender relationships in two twentieth-century urban Gothic tales: *Falling Down* (1992), and *Fight Club* (1999), based on Chuck Palahniuk's 1996 bestseller. By introducing and exploring the category of the "postfeminist man," I argue that the crisis in masculinity witnessed in these films reflects the complex negotiation of man's position within contemporary society. Although both *Falling Down* and *Fight Club* are saturated with aggressive violence, I maintain that it is the display of male anxiety, dissatisfaction and inefficacy that is the key to unlocking male identity in each film. As I contend, the postfeminist man is not the signifier of the re-masculinization of contemporary culture – a straightforward rejection of second-wave feminism that can easily be identified as part of the backlash – but, in contrast, an unstable and troubled subject position that is doubly encoded, as the sadistic forces of patriarchal violence are no longer turned solely against women.

For men, the re-scripting of the "rigid regulatory frame" of gender during the second half of the twentieth century has left them in conflicting subject positions. Within this context, I argue that the symbol historically associated with masculinity – the phallus – has become a ghostly form for men. This is, in part, the result of the severance of phallus from penis – through a kind of critical fellatio (using Butler's idea of "performativity as citationality" [*Bodies* 21]) that takes hold of the signifier and resignifies the phallus. The phallus's new mobility has left men haunted by the loss of its exclusively male signifying potential. In turn, the undermining of the essentialist nature of masculinity has left male identity unmoored and vulnerable.

So, if the phallus is a "transferable phantasm" (*Bodies* 86), I aim to repatriate and repudiate it, simultaneously re-erecting it for male use and undermining its ancestry and rejecting it as a symbol of patriarchy – the Father. This is not simply another act of "aggressive reterritorialization" but rather a re-membering of a non-severed phallus/penis in order to expose a ghost-ridden space at the centre of male identity (86). I maintain that the male subject is haunted by what I characterize as the "spectral phallus" – the signifier of the paradoxical shape of masculinity in contemporary society. The ghostly form of the spectral phallus is a symbol of presence and absence – the manifestation of an aggressive masculine identity and a lack thereof. It embodies the uneasy location of the male subject's relationship with his own masculinity, as emasculated and whole, impotent and virile. Male gender is now a ghostly performance of masculinity that is simultaneously hard and soft, macho and feminine. This severed signifier is spectral, haunting the male subject with its presence as a seemingly unobtainable symbol of monolithic proportions (what could be – delayed pleasure) while highlighting through its phantasmic form an absence at the very heart of male identity (expected pain – emasculation). In this way, I intend to develop Thomas Byers' argument that

> [a] major – perhaps *the* major – function and driving force of patriarchal narrative is the attempt to re-member a masculine body whose member has been "dissed." Thus sadism and violence directed against women are not in themselves synonymous with narrative; rather they are among the most common, and most virulently misogynist, strategies by which patriarchal narratives try to reconstruct an imaginary wholeness for the masculine subject – by which they try to disavow or repress that subject's castration. (422–3)

It is my contention that the spectral phallus is the new signifier of masculinity for the postfeminist man. It accounts for both the undermining of hegemonic masculinity and backlash scenarios as a symbol of masculinity that is paradoxically weak and aggressive. It also accommodates the potential for re-membering masculinity, at the same time incorporating the emasculation of men in the face of feminism's advances. As I argue in this essay, films such as *Falling Down* and *Fight Club* that are too quickly situated as part of the "white male backlash" need to be reconsidered in order to realize the possibility of conflicting readings of masculinity within these texts and within contemporary society. For instance, this multiplicity is exemplified by the ending of *Falling Down* (which I analyse in more detail later in this essay), which pinpoints the contradictory forces of masculinity at work. Although

"D-Fens'" showdown with Prendergast reinforces his victim status, it also confirms the spectral quality of the phallus as the phallic symbol of his gun is replaced by a flaccid water pistol – symbolizing the ineffectual male member. Yet the fact that "D-Fens" is shot by Prendergast with a gun taken back from his female partner also reinforces a backlash scenario, as phallus and penis are reunited. Likewise, the concluding scenes of *Fight Club*, while ultimately constructing a heterosexual coupling of Tyler and Marla, show the destruction of a series of phallic symbols as skyscrapers tumble before our eyes. In this way, the re-membering of hegemonic masculinity in the postfeminist era exposes the self-destructive potential of the phallus when placed in the wrong hands.

Re-membering the Gothic hero(ine)

> Feminist literary critics would like to reject any notion of women as inherently masochistic, indeed, as inherently prone to any essentialist quality. But more germane to our discussion is the need to recognize the female author's careful manipulation of the masochistic pose. That is, the gothic heroine indulges in what we would recognize as masochistic gestures for effect. ... These young women not only tolerate all manner of abuse; they actually seem to seek it out.
>
> Diane Long Hoeveler, *Gothic Feminism* (1998)

The Gothic heroine, as Diane Long Hoeveler has argued, adopts a subject position that embraces the abusive power of patriarchy, revelling in the violence exacted upon her. For example, as Hoeveler points out, Emily in *The Mysteries of Udolpho* employs "passive-aggressive strategies" that underline her masochistic tendencies as she manoeuvres herself into spaces that provide the potential for further oppression and abuse (13). In this scenario, the Gothic heroine performs or plays the role of the victim, Irigaray's strategy of "miming the mime," in order to take pleasure in the pain inflicted upon her and "wait for the oppressor to self-destruct" (14).

As Deleuze reminds us, the contrast between delayed pleasure and expected pain constructs the masochist's identity:

> The masochist waits for pleasure as something that is bound to be late, and expects pain as the condition that will finally ensure (both physically and morally) the advent of pleasure. He therefore postpones pleasure in expectation of the pain that will make gratification possible.

> The anxiety of the masochist divides therefore into an indefinite awaiting
> of pleasure and an intense expectation of pain. (63)

In what follows, I want to examine how the relationship between pleasure and pain that has historically defined the female Gothic heroine has been transferred in the late twentieth and twenty-first centuries on to the postfeminist man. I argue that an inversion has taken place, as the female Gothic heroine cedes her position and role to the postfeminist man. In other words, men's masculine identity has been transformed from sadism directed at women to masochism aimed at men. Instead of the female Gothic heroine performing her role of victim, it is the postfeminist man "miming" masculinity. In this sense, the postfeminist man's new status of victim is defined and delineated by his masculinity – he is trapped between the loss of his essentialist quality of masculinity and his attempt to reassert a strong masculine identity. As there is no place for phallic violence within contemporary Western society, the phallus has been both re-signified and displaced. This undermining of masculinity's essentialism and normativity has left male identity troubled by the parameters of the masculine self. In particular, the resulting backlash is proved to be ineffectual as the male subject who exacts his phallic revenge on women is ghostly, a performance of a spectral image of masculinity. Being a "wild man" is no longer a viable option in the postfeminist era – there is no place for Tyler, and "D-Fens" (whose name harks back to the decades of the cold war that had everyone on the alert) with his old-fashioned beliefs in safeguarding country and family is not needed. As a result of this redundancy, displays of masculine aggression have been either pushed underground or geographically/racially "othered."

In postfeminist Gothic texts, it is not enough to follow the scenario of the female Gothic that "make[s] the hero safe for the middle-class world by ritualistically wounding him" (Hoeveler 215) – he now must engage with his own masculinity in order to ultimately emasculate and "other" himself, retaining only a ghostly sense of the phallus, the echo of the amputated signifier. A shift has taken place as the feminized man of feeling from the eighteenth century – epitomized by figures such as Valancourt and St Aubert in Radcliffe's *Udolpho* – has developed into what could be characterized as the postfeminized postfeminist man. Whereas for Radcliffe "feminine sentimental virtues can reform masculine worldly energies" as Valancourt's experience of male libertinism is tamed by Emily's good character (Ellis 65), the postfeminist man is troubled by this legacy of "feeling." Although it is reconceived through a masculine lens, the postfeminist man deals with the same dilemma of "subjectivation" experienced by the Gothic heroine (Foucault; Butler).[3] For example, Emily in *Udolpho* uses "her body as a signifying surface" in order to "say things [that] the mind cannot admit" (Ellis 53). Likewise, in *Fight Club* the body becomes "a signifying surface" upon which male identities and sexualities are performed. The "New, New Man of feeling" reacts to this feminized version of masculinity by rediscovering "feeling" at the physical level of the body, rather than through the rhetoric of sensibility. For Tyler, "feeling" is associated with the physical pain experienced at Fight Club and the political activism of Project Mayhem, as meaning is deconstructed to the level of the male body. The inverted identities of the female Gothic heroine and the postfeminist man see "the dream of becoming masculinized" re-scripted, as the doubly encoded e/masculinization of man is achieved, not by "rising above the corrupt body," but by embracing it in a self-destructive act of definition (Hoeveler 245).

Masculinity re-done

> I'm the bad guy? How did that happen?
> "D-Fens,"
> *Falling Down* (1992)

In *Falling Down*, "D-Fens' " destructive journey across the social spectrum of American society maps out the decline of the white heterosexual male as an economically viable individual. "D-Fens' " violent rampage across Los Angeles as he heads "home," highlights the white heterosexual male's alienation and displacement from his central position within American society. Unemployed, divorced and considered a danger to the very society he was employed to protect, "D-Fens' " plight in the film echoes that of a black man seen protesting outside a bank who is refused credit because he too is not economically viable. In this unlikely association, the signifier of the racial other becomes the self through their meeting of eyes/"I"s, underlining the extent of "D-Fens' " estrangement.

"D-Fens" effectively becomes a ghost of the white heterosexual masculine male self he is meant to represent, as the alienated and emasculated white man returns to haunt America through his violent reclamation of the tools of masculinity. His anger is directed at American society/government in general because, as he asserts, "they lied to me." In particular, each encounter is directed against men – the Korean shopkeeper, Hispanic gang members, the neo-Nazi, and wealthy white men, for example. No longer the alpha male of American society, "D-Fens" resorts to guerrilla tactics in the urban jungle of Los Angeles in an attempt to take back control of his life. As he progresses on his destructive journey, "D-Fens" undergoes a transformation from white-collar worker (dressed in white shirt and black tie), to "GI Joe" – kitted out in combat dress. The estranged husband becomes the soldier on a mission to question American society and re-position himself at the head of the American family unit.

"D-Fens' " nemesis takes the shape of the retiring cop Prendergast. Disliked by his colleagues for "pretending to be a cop" (and by extension a man), Prendergast is chastised by his captain for his failure to curse: "I don't trust a man that doesn't curse. Real men curse." Facing the prospect of early retirement and a move with his wife to the middle of nowhere, Prendergast encounters "D-Fens' " rampage on his last day at work. Whereas his colleagues are unable to track "D-Fens' " violent trajectory "home" and recognize the threat this non-smoking, non-drinking white heterosexual man poses, Prendergast displays a sensitivity that allows him to pick up on important leads. In this way, Prendergast's feminized persona and alienation from his macho cop colleagues allow him to artic-ulate a better understanding of "D-Fens' " assault on American society.

Controlled by his wife and considered a coward by his captain, Prendergast acts as "D-Fens' " double. However, unlike in the case of the classic pairing of Jekyll and Hyde, "D-Fens" does not conquer his "weaker" half, as Prendergast reasserts his masculinity by shooting "D-Fens" dead. In this sense, "D-Fens" and Prendergast are not mirror images of each other. On the contrary, they are the same, but each chooses a different response to his emasculation by and alienation from American society. As their showdown at the end of the film reveals, their struggle is a metaphorical fight over who can re-appropriate and re-member the phallus for the white heterosexual male – who can define masculinity and male identity for the new millennium. Through Prendergast's victory, *Falling Down* makes the two options clear. On the one hand, Prendergast takes back his gun from his "partner," Sandra, in what seems to be a classic backlash scenario. On the other hand, "D-Fens' " gun is his child's water pistol, highlighting that his approach to the "crisis in masculinity" involves regressive strategies that have no future. Yet "D-Fens" tells Prendergast after he has been shot: "I would have got you" – thus reinforcing the sense that if his gun had been real, his "wild-man" masculinity would have prevailed. However, "D-Fens' " threat to the "Law of the Father" is misconceived, as the phallus is only symbolic – his inefficacy being confirmed by the simulacrum of the water pistol. This ending shows that there is no going back – the phallus cannot simply be re-membered through masculine might and aggression. At the same time, Prendergast's actions are not a straightforward backlash, as his victory involves a performance of masculinity. Prendergast "mimes the mime" in order to re-claim the phallus, stepping out from behind his feminized persona in order to re-establish the law against the invading father figure of "D-Fens." In this way, their encounter symbolizes male identity's negotiation of masculinity.

As Prendergast tells Sandra just before he heads out from behind his desk to apprehend "D-Fens," the spectral nature of his masculinity is defined by his wife, Amanda – the neurotic signifier of second-wave feminism: "She thought I was a ghost and I had to chase her all over the house." In this scenario, Prendergast's masculinity is made into a ghostly presence by Amanda through his perceived absence from the home – she believes that he has been shot. Although before he hits the streets he reasserts his masculinity by telling his wife to "shut up" – eliciting the single-word response, "shit" – this is all part of his gender performance. This is confirmed shortly after he has shot "D-Fens": as his captain sings his praises to the media, Prendergast responds by saying, "Fuck you ... Fuck you very much captain." Although Prendergast reclaims his masculine persona by killing "D-Fens," his performance is a gender parody, as his manhood is established and confirmed by cursing his captain. The backlash scenario is thus undermined by Prendergast's gender parody, as the phallus cannot fully re-materialize and remains spectral throughout his performance of masculinity. The result is a re-appropriation of the tools of masculinity for the white heterosexual man, not through an aggressive seizure of power, but by miming masculinity and, in so doing, assuming the position of the Female Gothic heroine.

Re-membering the feminized man

> Self-improvement is masturbation ... and self-destruction.
> Tyler Durden,
> *Fight Club* (1999)

The lives of men, as Tyler Durden tells us in *Fight Club*, have become nothing more than "by-products of a lifestyle obsession." As if he were reading straight from the pages of Susan Faludi's *Stiffed* (1999), Tyler defines man's predicament in terms of a postmodern malaise where "everything's a copy of a copy of a copy." Men, according to both Faludi and Tyler Durden, have lost their sense of purpose. As Tyler maintains, they have no "great war" or "great depression" – in fact, their "great depression is [their] lives." Men feel alienated and estranged from their own self-image as male identity and masculinity are shaped by the forces of consumerism. As Jack, gesturing to an advertisement for Calvin Klein underwear for men, asks Tyler: "Is that what men look like?" Jack does not recognize this image of "maleness," as signifier and referent have become detached. For Tyler this image represents the true horror of masculinity at the end of the twentieth century – the product of "ornamental culture" (Faludi 35).

This bleak account of the inefficacy of men in the postmodern era provides a backdrop to Jack's troubled negotiation of his own masculinity through his encounters with his schizophrenic alter ego, Tyler Durden. Tyler offers Jack multiple personalities and subject positions, being, as Tyler says, "all the ways in which you could be – that's me." Tyler transforms Jack through Fight Club from a white-collar worker living the "great depression" of his life to a leader of men who can offer salvation through pain. In fact, Fight Club becomes a self-help group for men whose masculinity has been undone.

The combat men endure at Fight Club redefines male identity through the physical experience of masculinity – a primeval embrace of Bly's "wild man." Fight Club becomes the first level of Tyler's plan for the "self-improvement" of men through the doubly encoded heterosexual/ homoerotic fist-fight, where the total embrace of the phallic violence of the fist-fight signifies a form of masturbation. At Fight Club, this metaphorical masturbation is played out on the body of the man – the site for the re-membering of phallus and penis – as the male body is "beaten" until it goes limp. Although charged with homoerotic tensions, it is the shared experience of masculinity that creates a community of men, not sexuality.[4] Fights climax in the exchange not of semen but of blood. Through the fist-fight, the postfeminized man of feeling is re-born as the masculinized man of action. In this sense, the signifying surface of the body redefines essentialist masculinity as something to be recognized and experienced by men. These indulgent acts of male self-improvement cannot be shared with women or society as a whole. Fight Club is set underground, a dark pursuit that cannot be discussed by its "members" out in the open – an indication of the fact that phallus and penis must remain severed in the postfeminist era. Its covert displays of the extremes of masculinity – and auto-eroticism – are horrific and yet cathartic for the men involved. Fight Club lays bare what Judith Halberstam in her essay in this collection calls "the horror of heteronormativity." However, the potentially dangerous power of the male identity constructed through Fight Club is withheld, as the horror remains repressed beneath the staged nature of each physical encounter. The men of Fight Club perform masculinity, substituting the laws of American society for the rules of Fight Club. Each member, whether inside or outside Fight Club, must engage in gender performance and mime masculinity. Heteronormative gender parody is at the heart of the Fight Club experience, as men are made into "Men" through the reiterated stylization of the body. Once again, the postfeminist man must be Janus-faced in his displays of masculinity – recognizing the threat that the phallic violence of Fight Club poses to the fabric of American society.

The second level, Project Mayhem, acts as a self-destructive riposte to the phallic pride of Fight Club. Whereas Fight Club turns flaccid male bodies into "wood," Project Mayhem aims to bring the system down, so that "we all go back to zero." Project Mayhem sees phallic violence and aggression turning on itself, as it attacks the institutions historically associated with patriarchal male identity – banks and credit card companies. This is graphically exposed by Jack in the final scenes of the film as he turns his gun on himself to "kill" Tyler, before witnessing the destructive conclusion of Project Mayhem while standing hand in hand with Marla. This apocalyptic finale marks a double-edged assault on masculinity and a return to "the horror of heteronormativity" as the phallic symbol of the gun is aimed at the self in order to destroy the alter ego of Tyler. Jack is left physically and emotional drained, pathetically dressed in a bath robe and boxer shorts as he displaces his own masculinity in order to re-establish a heterosexual/heteronormative bond with Marla. As Project Mayhem bears fruit and the symbols of capitalism and patriarchal male domination fall before them, Jack and Marla stand like the first couple – Adam and Eve – surveying the world before them. As events come full circle, the Gothic cycle is complete as the wounded hero of Radcliffe's female Gothic is transformed into the self-emasculated postfeminist man of *Fight Club*.

The reclamation and destruction of masculinity witnessed in *Fight Club* are not straightforward responses to second-wave feminism or a backlash against women. On the contrary, the men in *Fight Club* are defined by the absent father and the alienating images of male identity in contemporary culture. As Tyler tells Jack, "we're a generation of men raised by women." The dilemma for men in the postfeminist era is self-image – there are no "real" men, only copies, as the figure of the father has become spectral, a ghostly presence that still haunts the home even in his absence.

The postfeminist Gothic man

> The image of "man" that is unstable, that constantly needs to be re-created or re-told, is the image of the individual masculine subject who possesses the phallus – who occupies and is

adequate to the position of the paternal signifier – who is, in short, the Father.

Thomas B. Byers, "History Re-Membered" (1996)

It has been my contention in this essay that the masculinity on display in *Falling Down* and *Fight Club* is not a straightforward backlash, a one-directional assault on the women's movement. Both films depict an unstable and fractured image of masculinity and male identity that, in its attempt to re-member the phallus, "self-destructs" the self. The crisis in masculinity in these films does not simply result in phallic revenge against women, a "feminist bashing," as each film's protagonist directs his anger at men. Far from being in possession of the phallus, the post-feminist man has lost this "paternal signifier." In its place is a ghostly image of male "wholeness" – a male identity defined by the perform-ance of masculinity and through allusions to a spectral phallus. As a result, the backlash scenarios witnessed in *Falling Down* and *Fight Club* are problematized and ultimately proved impotent in their attempts to re-appropriate the phallus. This heterosexual and heteronormative gen-der parody of masculinity leaves the postfeminist man haunted by this spectral presence of the phallus while reinforcing its absence. As I have argued, the postfeminist man is a reconfiguration of the female Gothic heroine – relying on his performance of male gender identity to act as a substitute for the "real thing," he becomes the victim of his own mas-culinity. This heteronormative "subjectivation" sees the postfeminist man victimizing and victimized, acting and acted upon, as his subject position develops into a series of irreconcilable binaries. Male identity is left fragmented and confused as the "repeated stylization of the body" fails to "congeal" (Butler, *Gender Trouble* 33), leaving the "re-membered" postfeminist man struggling to keep a grip on the spectral phallus.

Notes

1. In *Stiffed: The Betrayal of the American Man* (1999), Faludi describes "ornamen-tal culture" as "constructed around ... image, glamour ... and consumerism," resulting in man's "loss of economic authority" (35, 595).
2. For more on the backlash, see Faludi's *Backlash: The Undeclared War against Women* (1992).
3. "Subjectivation" is the Foucauldian term used to describe the construction of the individual subject. Following Foucault, power should be understood not only as repressive but also as *forming* the subject. As he notes: "We should try to grasp subjection in its material instance as a constitution of subjects" (qtd. in Butler, *Psychic Life of Power* 1). In particular, see his *Discipline and Punish*

(1977). Judith Butler also offers an extensive discussion of the term in *The Psychic Life of Power: Theories in Subjection* (1997).
4. For more on the homoerotic tensions in *Fight Club*, see Robert Alan Brookey and Robert Westerfelhaus, "Hiding Homoeroticism in Plain View: The *Fight Club* DVD As Digital Closet" (2002).

Works cited

Brookey, Robert Alan, and Robert Westerfelhaus. "Hiding Homoeroticism in Plain View: The *Fight Club* DVD As Digital Closet." *Critical Studies in Media Communication* 19.1 (2002): 21–43.

Butler, Judith. *Gender Trouble: Feminism and the Subversion of Identity*. London: Routledge, 1990.

———. *Bodies That Matter: On the Discursive Limits of "Sex."* London: Routledge, 1993.

———. *The Psychic Life of Power: Theories in Subjection*. Stanford, CA: Stanford UP, 1997.

Byers, Thomas B. "History Re-Membered: *Forrest Gump*, Postfeminist Masculinity, and the Burial of the Counterculture." *Modern Fiction Studies* 42.2 (1996): 419–44.

Connell, R. W. *Masculinities*. Berkeley: U of California P, 1995.

Coward, Rosalind. *Sacred Cows: Is Feminism Relevant to the New Millennium*. London: HarperCollins, 1999.

Deleuze, Gilles. *Sacher-Masoch: An Interpretation*. Trans. Jean McNeil. London: Faber, 1971.

Ellis, Markman. *The History of Gothic Fiction*. Edinburgh: Edinburgh UP, 2000.

Falling Down. Dir. Joel Schumacher. Perf. Michael Douglas and Robert Duvall. Warner Bros., 1992.

Faludi, Susan. *Backlash: The Undeclared War against Women*. London: Vintage, 1992.

———. *Stiffed: The Betrayal of the American Man*. New York: William Morrow, 1999.

Fight Club. Dir. David Fincher. Perf. Brad Pitt, Edward Norton and Helena Bonham Carter. Twentieth Century Fox, 1999.

Foucault, Michel. *Discipline and Punish: The Birth of the Prison*. London: Penguin, 1977.

Hoeveler, Diane Long. *Gothic Feminism: The Professionalization of Gender from Charlotte Smith to the Brontës*. Liverpool: Liverpool UP, 1998.

Palahniuk, Chuck. *Fight Club*. 1996. London: Vintage, 1997.

5

(Re)Making the Body Beautiful: Postfeminist Cinderellas and Gothic Tales of Transformation

Stéphanie Genz

> There are no ugly women, just lazy ones.
>
> Helena Rubinstein

Gothic Changes

When Victor Frankenstein's creation emerged from his workshop in Ingolstadt to embark on his journey of knowledge and murder, the image of the Gothic monster was born. With his "black lips," "yellow skin," "watery eyes" and "shrivelled complexion," Frankenstein's hideous progeny was not only an aesthetic disappointment to his creator but also a reminder and embodiment of his unlawful and unnatural scientific pursuits (39). A deformed, physical "mess," the Gothic monster has come to represent a figure marked for his strangeness and excess, his difference from the norm-ality of social, cultural, moral, physical, psychological and human mores. He is undoubtedly other, unable ever to "fit in" and doomed to be repudiated and end his life "lost in darkness and distance" (191). The monstrous other has become a staple device of many Gothic novels and films, taking the shape of, for example, Stevenson's Mr Hyde, Wells's Beast People and Count Orlok in *Nosferatu* (1922). His very being, appearance and behaviour establish him as a reverse image of how *normal* people should be, look and act, a negative that turns light into dark, good into bad, self into other. These binaries have come under attack in recent Gothic criticism and writing that highlight the link, rather than the division, within the monstrous dichotomy. This generates a space for ambivalence that positions the monster at the heart of the self, an ambivalence that was already present in Shelley's text and gave

Frankenstein's creature a voice, albeit not a name. The monster becomes the site of what Fred Botting calls a "posthumane" identification; no longer symbols of deviancy and objects of animosity, monstrous figures now invite "sympathy and self-recognition" (286).

This movement towards a more "humane" monster takes a very specific turn in contemporary postfeminist tales of transformation that displace monstrosity onto not only a female body but also a stereotypically feminine one. Frankenstein's misshapen and horrifying offspring is replaced by the immaculately groomed and ultra-feminine protagonists of, to name but a few, *The Life and Loves of a She Devil* (1983, 1986), *Death Becomes Her* (1992), *Faustine* (1995), *The Stepford Wives* (2004), *To the Devil – A Diva* (2004) and *Adventures of the Artificial Woman* (2004). The new postfeminist monster is sexy, pretty, utterly confident in her display of and relentless in her quest for femininity. Importantly, however, her femininity does not turn her into the trapped and pursued "doll heroines" of the Female Gothic plot, nor does it transform her into a dangerously abject sexual predator or a phallic mother (Moers 138). What comes to the fore in postfeminist Gothic is not the monstrous feminine that has been the figure of subversion and excess in H. Rider Haggard's *She* (1887) and Angela Carter's *Nights at the Circus* (1984). Quite the contrary, the postfeminist Gothic monster is neither abject nor excessive, but strangely conventional and, dare I say, trivial. She is more *Pretty Woman* than *Bride of Frankenstein*, more patriarchal billboard than grotesque spectacle. In fact, I want to argue in this essay that postfeminist femininity has become a gendered postmodern monstrosity, not by becoming monstrous and adopting the appearance of otherness but by remaining normative and abiding by established images of womanhood. It is the fitting embodiment of a transgression-weary and desensitized postmodernity in which monstrosity has achieved a quasi-normal status that fails to shock or even stand out. In this process, femininity has been made available for a resignification that questions and undermines its associations with sensibility, chastity, humility and innocence that have been held up in earlier Gothic narratives. Whereas the Female Gothic in particular set out to test bourgeois and domestic femininity without ever severing its relationship to propriety and modesty, postfeminist Gothic engages with a paradoxical contemporary femininity that retains its outer trappings and looks but opens up a new line of signification to make it "monstrous." Its monstrosity lies precisely in its normality and its capacity to harbour new meanings and effect a catachresis that produces a subversive confusion over the feminine construct. It is only by "inhabiting" femininity that the postfeminist

Gothic heroine can go about her monstrous business and achieve a position of power and subjectivity.

The postfeminist Gothic monster performs the same cultural function as her visually other and excessive counterparts as she interacts with and reflects back onto the social structures that produce her. She draws close connections between postmodernity, Gothic, feminism and femininity, asking us to transcend the logic of non-contradiction and accept the inevitability of paradox and ambiguity. Postfeminism and Gothic are thus worthy companions as they both eschew easy categorization and definition. The Gothic remains notoriously difficult to pin down, evoking images of both barbaric freedom and modern order, and postfeminism similarly has been riddled with contradictions and questions regarding its meaning, outlook and position in contemporary society. Simultaneously denounced as a dangerous antifeminist backlash that harks back to a pseudo-Darwinian era of "retro-sexism" and celebrated as a postmodern/poststructuralist feminist stance that destabilizes fixed notions of gender, postfeminism is, as Coppock *et al.* and Projansky note, "a product of assumption" that "can be so many different things" (Coppock *et al.* 4; Projansky 68).[1] The term exhibits a motivational ambiguity and slipperiness whereby it refuses to adopt and be determined by a singular and definite signification. In this respect, Lotz bemoans that "we seem to have entered an alternate language universe where words can simultaneously connote a meaning and its opposite" (105). This firmly situates postfeminism within what Ang calls a postmodern "realm of uncertainty" in which one cannot avoid "living with a heightened sense of permanent and pervasive cultural contradiction" (1). Regardless of how various commentators have (ab)used the term, I maintain that the changeable life of postfeminism does not preclude the possibilities of its use. My point is that rather than trying to immobilize postfeminism in a rigid structure of meaning, we should interpret its polysemy as an integral part of its cultural force. As any attempt to define Gothic might be viewed as futile and even reductive, so postfeminism should not be constrained by a monological designation that impedes or rules out its other meanings and uses.

One of the most prominent sites of contradiction that postfeminism asks us to readdress is the relationship between feminism and femininity that has pervaded both feminist thought and the Female Gothic.[2] In feminist rhetoric from Mary Wollstonecraft in the late eighteenth century to Naomi Wolf in the late twentieth, women's quest for femininity has been associated with powerlessness and suffering.[3] In *The Feminine Mystique* (1963), Betty Friedan coined the term used as the book's title to describe women's unnatural imprisonment in a "comfortable concentration camp" that revolves around the traditional triangle of "Kinder, Küche, Kirche" (children, kitchen, church) (245). Friedan's uncovering of "the problem that has no name" was taken further by radical feminist critics in the 1970s who encouraged women to throw off socially constructed notions of femininity in order to discover the "wild woman" within.[4] This stance relies on an apparently definitive rupture between feminism and femininity, firmly situating the latter in a space of female subjugation and oppression. Femininity is described as a sexualized form of dehumanization, an institutionalized "form of obedience to patriarchy" that is constructed by disciplinary micro-practices of everyday life (Bartky 80). Joanne Hollows has commented on how feminist critiques are often dependent on creating "an opposition between 'bad' feminine identities and 'good' feminist identities" in order to assert a feminist selfhood and subjectivity (9). Accordingly, the adoption of one of these identities can be achieved only at the expense of the other, insofar as any articulation of femininity must inextricably be linked to a lack of feminist credentials. The *femme* is thus dismissed in much feminist writing as a *docile* body on which an inferior status is inscribed and whose energies are habituated to perpetual and exhaustive (self-) policing (Foucault).

The Female Gothic also engages with femininity and theories of female victimization and agency, depicting an innocent and virginal heroine pursued by patriarchal forces of oppression and ultimately triumphing over hardship and entrapment through a stoic adherence to her feminine sensibility and decorum. The Radcliffean romance in particular portrays femininity as a major resource that, under threat, provides the maiden in distress with the necessary stability and integrity to face her opponents. The interpretive possibilities inherent in this reinforcement of what Moers calls "proper English girlhood" have been developed in Gothic criticism that highlights the artificial and manipulative status of femininity in Female Gothic narratives (138). As Diane Long Hoeveler reveals in *Gothic Feminism* (1998), femininity is elevated to a "professional" art and ideology in the Female Gothic, propagating a new form of conduct for women centred around a "cultivated pose, a masquerade of docility, passivity, wise passiveness, and tightly controlled emotions" (xv). The passive–aggressive stance of pretended weakness allows the female characters and readers to gain "a fictitious mastery" over oppressive social and political regimes (xii). This amounts to "gothic feminism," a version of "victim feminism" described by Naomi Wolf in *Fire with Fire* (1993) as a "severe" and "self-denying" tendency in second-wave feminism to seek power through an identity of powerlessness (181).[5] The "gothic feminist" (or the professionally

LIVERPOOL JOHN MOORES UNIVERSITY
LEARNING SERVICES

feminine woman) offers the "appearance of compliance" while covertly seeking subversion, hence her "double character" (193).

Although the notion of "gothic feminism" begins to depolarize the long-standing dichotomy between feminism and femininity and to introduce some potential for feminine agency, it is still tied to a relatively static definition of femininity as passivity, weakness and acquiescence. Even though femininity might be consciously employed to achieve a position of strength and (material) power, it remains a given or constant in the Female Gothic, unchanging in its relationship to propriety and morality. In this essay, I propose that postfeminist Gothic goes beyond the Female Gothic in this respect as it destabilizes and "unmoors" the feminine construct itself, turning femininity into a space of resignifica-tion, of meaning in question. Postfeminist femininity is engaged in a process of what Judith Butler terms "reterritorialization" or "expropria-tion for non-ordinary means" that causes a citational slippage in the chain of feminine meanings (*Bodies That Matter* 231; *Psychic Life* 160). Butler's work is important for my understanding of both femininity and postfeminism as a whole as it emphasizes that "signification is not a founding act" but an enabling "site of contest and revision," character-ized by "strategic provisionality" rather than "strategic essentialism" (*Gender Trouble* 145; "Imitation and Gender Insubordination" 312). The Butlerian framework relies on a notion of reiterability, "a regulated process of repetition" that opens up the construction of meaning and creates the possibility of reconfiguration and redeployment (*Gender Trouble* 145). The reiterative nature of signification allows for postfemi-nism's multiple interpretations and plasticity that, in turn, make feasible a new understanding of femininity that loosens and undermines its associations with female victimization.

The most prominent example of this "reterritorialized" feminine subject position is undoubtedly the 1990s phenomenon of Girl Power, which reclaims once disparaged elements of femininity and resignifies them in feminist and emancipatory terms. Girlies insist that feminism and femininity are not mutually exclusive but can be combined in a new, improved blend (Baumgardner and Richards 137). They are adamant that they do not have to sacrifice "pick-packaged femininity" – the symbols of feminine enculturation (Barbie dolls and make-up) – but can reconstruct them as confident expressions of choice and self-differentiation (137). The defining factor in this resignification of femininity appears to be a feminist awareness that creates a signifying gap between image and identity, providing Girlies with the knowledge and capacity to "make girl stuff work for us" (136). Although I doubt that this is the emergence of a reliable and sound twenty-first-century politics of femininity, what one might call "femmenism," the Girlie stance does much to displace the essentialist and simplistic identification of femininity as unequivocally repressive and passive.[6] I prefer to describe this stance as a *pink power*, an intrinsically contradictory feminine subject position that does not reverse the victimization/agency diametric but increasingly obscures their differences.[7] In this respect, pink power is reminiscent of the paradox of subject formation delineated by Foucault in *Discipline and Punish* (1977) and later discussed by Judith Butler as a "subjectivation" (a translation from the French *assujetissement*). The term "subjectivation" itself carries a paradox as it denotes "both the becoming of the subject and the process of subjection – one inhabits the figure of autonomy only by becoming subjected to a power, a subjection which implies a radical dependency" (*Psychic Life* 83). This dialectic of subject formation describes the subject instituted through constraint whereby subjection is understood not only as subordination but also as "a securing and maintaining, a putting into place of a subject, a subjectivation" (90–1).

The postfeminist *femme* is not unlike Foucault's prisoner insofar as she is "subjectivated" through her body, simultaneously submitted to extensive rituals of normalization as well as "activated" or formed by them (84). Susan Hekman describes this state as an explosion of the dichotomy between the *constituting* subject of enlightened modernity and the *constituted* self of constructivist postmodernity (47). This polarization itself is the product of a modernist, subject-centred epistemology that relies on an oppositional, hierarchical structure to define the constituting self as autonomous and omnipotent and its constituted counterpart as wholly determined. The postfeminist subject breaks down these distinctions, adopting femininity as a liberating determinism that confines as well as creates, oppresses as well as relieves. To borrow Ien Ang's phrase, she is "free and yet bounded," inhabiting a contradictory space that is both constraining and emancipating (165).

What connects this postfeminist site with a specifically Gothic sensibility is the undeniable presence of a "haunting," a ghost of the past that continues to shadow the present and threatens to re-emerge. As David Punter reminds us, "the code of Gothic is ... not a simple one in which past is encoded in present or vice versa, but dialectical, past and present intertwined, and distorting ... each other with the sheer effort of coming to grips" (198). In postfeminist Gothic, the resignifications of femininity cannot rid themselves of the threat of phallocentricity, the spectre of heterosexism, as they still function within the same cultural imagery that transfers onto women the labels of inferiority and powerlessness.

The reterritorialization of femininity is not achieved by a flight from materiality and embodiment (such as in depictions of cyber-femininity) or by a "push to excess" of femininity that deconstructs into its opposite.[8] On the contrary, the female body is re-immersed in traditional gender formations and arrangements that continue to exert their power of signification over the feminine construct. This contradiction is inherent in the whole process of resignification that does not effect a radical "break with context" but instead brings forth "spectres" or echoes of the past that continue to haunt the new meaning (Butler, *Excitable Speech* 145).[9] The internal echo acts as an uncanny remainder, a Gothic presence that disrupts any sense of monosemy and uniformity. In this respect, postfeminism can undoubtedly be said to have a Gothic potential, torn as it is between backlash and innovation, female victimization and agency.[10] The new critical category of "postfeminist Gothic" engages with this spectral space in-between, making visible and materializing the ghosts of previous meanings. Oscillating between subject and object, victim and perpetrator, the postfeminist Gothic monster is the embodiment of these battles of signification, a site of meaning in question.

Postfeminist Gothic bodies

"To inhabit a woman's body is to be a gothic heroine," Donna Heiland notes in *Gothic and Gender* (2004), emphasizing that the female body has historically been seen as a means of entrapment that ties the protagonist to the limited role of a powerless and suffering *femme* (158). The only hope for women and way out of this Gothic prison were deemed to be an escape, denial and reinvention of the body.[11] The postfeminist Gothic heroine inverts this schema and turns it upside down by consciously and purposefully seeking a re-entrapment in feminine materiality. Born into or confined to a state of otherness and unfemininity, she employs every resource at her disposal to re-join the women's club and take up her place in the hierarchy of feminine appearance.[12] In this case, femininity is an actively pursued subject position that becomes available for a potentially subversive resignification that reinterprets the female body as an emblem of agency and empowerment. At the same time, femininity also gains darker, monstrous connotations by shedding its associations with modesty, chastity and innocence (held up in the Female Gothic) and instead becoming linked to unnatural and devilish pursuits and desires. What we are presented with are in effect "Gothicized" Cinderella stories that offer contradictory understandings of femininity as a means of both patriarchal enslavement and feminist emancipation.

These stories depict femininity's two-sidedness by reclaiming the female body as an ideological battlefield, a locus of ongoing controversy. In her act of bodily remoulding, the postfeminist Gothic Cinderella is victim and perpetrator, subject and object in one. Refusing to be branded as a freak, she attempts to cross into the realm of femininity by transforming her body, which is either too old, too big or generally too anomalous. In this sense, femininity works to bring the woman-as-subject into existence, simultaneously recreating her as a patriarchally determined object. I want to examine this paradox of femininity by focusing on what some might consider a relatively early representation of the category I have described as "postfeminist Gothic," Fay Weldon's *The Life and Loves of a She Devil* (1983), which was made into a television mini-series in 1986 and, more famously but less true to the book, the Hollywood film *She-Devil* (1989).[13]

Fay Weldon's satire focuses on the struggles and triumphs of a Cinderella persona who undergoes extensive cosmetic surgery in order to reinvent herself as a diabolically feminine subject bent on revenge against her unfaithful husband. Weldon's novel leaves the reader with several puzzles as, on the one hand, it is a feminist critique of female oppression and unequal power relations between the sexes, yet, on the other, it is a tale with a surprising twist as the female protagonist uses and resignifies her feminine position to regain control over her life and achieve self-determination. Weldon's text offers a scathing portrayal of feminine beauty norms that encourage women to alter their bodies and submit themselves to the excruciating pain and staggering expense of cosmetic surgery, without reducing the female subject to the position of a deluded victim and cultural dupe. The novelist repudiates monolithic notions of the docile female, trapped by the constraints of beauty regimes and blinded by social forces beyond her comprehension, in favour of a complex vision of a knowledgeable agent who assesses her situation and chooses to act. Weldon examines the postfeminist paradox and tensions between empowerment and disempowerment, subjectivity and objectification, deliberately refusing to endorse an either/or logic that relies on diametrically opposed stereotypes of the liberated feminist and the subordinated *femme*. Instead, the Cinderella/she-devil figure is positioned between these two poles, displaying a strong will and agency while employing this "feminist" energy to embody a highly restrictive norm of feminine appearance.

In particular, the heroine's body is surgically remoulded to mirror the physical image of her arch-rival, Mary Fisher, a successful writer of popular romances and her husband's lover. Weldon depicts the journey of her protagonist Ruth in several stages, from being a social freak, to becoming an entrepreneur and the epitome of a feminist success story, to finally transforming herself into a "blonde, simpering doll on stilts" (241). Importantly, the author does not represent Ruth's feminist and feminine achievements as irreconcilable or conflicting, and she undermines dualistic frameworks that do not allow for interpretive open-endedness and contradiction. Weldon criticizes simplistic and monological ideologies of appropriate female behaviour, and her heroine's metamorphosis can be understood as a combination of a feminist desire for autonomy with a patriarchally enforced urge to be beautiful and seductive. It is precisely at this "point of discomfort," this frontier between feminist and patriarchal discourses, that "Weldon shows how ambivalences can be embraced rather than dismissed or avoided" (Davis 67).

Weldon draws attention to and reworks a number of fairy tales and romance stories in order to deflate the notion of ideality that underlies patriarchal myths of feminine beauty. Ruth can be identified as a born Cinderella with a neglectful mother and favoured half-sisters (13). At the beginning of the novel, she is confined to the realm of sexual and physical unattractiveness: being six feet two inches tall, overweight and clumsy, Ruth is "fixed here and now, trapped in [her] body" (9). Her bodily extraordinariness marks her as a social outcast, a "dog," so far removed from the norms of desirability that she cannot aspire to approximate the cultural beauty ideal through the everyday maintenance work of femininity (12). Make-up and dieting will not be sufficient to transform her differences into sameness and to achieve her overall goal "to be like other women" and like Mary Fisher in particular (234). In fairy-tale terms, Ruth can be compared to the ugly stepsister who is determined to take over Cinderella's role, even to the extent of cutting off parts of herself to make the glass slipper fit. Devoid of supernatural guidance and help, she cannot hope for an instant and painless metamorphosis but has to become her own fairy godmother, employing the modern magic of cosmetic surgery and spending years and millions to change her appearance. Ruth has an even better blueprint for her eventual condition as she repeatedly invokes Hans Christian Anderson's little mermaid, who acquired legs instead of a tail and, with every step, felt that she was stepping on knives (254).

Ruth's journey also incorporates a popular romance formula, as the protagonist's progress can be interpreted as a quest to regain the love of Prince Charming, her husband Bobbo. However, in Weldon's version, the state of desperation, loss and separation that the heroine undergoes before being reunited with her beloved is situated after the traditional happy ending, marriage. Furthermore, Bobbo is far from being a stereotypical romance hero, since he is not only selfish, childish and irresponsible but also outwardly silly, his name supposedly being an intentional pun on the Spanish word meaning "stupid." In this way, Weldon provides the reader with the rough outline or silhouette of a Cinderella story and a romance happy ending as, after all, the ugly duckling turns into a swan and the princess is reunited with her prince, but she removes the elements of ideal love and magic from her novel. Ruth ostensibly follows in Cinderella's footsteps and achieves the same goals through the same means, but her victory has come at a high price, years of torture and millions of pounds, and it is also no longer axiomatic that the prince is worth fighting and suffering for. Weldon's reworking of the romance and fairy-tale scenario exposes the artificiality of these myths and represents a critique from within the norm (Hutcheon).

The novel also subverts feminist ideals of female comportment according to which women have to opt out of the patriarchal beauty contest. Initially, after Bobbo abandons her for Mary Fisher, Ruth appears to comply with the feminist call for political rejection of femininity as she sheds her dependent and passive nature and divests herself of all her motherly and wifely obligations by giving away her children and framing her husband to get him imprisoned. Moreover, she enters into a lesbian relationship with Nurse Hopkins, builds up a flourishing employment agency and even finds refuge in a separatist feminist commune. In Mary Daly's terms, Ruth can be discussed as a "natural witch" or a "wild woman" who privileges "real" femaleness over "false" femininity. Weldon uses a similar image to describe Ruth's psychological change into a she-devil who rejects patriarchal laws and conventions. As Ruth notes, instantly, "there is no shame, no guilt, no dreary striving to be good. There is only, in the end, what you want. And I can take what I want. I am a she devil" (49).

Ruth's personal and professional success takes place while she is still visually represented by her unfeminine body, and, in some ways, her final transformation into a plastic construct of femininity and "the show-girl type" seems redundant and contradictory (241). The protagonist's physical metamorphosis into "an insult to womanhood" has been interpreted as a denial and sabotage of her she-devil persona, and numerous commentators have criticized it as a "violent derailing of our expectations" and a "Sadean assault" on our beliefs (Weldon 239; Wilde 406, 414). The critics' objections relate to the fact that Ruth's evolution into an economically independent and supposedly disenthralled feminist role model does not engender a "raised" consciousness that might lead to the espousal of a political perspective and the rejection of beauty norms. Ruth's adventures in the world of the working woman and her various sexual encounters do not bring about a feminist liberation or a political viewpoint. Tellingly, the "Wimmin's commune" that Ruth temporarily joins ultimately seems "too denim-coloured and serviceable," lacking "glitter at the edges" (213).

Weldon refuses to locate her protagonist's diabolical conversion within the larger framework of an organized feminist struggle for collective liberation and emancipation. She problematizes Ruth's satanic change from the outset by depicting it as a matter of obedience to her husband rather than a self-willed feminist awakening. One could argue that Bobbo initiates his wife's black baptism by continually and strategically renouncing her feminine identity. Throughout their marriage, he denies Ruth access to "that other erotic world, of choice and desire and lust" in which women can have "power over the hearts and pockets of men" (28). Bobbo considers his wife to be "essentially unlovable" and reduces her self to her unshapely body, revealing that "he had married *it* perforce and in error and would do his essential duties by *it* but he would never be reconciled to *its* enormity, and Ruth knew it" (46, 37; my emphasis). Confined by her physical shape and the ensuing social position, Ruth is driven by a desire to fit in or "pass," if not as the epitome of beauty, then at least as a good housewife and mother. Yet these remaining pillars of traditional femininity are taken away from her in the course of her redefinition as a she-devil. According to Bobbo, Ruth is a "third-rate person," "a bad mother," "a worse wife" and "a dreadful cook" (47). Furthermore, he declares that "I don't think you are a woman at all. I think what you are is a she devil" (47). Ruth unquestioningly accepts this new identity as proof of Bobbo's superior knowledge, noting that "since he does so well in the world and I do so badly, I really must assume that he is right. I am a she devil" (49).

The novel eschews predetermined and monolithic conceptualizations of femaleness, feminism and femininity and, instead, puts forward an unresolved stance that favours ambiguity and contradiction. Weldon rejects the assumption that inside every woman, there is an authentic female or rather feminist self who is unconstrained by the pressures of the beauty system.[14] She refuses to portray Ruth as a feminist failure who is unable to find the "real me," the autonomous feminist subject who is positioned outside cultural restrictions. Acknowledging that "this is a slightly frivolous novel," Weldon sets out to undermine a pre-packaged feminist agenda that takes a uniformly negative view of beauty practices and cosmetic surgery (qtd. in Kenyon 123). Instead, she makes room for a more ambivalent interpretation that does not rob the feminine subject of her agency and determination but considers the paradoxical possibility whereby she is simultaneously a victim of the discourse of femininity and one of its most devastating critics.

Accordingly, we have to take into account Ruth's power and agency in her cultural signification and in the material reproduction of beauty ideals. The protagonist takes an active part in her Cinderella transformation as she becomes the driving force behind her self-correction and feminization. She is the agent who negotiates her body, using its cultural constructedness to re-inscribe the bodily text with her chosen writing. As her disheartened surgeon Mr Ghengis points out, "he was her Pygmalion, but she would not depend upon him, or admire him or be grateful" (230). Ruth employs cosmetic surgery as a source of empowerment, denying her doctors the position of godlike creators and, in Victor Frankenstein fashion, demanding this role for herself. Being completely in charge of her "extensive renovation," she is both monster and Frankenstein, creature and creator, at the same time (234). As she proclaims:

> Anyone can do anything ... if they have the will and they have the money. ... We are here in this world to improve upon [God's] original idea. To create justice, truth and beauty where He so obviously and lamentably failed. ... I will be what I want, not what He ordained. I will mould a new image for myself out of the earth of my creation. I will defy my Maker, and remake myself. (124, 170)

Ruth's reconstructive endeavour is conceived within particularly narrow parameters of femininity, as her perception of the imaginary feminine ideal takes the specific shape of Bobbo's lover, Mary Fisher, or rather the publicity image featured on the dust jacket of her romantic books. By selecting the conventional prettiness of Mary Fisher as her ultimate goal, Ruth reveals her involvement in and collusion with the stereotypes of feminine beauty and she contributes to the perpetuation of these bodily restrictions. She recreates herself as Mary's clone, a repetition of the fantasy image that the writer presents to the world.[15] Living in the High Tower far removed from the realities and injustices of the world, Ruth's nemesis is not a flesh-and-blood being but a symbolic construct, the personification of her own mass-produced, fictional heroines. The cosmetic surgeon Mr Ghengis objects to his patient's self-reduction and transformation into a caricature, the "feeble" and "absurd" incarnation of "the balding businessman's dream" (241, 249). Ruth's transformation into this artifice enables her to enter the erotic world from which she has been excluded and to fulfil her aspirations "to take everything and return nothing," "to be loved and not love in return" (29, 49). Once Ruth becomes the object of Bobbo's sexual desires, the sado-masochistic power relations between them are reversed. As she proclaims her *Schadenfreude*: "I have all and he has none. As I was, so he is now. ... Somehow it is not a matter of male and female, after all; it never was, merely of power" (256).

Ruth's erasure and re-inscription of her bodily material can be discussed as an act of gender parody, undermining the idea of an essential female or feminine identity.[16] Her metamorphosis emphasizes the possibility of "putting on" femininity, suggesting that it is also possible to remove it. She seizes the mask of womanhood from Mary Fisher and, in so doing, exposes its inauthenticity and artificiality. As Mr Ghengis declares, "there is no such thing as the essential self," "it is all inessential, and all liable to change and flux" (234, 235). Yet Weldon refuses to advance a straightforward espousal of parodic gender performances or present her protagonist as a consciously masquerading critic of Western beauty culture. Ruth notes that her "exceptionally adaptable personality" is not moulded by critical and/or political aspirations but by a desire for conformity and integration:

> I have tried many ways of fitting myself to my original body, and the world into which I was born, and have failed. I am no revolutionary. Since I cannot change them, I will change myself. I am quite sure I will settle happily enough into my new body. (217)

Ruth knows the rules of the game and she will play by them, following Mrs Black's advice that "if you can't beat them, join them" (239). Paradoxically, her agency and transformational powers are generated by the same ideological framework that defines and constrains her social position. Eluding a binary logic, she is neither an innocent victim paralysed by her structural confines nor the triumphant creator of a more authentic self, a volitional subject who adopts and elects a new identity at will. Catching her reader off guard using a literary ploy, "a comic turn, turned serious," Weldon examines the contradictory and multivalent aspects of female embodiment that are skipped over in monolithic discourses of feminism and femininity (256). The novelist puts forward both the reactionary and subversive potential of beauty practices, without privileging or committing herself to one side of the dualism. She portrays the complex intermingling of resistance and subordination as she explores the dilemmatic situation of a "free-yet-bounded" female subject who is simultaneously oppressed and liberated. Weldon's diabolical Cinderella is caught between old and new versions of femininity, inhabiting a space of haunted meanings, the spectral site that is "postfeminist Gothic."

Notes

1. For more on the different versions of postfeminism, see Susan Faludi's *Backlash: The Undeclared War against Women* (1992), Imelda Whelehan's *Overloaded: Popular Culture and the Future of Feminism* (2000) and Ann Brooks's *Postfeminisms: Feminism, Cultural Theory and Cultural Forms* (1997).
2. The links between feminism and the Female Gothic have been noted by a number of commentators. While the writers of Female Gothic narratives were influenced by early feminist voices in the late eighteenth century (the matrilineal connection between Mary Wollstonecraft and Mary Shelley being the most prominent example), its theorization in the late 1960s and 1970s can be related to the women's liberation movement and its task of raising women's consciousness about their subjugated status in society. See Ellen Moers's *Literary Women* (1976) for more on the connection between feminism and the Female Gothic.
3. In particular, see *A Vindication of the Rights of Woman* (1792) 113, and *The Beauty Myth* (1991) 10.
4. See Mary Daly's *Gyn/Ecology* (1979), Kate Millett's *Sexual Politics* (1970) and Shulamith Firestone's *The Dialectic of Sex* (1972) for examples of this radical feminist stance. Daly's account is particularly noteworthy as she distinguishes between "real" females whom she approvingly describes as "witches, nags and hags" and "plastic," "mutant," "painted birds." Daly exhorts her readers to reject conventional femininity in order to free the hag within and become a "wild woman."
5. Also see Rene Denfeld's *The New Victorians: A Young Woman's Challenge to the Old Feminist Order* (1995) for another description of this victim mythology.
6. Jeannine Delombard uses the term "femmenism" to describe a femininity politics that uses the signs and accoutrements of femininity to forge a political theory. In an ironic reversal of Audre Lorde's famous *bon mot*, Delombard explains that "femmenism is using the master's tools to dismantle the master's house" (22).
7. For more on *pink power*, see my forthcoming *Postfemininities in Popular Culture* (Palgrave 2008).
8. Susan Bordo discusses feminine excess in relation to anorexia, which, she argues, allows the female sufferer to "unexpectedly discover an entry into the privileged male world. ... At this point of excess, the conventionally feminine deconstructs ... into its opposite and opens onto those values our culture has coded as male" (179).
9. In this sense, one can compare the practice of resignification to the trope of recycling that incorporates the old into the new, preserving what it seeks to superimpose.
10. Gothic harbours a similar paradox with regard to women's status and position: whereas, on the one hand, Gothic novels expose a form of patriarchy

that "celebrates a male creative power that demands the suppression – and sometimes the outright sacrifice – of women," on the other hand, Gothic has also been described as a "myth" that "insist[s] upon female equality" and defines women as "partners and equals" in their relationships with men (Heiland 11; Miles 42).

11. This escape can be achieved in a variety of ways: either by a rejection of femininity in favour of masculine values and behaviour (as exemplified by some of the foundational texts of the second wave, most notably Betty Friedan's *The Feminine Mystique* [1963] and Germaine Greer's *The Female Eunuch* [1971]), or by Hoeveler's "gothic feminism" that "seeks to escape the female body through a dream of turning weakness into strength" (182).

12. In this respect, the postfeminist Gothic heroine resembles the overreacher of the Male Gothic plot who defies the rules of society and nature, symbolized in the archetypal Faust story by a pact with the Devil.

13. One notable difference between Susan Seidelman's Hollywood version and Fay Weldon's novel is that Ruth (played by a frumpy and mole-ridden Roseanne Barr) is not transformed into Meryl Streep's "pretty-in-pink" beauty but undergoes a prettification herself. As Susanne Becker has noted, this "feminist-heroic ending" denies the book's Gothic elements (191).

14. Noting in an interview that "I don't feel imprisoned by feminism" (qtd. in Kenyon 120), Weldon defends her protagonist's actions and her recourse to cosmetic surgery: "I'm glad she did it. I'm on Ruth's side though I get a lot of tuttutting from the right-minded readers. Irresponsible. Dangerous. Ruth should have done what she ought, faced up to things, not what she wanted. ... But that's always said of women, isn't it" (qtd. in Newman 199).

15. In fact, Ruth and Mary Fisher can be discussed as complementary figures who are set up as exact opposites and change place, character and face in the course of the narrative. Ruth's psychological and bodily metamorphoses are mirrored by the trajectory of her double as the more power the cheated wife gains by getting rid of her traditional feminine obligations, the more "real" her opponent becomes. Mary Fisher loses her idealized status as "the material world surges in" and she is forced to turn into a suburban housewife, becoming a mother to Ruth's children, a daughter caring for her senile mother and, ultimately, a betrayed wife to Bobbo (109). On a more physical level, there is a similar exchange as Ruth's beautification is diametrically opposed to and countered by Mary's bodily deterioration, which results in a painful death caused by cancer, the degenerative complement to Ruth's reconstruction.

16. For more on gender parody, see Judith Butler's *Gender Trouble* (1990). Also see Joan Riviere's 1929 essay "Womanliness As a Masquerade" and Mary Ann Doane's *Femmes Fatales: Feminism, Film Theory, Psychoanalysis* (1991) and "Film and the Masquerade: Theorizing the Female Spectator" for more on the concept of the masquerade.

Works cited

Ang, Ien. *Living Room Wars: Rethinking Media Audiences for a Postmodern World.* London: Routledge, 1996.

Bartky, Sandra Lee. *Femininity and Domination: Studies in the Phenomenology of Oppression.* London: Routledge, 1990.

Baumgardner, Jennifer, and Amy Richards. *Manifesta: Young Women, Feminism, and the Future*. New York: Farrar, Straus, and Giroux, 2000.

Becker, Susanne. *Gothic Forms of Feminine Fictions*. Manchester: Manchester UP, 1999.

Berger, Thomas. *Adventures of the Artificial Woman*. New York: Simon & Schuster, 2004.

Bordo, Susan. *Unbearable Weight: Feminism, Western Culture and the Body*. Berkeley: U of California P, 1993.

Botting, Fred. "Aftergothic: Consumption, Machines, and Black Holes." *The Cambridge Companion to Gothic Fiction*. Ed. Jerrold E. Hogle. Cambridge: Cambridge UP, 2002. 277–300.

Brooks, Ann. *Postfeminisms: Feminism, Cultural Theory and Cultural Forms*. London: Routledge, 1997.

Butler, Judith. *Gender Trouble: Feminism and the Subversion of Identity*. London: Routledge, 1990.

——. *Bodies That Matter: On the Discursive Limits of "Sex."* London: Routledge, 1993.

——. "Imitation and Gender Insubordination." *The Lesbian and Gay Studies Reader*. Ed. H. Abelove, M. A. Barale and D. M. Halperin. London: Routledge, 1993. 307–20.

——. *Excitable Speech: A Politics of the Performative*. London: Routledge, 1997.

——. *The Psychic Life of Power: Theories in Subjection*. Stanford, CA: Stanford UP, 1997.

Coppock, Vicki, Deena Haydon and Ingrid Richter. *The Illusions of "Post-Feminism" New Women, Old Myths*. London: Taylor & Francis, 1995.

Davis, Kathy. *Reshaping the Female Body: The Dilemma of Cosmetic Surgery*. London: Routledge, 1995.

Death Becomes Her. Dir. Robert Zemeckis. Perf. Goldie Hawn, Meryl Streep and Bruce Willis. Universal, 1992.

Delombard, Jeannine. "Femmenism." *To Be Real: Telling the Truth and Changing the Face of Feminism*. Ed. Rebecca Walker. London: Anchor Books, 1995. 21–33.

Denfeld, Rene. *The New Victorians: A Young Woman's Challenge to the Old Feminist Order*. New York: Warner Books, 1995.

Doane, Mary Ann. *Femmes Fatales: Feminism, Film Theory, Psychoanalysis*. London: Routledge, 1991.

——. "Film and the Masquerade: Theorizing the Female Spectator." *The Sexual Subject: A Screen Reader in Sexuality*. London: Routledge, 1992. 227–43.

Faludi, Susan. *Backlash: The Undeclared War against Women*. London: Vintage, 1992.

Foucault, Michel. *Discipline and Punish: The Birth of the Prison*. London: Penguin, 1977.

Friedan, Betty. *The Feminine Mystique*. 1963. London: Penguin, 1992.

Heiland, Donna. *Gothic and Gender: An Introduction*. Oxford: Blackwell, 2004.

Hekman, Susan. "Reconstituting the Subject: Feminism, Modernism and Postmodernism." *Hypatia* 6.2 (1991): 44–63.

Hoeveler, Diane Long. *Gothic Feminism: The Professionalization of Gender from Charlotte Smith to the Brontës*. Liverpool: Liverpool UP, 1998.

Hollows, Joanne. *Feminism, Femininity and Popular Culture*. Manchester: Manchester UP, 2000.

Hutcheon, Linda. *The Politics of Postmodernism*. London: Routledge, 1989.

Kenyon, Olga. *Women Novelists Today: A Survey of English Writing in the Seventies and Eighties*. Brighton: The Harvester Press, 1988.

Lotz, Amanda D. "Postfeminist Television Criticism: Rehabilitating Critical Terms and Identifying Postfeminist Attributes." *Feminist Media Studies* 1.1 (2001): 105–21.

Magrs, Paul. *To the Devil – A Diva*. London: Allison & Busby, 2004.

Miles, Robert. *Ann Radcliffe: The Great Enchantress*. Manchester: Manchester UP, 1995.

Moers, Ellen. *Literary Women*. 1963. London: The Women's Press, 1978.

Newman, Jenny. " 'See Me As Sisyphus, but Having a Good Time': The Fiction of Fay Weldon." *Contemporary British Women Writers: Texts and Strategies*. Ed. R. E. Hosmer. Basingstoke: Macmillan, 1993. 188–211.

Projansky, Sarah. *Watching Rape: Film and Television in Postfeminist Culture*. New York: New York UP, 2001.

Punter, David. *The Literature of Terror: A History of Gothic Fictions from 1765 to the Present Day. The Modern Gothic*. 2nd edn. Harlow, England: Longman, 1996.

Riviere, Joan. "Womanliness As a Masquerade." 1929. *Formations of Fantasy*. Ed. Victor Burgin, James Donald and Cora Kaplan. London: Methuen, 1986. 35–44.

She Devil. Dir. Susan Seidelman. Perf. Meryl Streep, Roseanne Barr and Ed Begley Jr. Orion, 1989.

Shelley, Mary. *Frankenstein or The Modern Prometheus*. 1818. Oxford: Oxford UP, 1998.

Tennant, Emma. *Travesties: The Bad Sister, Two Women of London, Faustine*. London: Faber and Faber, 1995.

The Life and Loves of a She-Devil. By Fay Weldon. Dir. Philip Saville. Perf. Julie T. Wallace, Patricia Hodge and Dennis Waterman. BBC. 8–29 October 1986.

The Stepford Wives. Dir. Frank Oz. Perf. Nicole Kidman, Matthew Broderick, Bette Midler, Christopher Walken and Glenn Close. DreamWorks, 2004.

Weldon, Fay. *The Life and Loves of a She Devil*. London: Sceptre, 1983.

Whelehan, Imelda. *Overloaded: Popular Culture and the Future of Feminism*. London: The Women's Press, 2000.

Wilde, Alan. " 'Bold, but Not Too Bold': Fay Weldon and the Limits of Poststructuralist Criticism." *Contemporary Literature* 29.3 (1988): 403–19.

Wolf, Naomi. *The Beauty Myth: How Images of Beauty Are Used Against Women*. London: Vintage, 1991.

——. *Fire with Fire: The New Female Power and How It Will Change the 21st Century*. New York: Random House, 1993.

Wollstonecraft, Mary. *A Vindication of the Rights of Woman*. 1792. *The Works of Mary Wollstonecraft*. Ed. J. Todd and M. Butler. 5 vols. London: Pickering and Chatto, 1958.

6

The Stepford Wives: What's a Living Doll to Do in a Postfeminist World?

Anne Williams

Since the publication of Ira Levin's novel *The Stepford Wives* (1973), his title has become proverbial in popular culture. One need not have read the book or seen the films to know that a Stepford Wife is a woman enslaved to a patriarchal definition of femininity, a wife who has no life, a wife who is almost literally an automaton. Levin's novel, like its predecessor *Rosemary's Baby* (1967), was an immediate best-seller. Like *Rosemary's Baby*, which was followed by Roman Polanski's spectacularly ominous film in 1968, this later novel was quickly made into a film. The first *Stepford Wives* movie (1975) did not match Polanski's masterpiece of urban Gothic, but it attained something of a cult status among horror-movie fans. It was recently re-released on DVD in a "Silver Anniversary Edition" that includes interviews with the director, Bryan Forbes, and several cast members, including Katherine Ross, who played the heroine Joanna, and Paula Prentiss, her best friend Bobby.

Frank Oz's *Stepford Wives* of 2004 was an expensive production with a high-profile cast, including Nicole Kidman, Matthew Broderick, Bette Midler, Glenn Close, Faith Hill and Christopher Walken. It was not, however, particularly successful with film critics. Many remakes fail to surpass their originals, of course, but it is quite clear from comments included on the DVD that the director and the screenwriter, Paul Rudnick, were *not* trying to reproduce the original in the usual way: that is, to remake it with up-to-the-minute special effects and more lavish production values. Both writer and director understood that the early versions of *The Stepford Wives* expressed the sexual politics of the early 1970s, the moment when "Women's Liberation" was becoming "second-wave feminism." Oz and Rudnick both recognized that that moment had passed. As a result, in the second film suburban Gothic mutated into a campy comedy. This mutation, I argue, offers unexpected insights into the changing faces of the Gothic and feminism.

I

In 1975 critics of *The Stepford Wives* film recognized that this faithful version of Levin's novel was concerned with feminism, but they disagreed about just what it was saying. From comments on the recent DVD release, we learn that the director, Bryan Forbes, intended to satirize the Stepford husbands, who were willing to murder their wives in order to transform them into robots performing a nostalgic, overtly Victorian notion of proper femininity. The word "archaic" (and presumably the concept) was not programmed into the robotic wives. Indeed, in the patriarchal paradise of Stepford, Connecticut, each man acquired his own mechanical "Angel in the House."

The plot of both novel and 1975 film would seem to support Forbes's interpretation. Walter and Joanna Eberhart, a couple with two young daughters, flee grimy Manhattan for the bucolic pleasures of suburban Connecticut. Walter is a highly successful lawyer and Joanna an aspiring photographer. In the time-honoured Gothic tradition, however, she begins to detect troubling signs of something sinister beneath the village calm. When Joanna takes the family dog for a walk one evening, she wanders into the grounds of the Men's Association and is warned away by the security guard, who tells her that they have painstakingly restored this imposing Victorian mansion. Meanwhile, she makes friends with Bobby, another woman new to Stepford, and even more of a free spirit than she. Both are surprised by the village housewives' placid domesticity. None of them seems to have interests beyond polishing floors, and they spend so much time and energy housekeeping that they refuse to participate in the consciousness-raising group Joanna and Bobby are trying to organize. When even Bobby is transformed into a domestic robot, however, Joanna realizes the town's terrible secret: the Stepford husbands are killing their wives and replacing them with machines. And it is too late for her, as well. As she tries to escape, her husband tells her that her children are being held in that Victorian mansion. Brave heroine that she is, Joanna enters the house to rescue them. There she is strangled with a stocking by "her" robot in a room decorated exactly like her own marital bedroom. In the last scene, we see "Joanna" and all the other wives dressed in flowery chintz frocks and garden-party hats, gliding vacantly through the supermarket.

As Elyce Rae Helford and Anna Krugovoy Silver have shown, the first versions of *The Stepford Wives* were rooted in the ideas of second-wave feminism. Just as Levin's story encodes feminist arguments about the subjection of women in contemporary American patriarchy, it also satirizes the emerging male backlash against feminists and feminism, expressing masculine nostalgia for the good old days when men were men and women were what men decreed they should be.

Surprisingly, however, the 1975 film evoked hostility from two viewers who might have been expected to be sympathetic: Betty Friedan and Pauline Kael. Friedan's *The Feminine Mystique* (1963) had delineated the pain that a wholly domestic existence caused middle-class suburban women, but she walked out of a screening arranged by several feminist writers. "I think we should all leave here. I don't think we should help publicize this movie. It's a rip-off of the women's movement" (Silver 111). *The New Yorker's* Pauline Kael, then the premier film critic in the United States, who often delighted in pop-culture genre movies, bitterly attacked this one as gratuitous male-bashing:

> If women turn into replicas of the women in commercials, they do it to themselves. ... if they go that way, they're the ones letting it happen. And as long as they can blame the barrenness of their lives on men, they don't need to change. They can play at being victims instead, and they can do it in the guise of liberation. (112)

Her diatribe concludes:

> I dislike "The Stepford Wives" for reasons that go beyond its being a cruddy movie: I dislike it for the condescension implicit in its view that educated American women are not responsible for what they become. Women, the abused, are being treated like the innocent potheads of the late sixties – as a suffering privileged class. This sentimentality is degrading. (113)

Kael also dismisses the film as a "sci-fi cheapo" (112). It may be "a cheapo," but is it really sci-fi? Though Levin's plot hinges on some sophisticated technology, its deepest generic affinity is with the Gothic, and reading *The Stepford Wives* as such also reveals the source of Friedan's and Kael's discomfort with the story. Acknowledging the novel and first film's Gothic identity also suggests why, a quarter of a century later, most viewers would no longer think of *The Stepford Wives* as a Gothic at all.

II

As a genre popular with women as readers and writers, the Gothic both implies the horrors of patriarchal control over women's minds and bodies and at the same time veils a proto-feminist celebration of female survival and even accomplishment. The so-called drugstore or mass-market Gothic of the 1960s featured the "Jane Eyre" plot, in which a young woman alone in the world finds herself in a dangerous space dominated by a mysteriously frightening and attractive older man whom she eventually marries, securing a place for herself in this world. Levin's earlier novel *Rosemary's Baby* (1965) was one of the first best-sellers to abandon the female Gothic for the equally old and conventional Gothic mode in which heroines are most interesting as bodies suffering at the behest of the powers that be, patriarchy in all its dimensions. *Rosemary's Baby* and *The Stepford Wives* both create a world in which male power, whether "natural" or "supernatural," is real, a world in which the damsel in distress cannot escape her painful fate. Masculinity defines and contains her within its prison of "the feminine," a process almost invariably violent. The Stepford husbands are basically high-tech Bluebeards.

But what was it about this Gothic manifestation of contemporary feminist ideas that so disturbed both Friedan and Kael? There may have been personal reasons for the two women to be offended by the film. Might Friedan have been angry to see her thesis enacted as a Gothic? This literary mode was then just beginning to be examined as a feminist phenomenon. She would almost undoubtedly not have known Joanna Russ's essay about the 1960s mass-market Gothic, " 'Somebody's Trying to Kill Me, and I Think It's My Husband': The Modern Gothic" (1973). If Friedan had any sense of this damsel-in-distress plot, she probably thought of it as archaic trash, which would nonetheless be congruent with Kael's most damning charge of sentimentality.[1] Neither Friedan nor Kael appears to want movies such as *The Stepford Wives* to rouse strong feelings about the plight of women violently redefined by their husbands. As Joanne Boucher observes, "Friedan was adamant that the women's movement present itself as reasonable, moderate, heterosexual, family-loving not family-destroying, man-loving not man-hating in its approach" (3).[2] Not only did the Gothic *Stepford Wives* violate several of these principles; it confronted Friedan's (and implicitly Kael's) liberal feminism with its most powerful taboo: the female body.

Similar to the Enlightenment claim that "all men are created equal," liberal or bourgeois feminism is founded on the so-called liberal self, the assumption that we are free to act independently according to our will and desires, free of any external determinants such as class, race or gender. All human beings are equal under the law. Founded on reason, liberal feminism is both the least threatening of feminisms and the most difficult to demonize. (This definition is the first to appear in the *OED*.) The perils faced by the Radcliffean heroine test her freedom and her autonomy, but also assert her identity as a member of a rationally ordered world free of ghosts and of tyrants; they celebrate the possibility of a woman of reason. Kael's disdain for the film is clearly based on a liberal feminist assumption that women are responsible for their own fates and must admit it: "If they go that way, they're the ones letting it happen."

But Enlightenment philosophers could proclaim "the rights of man" only when "woman" vanished into the generically male category of "the human." The Gothic, however, emphasizes the importance of suffering bodies, particularly female bodies. Radcliffe herself struggled with the problem of embodiment in her fiction, usually expressed in anxieties about her heroine's propriety – how could a Gothic heroine (or a Gothic author) remain a lady? – a question recently discussed in Yael Shapira's analysis of Ann Radcliffe, "Where the Bodies Are Hidden" (2006). M.G. Lewis and others, of course, had no such scruples: their heroines were simply bodies suffering in interesting ways, and Levin's horror plot makes the female body the battleground of female oppression.[3] The Stepford men's project acts out one of the most ancient and perhaps most fundamental of misogynistic fantasies: that women are nothing *but* body. In this view, the dimension we call "soul" or "self" or "identity" or "personality" is quite satisfactorily reduced to a collection of recorded words permitting rudimentary communication with a body that cooks the meals, washes the dishes and cares for the children. Furthermore, "she" is also always available and eager for sex. In evoking the Gothic tradition, Levin's narrative reiterates the genre's traditional emphasis on bodily harm, particularly when the body is female.

But even as Enlightenment philosophers were asserting that human beings are (or ought to be) free to determine their own destinies, others were recognizing that from a purely material perspective, the human body could itself be viewed as a form of machine. In 1747 Julien Jean Offray de La Mettrie published his treatise *L'Homme machine*, which argued that the mind is dependent upon and inseparable from the body, an idea congruent with the period's fascination with automatons of various kinds. A generation or so later, E.T.A. Hoffmann expressed this fantasy in a memorable tale involving a living doll. "The Sandman" tells the story of Olympia, an irresistibly attractive young lady who turns out to be entirely a construction of her "father," the watchmaker

Spalanzani. The protagonist Nathaniel falls in love with a female body that he thinks not only "real," but also ideal, a perfect woman. Delibe's ballet *Coppelia* (1870) and Offenbach's opera *The Tales of Hoffman* (1881) testify to the enduring popularity of this fantasy throughout the nineteenth century, though of course this most enduring expression of the man–machine appears as a specific, female body, the doll Olympia. Although there is no evidence that either Levin or Forbes was consciously remembering Hoffmann's story, the first *Stepford* film contains a nicely ironic moment that gestures towards it. As the family is about to leave Manhattan, one of the Eberharts' little girls sees someone carrying a nude mannequin down the street. She says, "There's a man carrying a naked lady." Her father replies, "That's the reason we're moving to Connecticut." The early versions of *The Stepford Wives* conflate two ways of confronting female embodiment: the female is the victim of patriarchal power, a culturally determined machine, and at the same time an entity easily reducible to a set of mechanical functions. Ironically, however, those functions do not include reproduction. (Even the Victorian "Angel in the House" was expected to give birth eventually, although this fantasy presumed that she was free of sexual desires.) Though patriarchy has sometimes diminished women by declaring that their bodies (and hence they) are, essentially, baby-producing machines, the Stepford robots seem to have had children before they are replaced. When Joanna confronts the newly transformed Bobby, she realizes that this version of her friend "does not bleed." After cutting her own fingers, drawing blood, Joanna stabs the robot in the abdomen (the uterus?), a wound that causes no pain and draws no blood. The only effect is a small malfunction of the mechanism: "Bobby" begins dropping coffee cups one after another in a futile attempt to serve Joanna the coffee she has already refused. In reducing their wives to housekeeping sex machines, the Stepford husbands also handily deny their wives the only female power patriarchy traditionally acknowledges: motherhood.[4] The Stepford wives are so many Athenas born from the brow of Dis (who used to build robots for Disney), the unmarried mastermind of these immaculate conceptions. "Why are you doing this?" Joanna asks Dis. "Because we can," he replies.

III

The "living dolls" of the first *Stepford Wives* were thus products of their times, and their Gothic story was founded on age-old assumptions about female difference and inferiority. Between 1975 and 2004, however, Friedan's liberal feminism had been challenged by bell hooks and others for seeming to assume that the subjection of women was a white middle-class phenomenon. By the 1990s the word "postfeminism" had begun to appear in print. In the popular press, the term almost invariably serves as a short-hand dismissal, suggesting that we have moved beyond feminism either because all its goals have been met and it is thus no longer needed or because women have discovered that the feminist promise that women could "have it all" is a delusion, and that those who naïvely believed in it invariably find themselves miserable.[5] But feminists themselves use "postfeminism" in a very different way, as a word indicating a feminist analysis that moves beyond binary oppositions such as male/female or virgin/whore, the binary structures in which the Gothic, like liberal feminism, is rooted. As the creators of the second *Stepford Wives* noted, however, times have changed, especially in regard to the roles of women. But could this story really be retold? What kind of story could it be? Does "postfeminism" inevitably generate a "post-Gothic"?

Some elements of the 2004 film are familiar – the setting in a Connecticut village, the Stepford husbands' dastardly deeds, the Victorian mansion belonging to the Men's Association. But the men's secret project is revealed about halfway through the film. The population of Stepford now includes a gay couple, and in a climactic revelation, the male president of the Men's Association turns out to be a robot himself, created and controlled by his wife, who is played by Glenn Close as a rigidly coiffed blonde who might well remind American audiences of Phyllis Schafley, the woman who campaigned successfully for the defeat of the Equal Rights Amendment to the US Constitution. But, most significant, these Stepford wives' transformations are reversible.

Though the second film is not primarily a Gothic, Paul Rudnick, the screenwriter, creates a frame for the narrative that both invokes and relinquishes the Gothic order of the 1975 film. *This* Joanna Eberhart is the highly successful director of programming for a television network apparently aimed at a female audience. As the film begins she presents her new shows at a company meeting. These include a game show, "Balance of Power," that pits a man against a woman. In the episode shown, the woman wins handily. A second is a "reality" show called "I Can Do Better!" where a happily married couple are separated for a week to explore other sexual possibilities with "professional prostitutes." In the pilot episode, after a week of resisting temptation, Hank the husband declares that he simply wants to return to his life in Omaha with his "lovely wife Barbara." She, however, declares that "she can do better," and announces that she is leaving him. Just as the screening concludes, however, Hank appears at the convention and starts shooting – reminiscent of the all-too-real episode in Montreal in 1989, where a gunman slaughtered several women, shouting that they were feminists.

In the frame narrative Manhattan looks gloomy and Gothic. The network representatives meet in a dark, cavernous auditorium. Joanna is garbed in the professional woman's chic but severe black. She lives in a world that has in many ways fulfilled the promises of liberal feminism. It is, however, still organized around the binary pair of male and female: their relative powers have simply been reversed. Joanna has an influential and well-paid career; her husband has a lower position as a vice-president in the company she heads. Joanna has retained her "birth name" Eberhart; her husband is Walter Kresby.[6] As a powerful TV executive, she has in effect colonized the male gaze. But the object of that gaze has not really changed. Though women are offered and allowed the freedom to choose their own lives, their possibilities still remain poised between the either/or of conventional versus unconventional behaviour, those "conventions" still predetermined by patriarchy. After the shooting, the network fails to have the courage of its convictions about empowering women. Joanna escapes injury but loses her job. Like a good Gothic heroine, she suffers a complete mental collapse. Thus the frame narrative implies that without escape from the imprisoning constraints of binary structures, a redistribution of power will only lead to more violence.

In an attempt to rescue Joanna from a depression that shock treatment has barely affected, Walter buys a house in Stepford. But the Stepford that this Joanna and Walter move to has also changed since 1975. It is now a gated community of McMansions, fully automated "smart houses." In this Stepford, the women as well as the men have a centre for their activities, the Simply Stepford Day Spa. Whereas the male mastermind of the first *Stepford* was unmarried, here "Mike" (Christopher Walken) is a devoted husband. Indeed, his wife Claire virtually runs the community. She sells houses, welcomes new residents, creates exercise routines for the wives (based on housekeeping movements that they perform in bouffant skirts and high heels) and presides over the town's social events, including a Fourth of July picnic with square dancing and a formal ball at which everyone waltzes in tuxedos and evening dresses. Furthermore, a gay couple, Jerry and Roger, now reside in Stepford. In this culture, gender is no longer straightforwardly congruent with male power and female subordination. Superficially, at least, it presents itself as a postfeminist utopia in both the popular and specialized senses: women have returned to their proper domesticity, but the male/female binary has lost some of its power.

Joanna finds everything about this affluent suburb weird, but she and Walter agree that they must attempt to salvage their marriage by trying to return to the old model of separate spheres, which had been damaged by Joanna's high-powered career. She takes to wearing pink and baking cupcakes by the hundreds. She makes friends with Bobby Markowitz, played by Bette Midler, a successful author of self-help books such as *I Love You, but Please Die* (about her mother), and with Roger, the flamboyant member of the gay couple and a successful architect. Walter is immediately seduced by the pleasures of the Men's Association, a kind of frat house where the Stepford husbands indulge in adolescent camaraderie. (The director, Frank Oz, remarked that he envisioned them as "dot com nerds" who have the technical know-how to create the female robots but are clearly acting on ideas about women and the relations of the sexes appropriate for sixteen-year-olds.) About halfway through the film, Joanna and Bobby sneak into the Men's Association house when the group is meeting, thus disrupting the first version's Gothic congruence of the mysterious house and the plot's climax. They find nothing more distressing than a portrait gallery depicting all the men and their families and escape undetected except by Roger. But shortly afterwards, Roger vanishes, only to reappear as a robotic right-wing, Brooks-Brothers-suit-wearing candidate for Congress running on the plank of Christian family values.

As in the earlier versions, Bobby is also transformed and Joanna is spurred to go to the Men's Association mansion, where she apparently meets her fate. But the film continues. The climactic revelation occurs at a ball attended by all of Stepford where the new Joanna is introduced, clothed in chiffon with flowing blonde curls. Walter leaves her to dance with Mike while he sneaks into the vaults below that contain the computers controlling the robots. He de-programs them, so that suddenly all the wives (and Roger) return to their former selves. In fact, in a joint cooperative effort, Joanna and Walter have only pretended that she has been transformed; she has been merely masquerading as a robot. When Mike realizes what Walter has done, he attempts to attack him, but Joanna strikes out at Mike, neatly decapitating him – neatly, because he does not bleed, either. Claire discloses the Gothic history of this Stepford, confessing that she, a brilliant scientist, had returned home one evening to discover her husband having an affair with her lab assistant. She kills them both and transforms Mike into a robot who will preside over the community of Stepford, which espouses old-fashioned sex roles. In a passionate outburst she declares her motives. She yearned for "a perfect world in which men were men and women were cherished," a life that was beautiful and orderly, a world of "tuxedos and chiffon." Hence her desperate, nostalgic scheme.

Thus Oz and Rudnick clearly believe that changed conditions in the cultural status of women support a comic optimism. Reviewers were often confused, however, complaining that the film is "an empty comedy that takes hackneyed potshots at consumerism" (Thomson) or a dark comedy belonging to "the most bedeviling category of all – trying to make death, destruction, and dismemberment funny" (Griffin). What is interesting about this last comment is that it clearly constitutes a mis-reading of the second film. The only dismemberment that occurs is at the very end, when Joanna accidentally knocks the robotic Mike's head off. That moment, and Claire's confession that follows it, coincides with the disclosure of Stepford's Gothic history, and one that is rooted in sexual violence. Even more oddly, perhaps, Claire's story ends by evoking two extravagantly operatic love deaths. Similar to Salome at the end of Richard Strauss's opera, she crawls towards Mike's head, seizes it and kisses it. Electrocuted, she dies with Mike in a Wagnerian *Liebestod*.

But that denouement is not the final revelation and not the last word either, as it would be in a Gothic tale or a tragic opera. The last scene returns to Manhattan. Here, Joanna, Bobby, and Roger are being interviewed on "Larry King Live." Roger's political career is thriving; Bobby is writing poetry advocating hope and compassion, or so she says. (The title she mentions is "Wait Until He's Asleep, and Cut It Off.") Joanna and Walter (who's waiting proudly off-camera) affirm the renewal of their marriage on more equitable terms. Thus the last scene fulfils the comic formula in which the protagonists are thriving, even as it satirizes a celebrity culture in which an appearance on "Larry King Live" truly seems to affirm a real happy ending.

But is this conclusion really convincing as a happy ending? We do know that this scene was an afterthought. According to Nancy Griffin, Paramount made an "unpleasant decision" that the "new footage was necessary to add a comic coda" (3). The cynical feminist viewer of the second film might want to point out that despite the happy ending and the salvation of all the robots, this narrative is still uncomfortably grounded in the old opposition of male versus female. For just as an unexpectedly Gothic story lies behind the history of Stepford, so some familiar Gothic elements, including misogyny and a desire for power, remain. Men are still trying to transform their wives into automatons. (One of the more disturbing scenes is the demonstration that impresses Walter and tempts him to agree that transforming Joanna would be a good thing: one of the wives is an ATM, spitting out twenty dollars in singles on command.) This time we are asked to blame a woman for all the mischief, a commonplace in "backlash" arguments. And there is something alarming in that though Bobby has taken to writing a poetry of "love and affirmation," her new title is still violent and still implies an eternal battle between the sexes. It might seem that the Gothic is not so easily left behind and that leaving the old but fixed polarities results in a good deal of generic confusion.

Though Gothic and comedy might superficially seem far apart, Avril Horner and Sue Zlosnik have shown in *Gothic and the Comic Turn* that comic materials have often appeared in Gothic fictions from Walpole onwards. Our tendency to ignore them may be caused or at least encouraged by our tendency to think of Gothic and comic as opposites. "Rather than setting up a binary between 'serious' and 'comic' Gothic texts," they suggest, "it is perhaps best to think of Gothic writing as a spectrum that, at the one end, produces horror-writing containing moments of comic hysteria or relief and, at the other, works in which there are clear signals that nothing is to be taken seriously" (4). The first and second *Stepford Wives* are located at these two ends of this spectrum.

Thus the second film's comic turn may in itself be a symptom of a kind of postfeminist sensibility. Its comic elements are complex, and perhaps ultimately incommensurate. The second film is a parody of the first – we laugh to see familiar elements twisted in different directions. This type of self-reflexive parody is also a marker of a camp sensibility, that is, a parade of the ostentatious, exaggerated, affected, theatrical and effeminate, according to the *OED*. But this viewpoint of the "queer eye" might be seen as a first step towards a truly postfeminist perspective, an eye that sees the world not from either the "male" or "female" position, but from an altogether different angle. This perspective also makes sense of the film's curiously operatic qualities. "Everyone is over the top here," notes Nigel Andrews. This fact would account for Claire's improbably operatic death, which turns out to fit into the film's broader pattern of appropriating and rewriting Gothic conventions. In *After the Love Death: Sexual Violence and the Making of Culture*, musicologist Lawrence Kramer argues that this high Romantic convention is founded on the logic of gender polarity, the familiar male/female dichotomy. Kramer argues that the notion of the love death, no matter how disguised by, for instance, Wagner's seemingly transcendent music, cannot be escaped until culture and, in particular, the cultural roles assigned to men and women themselves change.

Perhaps the second film is still too tightly controlled by its inherently Gothic foundations to be authentically postfeminist. (And, indeed, this term itself needs to move away from its own inherent binary pair, feminist/postfeminist.) But it seems to me that the most strikingly postfeminist element in the plot derives less from cultural changes in men's and women's social roles than from technological developments that enable one to imagine other modes of being a robot. If the condition is reversible, a living doll need not remain one for ever. In the first film, Stepford wives were still like Hoffmann's Olympia, dolls who could not die but could be dismembered. But by 2004, audiences were familiar with computers: they are robots that can be programmed, and such programs can also be deleted. The metaphor of body as mechanism familiar in the eighteenth and nineteenth centuries, however, also foreshadows another idea recently analysed by postmodernist theorists and congruent with modern experience with computers: the notion that even seemingly "natural" events, such as sexual attraction, are also cultural constructions. In other words, there are ways in which the mind is a machine as well. Mladan Dolar argues that Mozart and DaPonte's famously misogynistic opera *Cosí fan tutte* ("thus do all women" or "women are like that") approaches this insight from this psychological angle; two sisters fall in love with each other's fiancés when the two men depart and reappear in disguise. While the plot is psychologically unconvincing (in the libretto at least if not in the music), Dolar argues that the logic of DaPonte's plot rests on the notion of the *femme machine*, that women are controlled by their culture's determinations regarding romantic love. They fall in love with the other man because, in effect, they have been programmed to do so:

> There is something in love that is more like a machine than a mere set of predictable emotions; there is a mechanical predictability in its emergence that can be experimentally induced. Women, proverbially unstable and unpredictable, are yet the best embodiments of this mechanical part, the *femmes machines*, the puppets. (63)

Thus Frank Oz's *Stepford Wives* also gropes towards an insight that has been articulated by various feminisms over the past three decades: the notion that if women have been culturally programmed into domestic, passive roles, the logic of the male/female binary also requires that men be programmed to perform the opposite type of role. The Stepford husbands have been taught to expect certain things from their wives, and can wield their cultural power to enforce their ideal. But Walter's refusal ultimately to participate in the second Joanna's transformation is intended, I think, to suggest that both sexes may eventually escape the prison house of gender. If so, Gothic stories will become very hard to read because they seem so strange and so foreign. Living dolls will languish, beside corsets and farthingales, on the shelves of antique shops.

Notes

1. Friedan may also have a blind spot in regard to Gothic in general. In *The Feminine Mystique* she disparages Shirley Jackson's "housewife humor," appearing to be unaware of Jackson's fiercely Gothic critiques of mid-century American domesticity (57). Thanks go to my colleague Tricia Lootens for pointing out Friedan's remarks about Jackson.
2. Jeanne Boucher points out that in *Betty Friedan and the Making of* The Feminine Mystique: *The American Left, the Cold War, and Modern Feminism* (1998), Daniel Horowitz excavates Friedan's radical past as a left-wing journalist. He speculates that she deliberately concealed this past, which included association with communist causes, as a result of McCarthyism's witch hunts in the 1950s. To bury that past was a necessary gesture that may have intensified her desire to have feminism seem unthreatening and respectable.
3. It is interesting to consider the very different fate of another "sci-fi cheapo" that successfully plays with the same essentially paranoid theme: *Invasion of the Body Snatchers* (1956). In it, "real," "natural" human bodies are being replaced by nearly identical substitutes by aliens. But the victims are both male and female. It was successfully remade in 1978.
4. In *Rosemary's Baby*, Levin exploits the presumably inexorable maternal instinct as a source of Gothic horror. Driven to nurture her diabolical infant, Rosemary accepts him and rationalizes that he cannot be all bad, since he is half hers – a supposedly "human" response that merely intensifies our horrified reaction.
5. Newspapers and news magazines regularly publish articles about sociological studies purporting to demonstrate that highly educated women are choosing to be stay-at-home mothers. Lawrence Summers's recently forced resignation from the presidency of Harvard was cast as a disagreement between feminists imposing their "politically correct" taboo against voicing the (manifest) differences between men and women. In fact, feminists were probably more incensed by his ignoring the masses of scientific research that have failed to document these supposed differences.
6. In the novel and 1975 film, Eberhart is Joanna's married name. But in a sense, Eberhart *is* the name that she was born with in Ira Levin's imagination.

Works cited

Andrews, Nigel. "Time to Have Fun with the Robot Bimbos." *The Financial Times* London edition 29 July 2004. 30 June 2005 <http://web.lexis-nexis.com/universe/printdoc>.

Boucher, Joanne. "Betty Friedan and the Radical Past of Liberal Feminism." *New Politics* ns 9.3 (2003). 20 April 2006 <http://www.wpunj.edu/~newpol/issue35/boucher35.html>.

Friedan, Betty. *The Feminine Mystique*. New York: W.W. Norton, 2001.

Griffin, Nancy. "Can This Film Be Fixed?" *New York Times*, 6 June 2004. 20 June 2005<http://web.lexis-nexis.com/universe/printdoc>.

Helford, Elyce Rae. " 'It's a Rip-Off of the Women's Movement': Second Wave Feminism and *The Stepford Wives*." *Disco Divas: Women and Popular Culture in the 1970s*. Ed. Sherrie A. Inness. Philadelphia: U of Pennsylvania P, 2003. 24–38.

Hoffmann, E. T. A. "The Sandman." <http://www.fln.vcu.edu/hoffmann/sand-e_pics.html>.

Horner, Avril, and Sue Zloznik. *Gothic and the Comic Turn*. New York: Palgrave Macmillan, 2005.

Horowitz, Daniel. *Betty Friedan and the Making of* The Feminine Mystique: *The American Left, the Cold War, and Modern Feminism*. Amherst: U of Massachusetts P, 1998.

Kael, Pauline. "The Current Cinema: Male Revenge." *The New Yorker* 24 February 1975.

Kramer, Lawrence. *After the Love Death: Sexual Violence and the Making of Culture*. Berkeley: U of California P, 1997.

La Mettrie, Julien Jean Offray de. *L'Homme machine*. 1747. 8 April 2006 <http://www.fhaugsburg.de/~harsch/gallica/Chronologie/18siecle/LaMettrie/met-hom0.html>.

Levin, Ira. *The Stepford Wives*. New York: Random House, 1973.

Russ, Joanna. " 'Someone's Trying to Kill Me and I Think It's My Husband': The Modern Gothic." *Journal of Popular Culture* 6 (1973): 666–91.

Shapira, Yael. "Where the Bodies Are Hidden: Ann Radcliffe's 'Delicate' Gothic." *Eighteenth-Century Fiction* 18.4 (2006): 433–55.

Silver, Anna Krugovoy. "The Cyborg Mystique: *The Stepford Wives* and Second Wave Feminism." *Arizona Quarterly* 58.1 (2002): 109–26.

The Stepford Wives. Dir. Brian Forbes. Palomar Pictures, 1975.

The Stepford Wives. Dir. Frank Oz. Paramount Pictures, 2004.

Thomson, Desson. "An Old Wives' Tale." *The Washington Post* 11 June 2004. 20 June 2005 <http://web.lexis-nexis.com/universe/printdoc>.

Žižek, Slavoj, and Mladen Dolar. *Opera's Second Death*. New York: Routledge, 2002.

7

The Postfeminist Filmic Female Gothic Detective: Reading the Bodily Text in *Candyman*

Diane Long Hoeveler

"Sadism demands a story" – Laura Mulvey

In an essay published more than twenty years ago, "When the Woman Looks," Linda Williams asks what happens when women view horror films, and she observes that "the female look – a look given pre-eminent position in the horror film – shares the male fear of the monster's freakishness, but also recognizes the sense in which this freakishness is similar to her own difference" (87–8). In other words, when a woman looks at a black or monstrous male body, she recognizes her own socially constructed sense of bodily deformity and freakishness. Projection, introjection, cannibalization and identification – such have been the psychic contortions that have characterized women as subjects and objects in contemporary American horror films. This essay examines the evolution of the filmic postfeminist female Gothic detective in Clive Barker's short story *The Forbidden* (1985), the literary source for the first two *Candyman* films (1992, 1995). It focuses specifically on the woman's pursuit of the meaning and identity of the monstrous black male body that eerily begins to resemble her own.

To begin, I would claim that both *Candyman* films suggest that the dominant culture has a strong investment in a racial hierarchy, and in asserting the supremacy of whiteness, the dominance of white masculinity, and that both of them play with the tropes used much earlier in *Birth of a Nation* or *King Kong*: the ritual sacrifice of a virgin to a black potent male, the "brutal black buck." As such, both films have to be recognized as replicating in their very tropes the stereotypes that they appear to be critiquing.[1] In focusing on the postfeminist female Gothic detective, however, both films actively position and reify the power of the female *gaze* against the sexual violence inherent in the black male body while also focusing on the destructive heritage that this male body has both caused and suffered. To put it another way, the black male body is split between being portrayed as both a victim and a victimizer of white male violence, just as the female body traditionally has been bifurcated in the many virgin/whore depictions of women in Western cultural works.

There are many graphic and grotesque murder scenes in Bernard Rose's first *Candyman* film (1992), some so bloody and garish that viewers are forced to cover their eyes out of sheer self-protection. But if one's tastes run to the more psychologically complex forms of terror, perhaps the most frightening scene in the first *Candyman* film occurs in the parking lot when the heroine is accosted by the ominous and ruggedly handsome black man, known as the Candyman, who pins her against her car and sneers, "be my victim." What is most horrific about the demand is not simply its baldness, its sheer blunt, brazen, unsubtle wording; instead what grips the viewer (at least this female viewer) is the heroine's eyes, the ambivalent combination in them of willingness and fear, desire and loathing. The film, in other words, ostensibly presents a black man's attempt to seize the power of the *gaze*, to seize the meaning of the narrative for himself, to make the film about him, his erotic pain and history. The white woman as academic researcher and postfeminist female Gothic detective, however, gazes back in such a dominating manner that instead she appears to take control of the *gaze*. Effectively, she turns the black man into the castrated object of the film's – and her – visual desire. But both are destroyed by the conclusion of the first film and the story on which both films are based. In fact, examining what I would call the nexus of *Candyman* texts reveals how difficult it is to tell anything but thoroughly sexist, racist and classist narratives, even when the authors are well-intentioned liberals who ostensibly want to expose those very crimes in their works. What this nexus of texts reveals, finally, is the power of the sheer negative weight of ideologies about the connection between white women and black men.

First, a few words about postfeminism in the context of Candyman's blatant demand, "be my victim." As Sarah Gamble has noted, "the postfeminist debate tends to crystallize around issues of victimization, autonomy, and responsibility" (43), with young women rejecting one of second-wave feminism's chief claims, that women are always already victims of forces beyond their control. In its repudiation of victim status, postfeminism seeks instead to position women as canny, flexible survivors of a patriarchal system that they actually dominate and manipulate through a variety of passive–aggressive behavioural strategies that are passed on through cultural systems such as female Gothic novels (cf. Hoeveler, *passim*).

As for filmic theory, in her classic essay "Visual Pleasure and Narrative Cinema" (1975), Laura Mulvey has claimed that Hollywood cinema has succeeded so spectacularly because it has constructed a series of patriarchal and sexist visual codes that produce the fantasy that the white male subject is not essentially a fragmented being but instead possesses an imaginary unified ego, thereby giving rise to his erotic and sublimated pleasure. Male hegemony, according to Mulvey, is built on the back of those fragmented beings – women and minorities – whose subjectivity is effaced so that the white male viewer can experience himself and his world as unitary (432). Film, she argues, functions as "the unconscious of patriarchal society," while "phallocentrism in all its manifestations depends on the image of the castrated woman to give order and meaning to its world" (432). For Mulvey, the castrated woman can transcend her "lack" only through the production and visual display/presentation of a child, the vehicle through which she can enter, however tenuously, the realm of the symbolic: "she turns her child into the signifier of her own desire to possess a penis ... Either she must gracefully give way to the word, the name of the father and the law, or else struggle to keep her child down with her in the half-light of the imaginary" (432–3). Keep that image of "half-light" in mind as we discuss the woman and child who enter the inferno at the conclusion of Clive Barker's story *The Forbidden*, and its first filmic adaptation, with only the child escaping in the film version and the heroine going up in flames as a sacrifice to the patriarchal order.

In addition to a fairly standard Lacanian approach, Mulvey's analysis neatly posits two modes of looking at film: (1) identificatory voyeurism based on sexual drives or (2) gazing based on narcissism and controlled by ego instincts. She notes that for male viewers there are only two ways to escape the castration anxiety provoked by gazing on the woman's sexual difference: demystifying her mystery and saving her (as in *film noir*) or overvaluing and fetishizing her (as in star vehicles and cults; 438). As she observes, "sadism demands a story[; it] depends on making something happen, forcing a change in another person, a battle of will and strength, victory/defeat, all occurring in a linear time with a beginning and an end" (438). Mulvey advocates in place of this sexist monopoly a "new language of desire that would disrupt the pleasure of a male gaze directed at a female object." This new "language of desire" would be known instead as a "female gaze," and presumably would reverse patriarchal and sexist visual imagery with egalitarian tropes that would please women viewers. But Mulvey's pat formula has not gone unchallenged, and many recent film critics have complicated our understanding of how women view film, and indeed how they read texts.[2] Mary Ann Doane has, for instance, attempted to use Joan Riviere's theory of "feminine masquerade" to explain the female gaze: "what might it mean [for a woman] to masquerade as spectator? ... to assume the mask in order to see in a different way?" (82). She goes on to note that the female spectator of film is given two options: "the masochism of over-identification and the narcissism of becoming one's own object of desire, in assuming the image in the most radical way. The effectivity of the masquerade lies precisely in its potential to manufacture a distance from the image, to generate a problematic within which the image is manipulable, producible and readable by the woman" (87). It seems fair to say that a certain sadism as well as masochism permeates the presentation of women in horror films, but the same is true of the fetishizing of people of colour. What happens, however, when a white woman and a black man vie for the status of legitimate victim in literature and its ideological helpmate, film? This essay attempts to address that question by focusing alternately on the figure of the white female detective and her demonized alter ego, the tortured black male body, in the first two *Candyman* films.

"She fought to resist the rapture, though. There was a monster here" – Clive Barker, *The Forbidden*

When Clive Barker published his story *The Forbidden* in 1985, he set the action in a public housing project in Liverpool – the Spector Street Estate – inhabited by lower-class white residents in urban England. And note the name of the development – Spector – these are lower-class people who are not allowed to look at themselves and hence are powerless to transform their economic and social situations. Instead, they are the objects of study for others. Or, even worse, they are transfixed and held in the grip of a spectre, the evil presence they name "Candyman" out of a mixture of irony and desperation. Further, they are the objects of futile speculation by others, including Helen, the white academic researcher who cannot improve their lot but only puzzle about it as a subject for her thesis. Barker's political agenda is clearly liberal, as he presents a dehumanizing concrete block hell in which hundreds of poor white people are forced to live, like so many drones in a capitalistic machine-hive. The story *The Forbidden* had for Barker an original and specific political purpose: to reveal the class prejudice and institutionalized poverty that permeated and polluted British society. Barker and his later film collaborators revised and recast this story in two American filmic adaptations, both of which moved the focus away from white lower-class Britons to a more relevant topic for American audiences: the continued traumatic effects of miscegenation and slavery in the United States.

In Barker's story his heroine, Helen Buchanan, is engaged in writing a thesis on the subjects of sociology and aesthetics, "Graffiti: The Semiotics of Urban Despair," a rather trite subject as her professor–husband, Trevor, informs her. But Helen has grandiose ambitions; she seeks nothing less than the discovery of "some unifying convention ... the lynch-pin of her thesis" (2). What Helen discovers instead is a large head painted around a door, so that the door functions as the head's mouth and, in order to enter the room, people are forced to step through the mouth as if into the figure's head. Scrawled around the head is the phrase "Sweets to the sweet" (7). But before Helen can make any sense out of the cliché, she is informed that there is a murderer in the complex, and that one of his most recent victims was an old man who was found cut to pieces, with his eyes sliced out (9). Lest we miss the blatant castration imagery here, we are next informed via some local women that another of the recent victims was a retarded man who had been attacked in a public toilet: "and they'd cut off his private parts. Just cut them off and flushed them down a toilet. No reason [on] earth to do it" (15). But in any discourse system ultimately concerned with male potency, and threats to it from women and black men in particular, there is every reason to "do it."

As a contemporary version of the female Gothic detective, Helen employs these tales of mutilation and horror as dinner-party conversation with her insufferably unfaithful and aloof husband and his gay colleague–rival, Archie Purcell, who condescendingly dismisses them as variations on an old gothic staple, the bleeding nun narrative, which he describes in modern-dress form: "What about the lovers and the escaped lunatic ... the lover is disembowelled – usually by a hook-handed man – and the body left on the top of the car, while the fiancé cowers inside." As Archie notes, this staple of folklore is actually a "cautionary tale, warning of the evils of rampant heterosexuality" (18). Helen presses Archie on the sheer prevalence of the tales, and finally he concludes that such persistence suggests that the subject of sudden and violent death "is simply taboo material," and another guest chimes in, "maybe [it's] just that death has to be *near*; we have to *know* it's just round the corner. The television's not intimate enough" (19). Nor, presumably, are films. And later, when Helen is informed by a police detective that the murders and mutilations had never occurred, she muses, "was there a place, however small, reserved in every heart for the monstrous?" (28). Barker would, I think, answer in the affirmative.

In Barker's story, Candyman is a mysterious force of evil who demands the periodic sacrifice of small children to stave off his murderous attacks on the inhabitants of a lower-class housing project. Everyone in the story is white, and race never figures in the text's production of horror; however, death does. For some inexplicable reason, a young mother has allowed her baby to be this year's sacrifice, and Helen stumbles on the dead baby while hunting for the source of murder and mayhem in the complex. When Helen finally confronts the Candyman in his lair, she finds him wrapped in a cloak that conceals razor blades as well as candies. He is every child's imagining of the bogeyman come to life, the stranger who lures you with candy only to slash your throat and possibly drink your blood. And such a scenario seems, in fact, to be operative, for Helen finds Candyman with the dead and mutilated baby at his feet, and she describes him as a cross between the Frankenstein monster and Dracula, with something of the risen Christ thrown in for ironic measure:

> He was bright to the point of gaudiness: his flesh a waxy yellow, his thin lips pale blue, his wild eyes glittering as if their irises were set with rubies. His jacket was a patchwork, his trousers the same. He looked, she thought, almost ridiculous, with his blood-stained motley, and the hint of rouge on his jaundiced cheeks. But people were facile. They needed these shows and shams to keep their interest. Miracles; murders; demons driven out and stones rolled from tombs. The cheap glamour did not taint the sense beneath. It was only, in the natural history of the mind, the bright feathers that drew the species to mate with its secret self. (32)

In this final climatic confrontation between Helen and Candyman, he asks her whether she believes in him, as if he were some sort of a god. Next he asks her why she wants to continue living if she admits his existence: " 'Be my victim ... I won't force it upon you. I won't oblige you to die. But think; *think*. If I kill you here – if I unhook you,' – he traced the path of the promised wound with his hook. It ran from groin to neck" (33).

As Candyman very reasonably points out, if Helen were to be slaughtered as yet another of his infamous victims, she would live forever as part of his legend, "in people's dreams."[3] Helen, however, resists what she recognizes as a "seduction," and instead states that she would "prefer to be forgotten than [to] be remembered like that" (33). But she has lied. She attends the complex's celebration of the bonfire night – 5 November – already scheduled for that evening, a ritualistic re-enactment of the foiling of Guy Fawkes's "Gunpowder Plot," with a bonfire composed of cast-off furnishings from the complex rather than the gunpowder that Fawkes intended to use to blow up the English Parliament in 1605. By continuing to commemorate an event of which they have forgotten the meaning, the people of the housing project mirror Barker's sly presentation of Christians, who fail to grasp the horrific significance of their own ritualistic sacrifice of what was once a baby born in a precarious outpost. The baby in Barker's story mimics the baby Jesus; both are sacrifices to social, economic and political orders that they cannot redeem, even with their blood.

But Helen is determined to play the role of saviour herself, and she enters the bonfire in a futile attempt to rescue the already dead baby from burning to cinders in the flames. She fails and instead is taken deeper into the fire by the omnipresent Candyman: "perhaps they would remember her ... Perhaps she might become, in time, a story with which to frighten children." Seeing her husband in the crowd, searching vainly for her, she muses that it would be lovely for him to see her burn and then she would finally have something of value to give him, "something to be haunted by. That, and a story to tell" (37). The story that Barker tells concerns not simply the taboo topics of castration anxiety, the fear of death and the irrational desire for immortality – even if all these are treated only as literary *topoi*. No, Barker is telling another, more cryptic and much darker tale, and it concerns the human need to invent divinities that embody our worst fears and imaginings. Candyman the stranger is somehow another version of Christ the redeemer, the superhuman who holds out the promise of sweets but delivers instead only the stinking tomb.[4]

"The emotional terrain of the slasher film is pretechnological" – Carol Clover

The first two filmic adaptations of Barker's story, both executively produced by Barker himself, accomplish different cultural work that his earlier story does not attempt. The American films transform the quasi-religious British Candyman into a black man, a victim of vicious racism himself and the subject of torture and murder, and it is this dichotomy between his victimization and his vicious treatment in turn of his victims, white women, that constitutes the urban legend at the heart of this sequence of texts. In the second film he is provided with a name,

"Daniel Robataille," but his story is the same in both films (although the location of the events very noticeably changes from Chicago to New Orleans). The son of a former slave who becomes a successful designer of mass-produced shoes, Daniel is sent to the best schools and has been raised in polite society. His native talent as an artist is nurtured and he becomes so successful that he is hired by a prominent landowning family to paint the portrait of their beauteous white daughter. During the portrait sittings the inevitable occurs, and the woman becomes pregnant with the black man's child. Begging for permission to marry him, the daughter is forced instead to witness a white mob torture and mutilate the man. First, his right hand is chopped off and replaced with a hook, signifying his castration and ensuring his inability ever to paint again. The hook, of course, later becomes his murder weapon, as he attacks the bellies of his victims with one fell swoop and rips them open just as he had been ripped open. Next, his body is smeared with honey (hence the origin of his name) and then hundreds of bees are set loose to feed on his flesh. Once his body has been eaten away, he – an artist so sensitive to portraiture himself – is asked to look at his face in his beloved's mirror, to see reflected there his freakish monstrosity.

The mirror, as we might expect, comes to hold special powers, and as long as it remains in his possession his immortality is assured. Using a mirror in a film to signify the interconnection of narcissism, the *gaze* and exhibitionism is not exactly original, but the mirror in this film finally represents something more; that is, it tropes the act of looking at and recognizing the undead history of racism and miscegenation in America. As its penultimate act of torture, however, the mob burns Daniel's body and scatters his ashes over the land that will eventually become the infamous Chicago housing project Cabrini Green. In the first *Candyman* film, Helen Lyle, a researcher attempting to document the persistence and cultural meanings of urban legends such as the Candyman, finds herself drawn to the several competing versions of the tale: the popular versions told by students, janitors and residents of the Cabrini Green housing project, as well as the professional versions told by her husband, sociology professor Trevor, and his professional rival, Archie. Hoping to synthesize all of these rival versions of reality into one overarching theme of meaning, Helen is very much the modern-day liberal mythographer, a contemporary Causabon, seeking the key to all mythologies – Joseph Campbell in drag. Helen begins her investigation certain of the non-existence of Candyman, for, as she tells a young boy in the housing development: "Candyman isn't real. He's just a story, you know, like Dracula or Frankenstein. A bad man took his name so he could scare us, but now he's locked up, everything's going to be okay."

Unfortunately, however, Candyman is real, and what is even more alarming, he informs Helen that she is the reincarnation of his former white lover, the woman he has been waiting for on the site of his torture and murder. "With my hook for a hand I'll split you from your groin to your gullet," Candyman's persistent refrain echoes throughout the films as his horrific promise to link the reality of the body and its sexuality with the reality of death. As Hill notes, the legend is centred on the fact of the groin, while "also part of negotiating a woman's identity in response to heterosexual objectification" (171). *Candyman* is, for Hill, "a horror film in which the monster wins" (170). But does he? He loses his hook to Helen in the first film, and his mirror to Helen's replacement, Anne, in the second film. Women finally castrate the black man and seize the power that he had possessed, won by virtue of his intense sufferings and victimization. In winning the status of the privileged purveyor of the hook, the white woman rewrites the realities of American history and installs herself in the rightful position of both victim and victimizer. In this way, the *Candyman* films invert the white liberal ideology of Barker's original story and present to the masses a more palatable fare: white liberal guilt is rewarded with the very real power to do something about discrimination. It is white women who seize the power to strike back, but they do not do so in a way that renounces racism; they do so instead in a manner that actually reifies racism.

The academic woman, forced to forgo maternity in her manic pursuit of a career in the safe confines of the university, the ultimate patriarchal approval system, understands too late that women are finally bodies on which men (their husbands and colleagues and even the subjects of their research) can write only one script: seduction. When Trevor rejects Helen for a young student, an earlier version in fact of what Helen had been before she thought she could think for herself, he enacts patriarchy's denunciation of the dangerous intellectual woman. So is it the blackness of Candyman that is figured as monstrously repressed, or is it the whiteness and intellectuality of the beleaguered Helen?

If women can function in ideological formations only as objects to be saved or punished, or exalted and fetishized, then what does this make of Helen? Very significantly, she has no child, nor is she likely to bear one given her husband's very blatant interest in other (and younger) women. Helen functions in the story as the ineffectual saviour of the sacrificed baby, perhaps even the cause of the baby's death. In the first film version, however, Helen goes into the fire to bring the baby out alive, but she returns voluntarily in place of the baby and is consumed by the flames, a substitute sacrifice to Candyman's insatiable demands for more victims, more "sweets" to consume. Finally, Helen is coded as an intellectual not a physical woman, and in the universe of male-created ideology, women cannot be both. As an intellectual, Helen is expendable; in fact, she is actually an anomaly that has to be eradicated if male hegemony is to be ensured. A woman without a fertilizable body can stand only as a threat, a potential castrator, a woman with a hook rather than a womb. Helen has to be eliminated because she can only be an empty signifier of the sterility and danger of the academic female. But if Helen's whiteness and intellectual status have marked her for elimination, what does this mean for Candyman? Can he survive in her place, if, in fact, the white hegemonic system accepts her as the sacrifice? Another way of asking this question is to wonder how black men can rewrite or recreate themselves in a culture that can see them only as sexual predators. And how do white women collaborate with black men in their own subjection and subjugation?

The miscegenation-as-nausea theme, so prevalent in American culture, can actually be traced back to the Gothic genre that originated and flourished in late eighteenth- and early nineteenth-century Britain. Dark men ravaging white women has been a staple of the Gothic imagination, beginning with Matthew Lewis's presentation of the black slave Hassan in his Gothic drama *The Castle Spectre* (1798) and culminating most notoriously in Charlotte Dacre's *Zofloya* (1804), a novel that depicts the seduction of a white woman by a black servant who is actually Satan in disguise. Samuel Arnold and John Fawcett's *Obi, or the three fingered Jack* (1800) was another popular British melodramatic work; it depicts the social transgressions of a mutilated black Jamaican slave who leads an ill-fated rebellion, and the play ends with the decapitation of Obi and the triumphant display of his head on the stage. Mary Shelley's *Frankenstein* (1818) presents a monstrous eight-foot-tall man with yellow skin preying on men, women and children indiscriminately, and Bram Stoker's *Dracula* (1897) concerns a Transylvanian aristocrat who sucks the blood from his preferred victims, women with very white skin. And their skin is a good deal whiter after the sucking.

One need not look much further than the realities of British imperialism and its results to explain the intense anxiety that surrounded the association of black men and white women. In a culture where citizens were encouraged to travel and appropriate the goods and lands of other, darker peoples, one is forced to recognize that fairly quickly one of the unmistakable and unavoidable products of this travel was the appearance of mixed-race children. Tremendous anxiety surrounded the existence of these children, and one might even be tempted to claim that the Gothic functioned as a genre that brought the culture face to face with its worst imaginings: sexual relationships not between black women and white men, but between white women and black men. Preserving the pristine whiteness of British women – and by extension the British population – was the unstated goal of much of the cultural work of Gothic fiction and later horror films.[5]

"Hysterics suffer mainly from reminiscences" – Freud

In the second *Candyman* film adaptation, *Candyman 2: Farewell to the Flesh* (1995; dir. Bill Condon), the action is moved to New Orleans, and in this version we are given much more graphic detail about the life and supposed crime of Candyman. As Barker himself explained, "the whole point of *Candyman 2* is to enrich the mythology of the first film. I think it's going to end up more baroque than the first one; as much a consequence of locations than anything else. I think this movie will answer a lot of questions that were left unanswered at the end of the first *Candyman* picture."[6] In this second film we are literally shown the amputation of Candyman's hand, as well as the mob mutilation with the bees and a lynching added for good measure. We are also informed that Daniel Roboutille was murdered during the Mardi Gras celebration for his seduction and impregnation of Caroline Sullivan, recalling Christian associations with the crucifixion and penance. In fact, the ambivalent carnival atmosphere of Mardi Gras – the combination of licentiousness and abstinence – is invoked as the leitmotif of the film. Giving up the claims of the flesh is something that is impossible for all human beings, as Candyman's ironic name implies. "Candyman," after all, could refer to the sugarcane that slaves harvested in the colonies, although it has modern connotations of cocaine dealing, as well as of a man guaranteed to deliver sexual satisfaction.

The viewer of this second film is given even more information about the black man in an effort to humanize and position him as the true victim in the film, and this work culminates with Candyman demanding of the female Gothic detective, Annie Tarrant, "Be my witness." This request is a significant shift and it suggests that the black man has moved from the subject to the object position. He can no longer victimize the woman; instead he can only ask her actively to record his sufferings and pain, to bear witness to his crucifixion and ultimate demise as the mirror, which had held the power of his immortality, cracks and he finally dies. *Candyman 2*, in fact, reveals how ideology triumphs as a representational system of repression, while also recuperating the anxieties of its purported audience. If the first *Candyman* film was suffused with racial fears and white ambivalence towards Black encroachment on Northern cities, the second film comes down firmly on the side of liberal acceptance of miscegenation and the intermixing of the races. But notice that the action this time is set very specifically in New Orleans, about as Southern an outpost as one can find in America.

Candyman 2 is predicated on the claim that Annie Tarrant is the descendant of Candyman, his great-great-granddaughter. He has returned, not for revenge or wanton murder and sacrifice, but for recognition and acknowledgement by his "white" family. When Octavia, Annie's mother, refuses this act, she is killed with Candyman's infamous hook, while Annie is framed for the murder (a scenario that repeats the earlier framing of Helen for her black assistant's murder in the first film). Both films continually suggest the alliance of women and blacks, but finally both films refuse to do anything but present the association as monstrous, murderous, unnatural and a manifestation of the horror-producing perverse. When Annie and Candyman have their final climactic confrontation, it occurs in the slave shanty behind the old plantation of the Sullivan family, the white enclave of power that had excluded and then exterminated Daniel. His final plea, "Be my witness," is a poignant statement of his longing for acceptance by a society that had written him out of their genetic record book. The monster is not, in fact, as monstrous as his white relatives, who have erased him and seek nothing more than to obliterate any rumour of his blood flowing in their veins. But the mirror that holds the magic of his immortality shatters, and he dies unaware that yet another descendant, a baby girl, will be born into his and Annie's family.

Candyman 2 concludes with Annie sitting in the bedroom of her very white and very blonde daughter, instructing the little girl that yes, she did once upon a time have a black man for a great-great-great-great-grandfather. It is all so long ago that the little girl, as well as her mother, can talk about the butchered Candyman as almost a fairy-tale figure, a distant and non-threatening detail of their lives. But after the mother leaves the room, the girl begins to conjure up Candyman in her mirror, and the mother quickly appears, putting a stop to such potentially dangerous games. The film attempts, I think, to present an allegory of the hidden life of miscegenation in American society, but its dishonesty and its obsession with special effects and horror spectaculars ultimately detract from what could have been a serious meditation on racism and sexism, and their unfortunate ideological marriage.

And setting the film in New Orleans is a particularly telling slip. Miscegenation in the South has long been an established fact of life, so the Sullivan clan's attempt to conceal Daniel's paternity of Caroline's daughter is farcical and pathetic, and also ultimately doomed. Moving the action away from Liverpool, the bleakly industrialized England, to Chicago, the prosperously industrialized North, to New Orleans, the wanton, lustful capital of sin in the South, reveals the dishonesty of the second film's vision. Whites in the rural South are allowed to cavort with blacks, but whites in industrialized areas are to be kept from contact with them. So "be my victim" can only be a threat in the North, where black migration from the South poses a very real threat to the more prosperous economy of white America. But "be my witness" is a far more palatable and safer statement, particularly in the South, where all the beleaguered Daniel wanted was to be acknowledged as part of a corrupt and ineffectual dying Southern family. The ideology that triumphs in the second film, as I noted above, is not positive, nor is it liberal. As an examination of this cycle of texts suggests, "sadism demands a story." And when that story is about black men and white women, the story can only be very sadistic indeed.

Notes

1. See Schneider, Wartenberg and Modleski for discussions of mixed-race couples, *King Kong*, and race in contemporary films, in particular *Candyman*.
2. Revisions of Mulvey's essay are numerous, and include de Lauretis, Doane, and Mulvey herself (1988).
3. As Barker himself noted, in talking about the first film version of the Candyman character: "He's very sympathetic. And there's a great seduction to him. He invites his victims. He's quite polite about it: 'Be my victim.' Of course he pursues them relentlessly and of course he's going to get what he wants. He's probably more like Dracula than any other monster: he does seduce, and he does offer a kind of immortality, which is what Dracula does. He says, 'Be part of my legend.' And what Dracula says is, 'Allow me to bite you and live forever.' But yes, I think the appeal is definitely one of immortality" (qtd. in "Clive Barker's *Candyman 2*," *Cinefantastique* 26 [1995], 9).
4. A somewhat similar conclusion has been reached by Hoppenstand, who reads the Spector Street graffiti as "the religious language of a new god, a god born from folklore legend, a god who accepts sacrifices of blood and candy, a god emblematic of the contemporary urban experience ... The Candyman's stock-in-trade is true immortality, an immortality that sacrifices the physical body in favor of notoriety, an immortality powered by the oral tradition of legend that is part of the same life force that animates the dreaded Candyman himself" (135).

5. For a sample of the very diverse and interesting approaches to the *Candyman* films, see Briefel and Ngai, Botting, Halberstam, and Wyrick.
6. Interview with Clive Barker in "Candyman: Interview with the Monster," *Cinefantastique* 26 (1995), 43.

Works cited

Barker, Clive. *The Forbidden. Books of Blood*. Vol. 5. London: Weidenfeld & Nicolson, 1985. 1–37.
Botting, Fred. "Candygothic." *The Gothic*. Ed. Fred Botting. Cambridge: Brewer, 2001.133–51.
Briefel, Aviva, and Sianne Ngai. " 'How much did you pay for this place?': Fear, Entitlement, and Urban Space in Bernard Rose's *Candyman*," *Camera Obscura* 37 (1996): 71–91.
Candyman. Dir. Bernard Rose. Screenplay Bernard Rose. 1992.
Candyman 2: Farewell to the Flesh. Dir. Bill Condon. Screenplay Rand Ravich and Mark Kruger. 1995.
Clover, Carol. *Men, Women, and Chain Saws: Gender in the Modern Horror Film*. Princeton: Princeton UP, 1992.
de Lauretis, Teresa. *Alice Doesn't: Feminism, Semiotics, Cinema*. Bloomington: Indiana UP, 1984.
Doane, Mary Ann. "Film and the Masquerade: Theorizing the Female Spectator." *Screen* 23 (1982): 74–88.
——. "Masquerade Reconsidered: Further Thoughts on the Female Spectator." *Discourse* 11 (1988–9): 42–54.
Gamble, Sarah. "Postfeminism." *The Routledge Companion to Feminism and Postfeminism*. Ed. Sarah Gamble. London: Routledge, 2004. 43–54.
Halberstam, Judith. *Skin Shows: Gothic Horror and the Technology of Monsters*. Durham, NC: Duke UP, 1995.
Hill, Mike. "Can Whiteness Speak: Institutional Anomies, Ontological Disasters, and Three Hollywood Films." *White Trash: Race and Class in America*. Ed. Matt Wray and Annalee Newitz. New York: Routledge, 1997. 155–76.
Hoeveler, Diane Long. *Gothic Feminism: The Professionalization of Gender from Charlotte Smith to the Brontës*. University Park, PA: Penn State Press, 1998.
Hoppenstand, Gary. *Clive Barker's Short Stories*. Jefferson, NC: McFarland, 1994.
Modleski, Tania. "Cinema and the Dark Continent: Race and Gender in Popular Film." *Feminism without Women: Culture and Criticism in a "Postfeminist" Age*. New York: Routledge, 1991.
Mulvey, Laura. "Afterthoughts on 'Visual Pleasure' Inspired by *Duel in the Sun*." *Feminism and Film Theory*. Ed. Constance Penley. New York: Routledge, 1988.
——. "Visual Pleasure and Narrative Cinema." Rpt. in *Feminisms*. Ed. Robyn R. Warhol and Diane Price Herndl. New Brunswick, NJ: Rutgers UP, 1991. 432–42.
Schneider, Steven Jay. "Mixed Blood Couples: Monsters and Miscegenation in U.S. Horror Cinema." *The Gothic Other*. Ed. Ruth B. Anolik and Douglas Howard. Jefferson, NC: McFarland, 2004.

Wartenberg, Thomas E. "Humanizing the Beast: King Kong and the Representation of Black Male Sexuality." *Classic Hollywood, Classic Whiteness.* Ed. Daniel Bernardi. Minneapolis: U of Minnesota P, 2001. 157–77.

Williams, Linda. "When the Woman Looks." *Re-Visions: Essays in Feminist Film Criticism.* Ed. Linda Williams, Mary Ann Doane and Patricia Mellencamp. Frederick, MD: University Publications of America and the American Film Institute, 1986.

Wyrick, Laura. "Summoning Candyman: The Cultural Production of History." *Arizona Quarterly* 54 (1998): 89–117.

8
Moving beyond Waste to Celebration: The Postcolonial/ Postfeminist Gothic of Nalo Hopkinson's "A Habit of Waste"

Gina Wisker

> It had begun with the Christmas and the gift of dolls. The big, the special, the loving gift was always a nice blue-eyed Baby Doll ... Adults, older girls, shops, magazines, newspapers, window – signs – all the world had agreed that a blue-eyed, yellow-haired, pink-skinned doll was what every girl child treasured.
>
> Toni Morrison, *The Bluest Eye*

> These are the latitudes of ex-colonised, of degradation still unmollified, imported managers, styles in art, second-hand subsistence of the spirit, the habit of waste, mayhem committed on the personality, and everywhere the wrecked or scuttled mind.
>
> Slade Hopkinson, "The Madwoman of Papine: Two Cartoons with Captions"

These quotations from Toni Morrison's *The Bluest Eye* (1970) and a poem by Nalo Hopkinson's father, Slade Hopkinson, focus on ways in which once-colonized people can be seen to internalize worldviews and behaviours that limit their development, stunt their identities. A call to recognize, challenge and move beyond such destructive limitations runs throughout Canadian/Trinidadian/Jamaican Nalo Hopkinson's "A Habit of Waste" (2001), as it does through much postfeminist, postcolonial Gothic fiction. This essay explores ways in which post-feminist, postcolonial Gothic women writers engage in a critique of oppressive versions of history and self, inflicted from the colonial past.

In so doing, it investigates how their critical and imaginative use of Gothic and postcolonial writing, intersecting at the issue of abjection and body image, rises above colonialism's negative effects, laughing off and rejecting denigrating constraints embedded in myth, history, story and everyday behaviour.

Becoming woman

Hopkinson's "A Habit of Waste" embodies and dramatizes how the texture and texts of colonial and imperial powers manipulate colonial and once-enslaved peoples. By renaming and rewriting both the limiting historical narratives and versions of the self, the young woman at the heart of this tale emerges renewed and re-empowered. Hopkinson's short story dramatizes collusion with internalized reflections of white cultural versions of women in terms of bodily shape and values. In so doing, it focuses on Cynthia, an African American woman who buys a new skin, a white body, but realizes gradually she prefers her own self – larger, black. Lying behind this tale is Toni Morrison's earlier *The Bluest Eye*, which engages with the damage done by internalizing denigrating representations of black women, emphasizing how crucial body image and performance are in terms of identity, history and self-respect: "It was a small step to Shirley Temple. I learned much later to worship her, just as I learned to delight in cleanliness, knowing, even as I learned, that the change was adjustment without improvement" (25). For Morrison's Claudia, reflection enables some distance, but for Pecola Breedlove, the silencing and abuse that follow her mere existence as not pretty, not white, not rich destroy her.

Deleuze and Guattari's notion of "becoming woman" can be useful to our reading in considering postcolonial women as a site for development and change (1988). One of their arguments is to see women as a force for postcolonial change – as David Punter puts it, "the only alternative to masculinist reinterpretation" (151). In a positive reading, we can see that although gender roles are unstable, women can move on from established readings and roles in "an abandonment of the already empty site of the male," with "various trajectories, the various lines of flight, that women might take if they are to flee from the ruins" (Punter 154). Each of these moves is variously successful or unsuccessful, but in the midst of the change left by colonialism there is no choice of remaining still.

Hopkinson's protagonist gains self-awareness and moves away from established roles offered to her by men and colonialists. The short story focuses on ways in which women change and move towards a sense of owned identity. In this respect, several theories help to interpret the text and also to offer ways forward for readers. In particular, we can draw on "becoming woman" as a theory, the ways in which the literary Gothic confronts contradictions and paradoxes, postcolonial theory, which exposes silencing and celebrates revaluing of difference, and the ways in which postfeminism foregrounds gendered inflections of recognitions of self in cultural contexts. Together these theories help to explain the trajectory of "A Habit of Waste" by focusing on the conflict, reflection, rejection, rebuilding of the self and self-image – the renaming of versions of the past, present and future, and the suggestions of recognition of self-worth and of agency enacted in the tale. Shape-changing can here be seen to be both a characteristic of the literary Gothic and a postfeminist postcolonial strategy to embody celebratory, insightful change for the women concerned. A postfeminist Gothic concern with rejecting negative self and identity constructs and developing more positive, owned versions of self (without any essentialist sense of "a true self") aligns it with the reinterpretation offered by postcolonial perceptions. Cynthia, like Morrison's Claudia, does not have to remain stuck with negative self-perception, the zombification of the colonized. She moves on. The strategies of postfeminist, postcolonial Gothic enable a rewriting and a re-visioning.

David Punter establishes a link between the disgust, abjection and haunting of much literary Gothic and the postcolonial: "The process of mutual postcolonial abjection is, I suppose, one that confronts us everyday in the ambiguous form of a series of uncanny returns" (vi). For some, the questioning of hidden or disempowering aspects of self-image using the speculative, fantastic strategies of the Gothic could be seen as less "serious" than the strategies of realism. In this respect, postcolonial postfeminist Tananarive Due identifies the use of strategies of fantasy, horror, and the literary Gothic as a risk: "I needed to address my fear that I would not be respected if I wrote about the supernatural." Fantasy is a form that often does not gain its rightful respect and approval. Where Due voices her concern that her work should be taken seriously, Toni Morrison asserts the importance of re-engagement with the powerful, historically, culturally inflected mythic and magical dimension of black consciousness and imaginative history. Morrison places the imaginary as expressed in the literary Gothic in fantasy, the supernatural and horror centre stage, as creative ways in which postcolonial people see the world and express their visions. She talks of finding "the tone in which I could blend acceptance of the supernatural and a profound rootedness in the real time at the same time with neither taking precedence over the other" ("Rootedness" 342). One of her reasons for this is a re-engagement with the "discredited" worldview and expression found in once colonized or enslaved cultures. She notes that

> [i]t is indicative of the cosmology, the way in which Black people looked at the world, we are a very practical people, very down to earth, even shrewd people. But within that practicality we also accepted what I suppose could be called superstition and magic, which is another way of knowing things. But to blend these two works together at the same time was enhancing not limiting. And some of those things were "discredited" only because Black people were "discredited" therefore what they knew was "discredited." And also because the press upward towards social mobility would mean to get as far away from that kind of knowledge as possible. That kind of knowledge has a very strong place in my world. (342)

Postcolonial postfeminist women's Gothic fantasy and horror offer an imaginative space in which to engage, explore and critique the constraints and effects of material human processes, experiences and possibilities, seeking alternative ways of being, behaving, thinking and acting. In this respect, postfeminist Gothic fantasy and horror present a challenge to more conventional realist, social, feminist fictional engagements with material practice, social, historical and culturally inflected construction and experience. In other respects, it is fully in line with established feminist and postfeminist enterprise – liberation, enabling articulation of being in the world from different perspectives, engaging with the imaginary, the felt experience of the mind, which affects that of the self in the world.

Creative writers, such as Angela Carter, Doris Lessing and Margaret Atwood, and critics, including Rosemary Jackson and Lucie Armitt, have been engaging since the days of second-wave feminism (early 1970s onwards) with the potential of Gothic fantasy and horror fictions for the feminist enterprise of cultural critique and the exploration of new visions and versions of what it can mean to be women in differing contexts. For many postcolonial women writers and women of African descent, forays into the Gothic fantastic and horror are still relatively recent. Nalo Hopkinson, Tananarive Due, Erna Brodber, Toni Morrison, Jewelle Gomez and Octavia Butler, among others, have engaged with postfeminist Gothic fantasy and horror, which are critically recognized as forms of powerful expression providing space and discourse to explore a liberating movement beyond colonial, imperial and gendered silencing and oppression.

Postcolonial/postmodern/postfeminist

In exploring the expression and use of postfeminism and other "isms" in our reading of these texts, it is helpful to clarify the use of these contested terms. "Postcolonialism" suggests both a reaction *against* colonialism and a response *after* it, taking "post" to mean in the one instance "anti" and moving on ideologically, and in the other merely a historical moment. My own use of "postcolonialism" favours the "moving on" and "anti" version of the term (Wisker 2006), whereas my reading of another "post," "postmodernism," sees both a historical development and many continuities. Modernism problematizes received views of "reality" and uses fragmentation as motif and form. So too does postmodernism, which elaborates on the breakdown of certainties and questions notions of continuity and wholeness of self.

So what can be said of the third contested term, "postfeminism"? Some might argue that it means "after" or "anti" feminism, as do the "after" or "anti" versions of postcolonialism and postmodernism. However, as with my reading of "postmodernism," I see many continuities and productive metamorphoses rather than complete breaks. Feminism is far from dead or over, since its fundamental aims of equality are but a few visible steps down the line to achievement in many instances, especially following the backlash against feminism and the accompanying and worrying (to my mind dangerous) complacency about its achievements. This can be seen, perhaps, as a few steps forwards and a few steps back. Critics exploring postfeminism frequently comment on the backlash against the feminist movement. In this context, Susan Faludi (2001) identifies four versions of the use of the term "postfeminism." One version sees a dramatic erosion of the women's movement among young women; some women are resolutely "antifeminist" and consider the movement as over, whereas the final version sees it as not dead, but as having *changed*. Some critics of feminism note that in its zeal to stop pornography and violence against women it has supported censorship, curtailed sexual freedoms and portrayed itself as anti-sex. Ironically, then, sexual harassment and "anti-pornography" laws championed by some feminist contingents are viewed as being anti-sex and empowering the patriarchy. Not surprisingly, feminists who do not want to be associated with such positions have re-identified themselves as "post" feminist.

Aligned with the arguments of C A E (an avant-garde writing and performance collective, 2006), I would argue against any monolithic view of feminism, and favour versions of postfeminism that seek to identify developments, attempts at resolutions to some established feminist tensions regarding sexuality, body image, individual subjectivity and priorities related to ethnicity and difference, and that deal with challenges rather than radical breaks. In this respect, the postcolonial postfeminist Gothic of Hopkinson moves beyond the historically powerful assertion that feminism is a white Western construct that marginalizes black women. Replaying and reminding us of this argument, Wallis and Vaid *et al.* suggest that, in terms of women of colour undermining feminism, "minority women feel their needs and values have been largely ignored by the organized women's movement, which grew out of white, middle-class women's discontent" (Wallis 82), and racial-minority women feel they cannot participate in the feminist movement because of white women's racism (Vaid *et al.*).

Hall and Rodriguez historicize this position as a process during second-wave feminism, and they also avoid falling into the trap of presuming that contemporary versions of feminism are able to encompass the wide diversity of women's lives and needs. In some instances, black and Asian women's critiques of second-wave feminism as Western-centric, ignoring and silencing their very different experiences, sufferings, values and celebrations, have also led to identifying as postfeminist, black and Asian postcolonial women's engagement with and assertion of women's equality and right to identity and voice. Not surprisingly, there is no consensus here, and actually postfeminism, like "becoming woman," can be seen as metamorphosing, not merely stuck, rigidly, as a backlash against the 1970s and 1980s.

I would argue that celebrations of the sexual self (heterosexual, bisexual, lesbian, gay, transgendered) and of culturally different needs, challenges and achievements are all part of the way feminism has moved on, part of a new stage in its development. I do not have a problem with calling postfeminist, rather than feminist, those creative and critical views that emphasize the value and equality of cultural differences, move on from silencing and subaltern positioning, expose the performativity rather than any fixity of our variously gendered and sexual selves while celebrating rather than shutting them down.

In terms of the discussion of Hopkinson's "A Habit of Waste," the location of the text, at the intersection of postcolonialism, postfeminism and the Gothic, enables us to consider ways in which it uses literary Gothic strategies – doubles, the supernatural, fantasy, futures, transformation – to express postcolonial and postfeminist reclamation of identity, history, voice and the body. It develops a postfeminist focus on performativity and moving beyond artifice and simulacra to conscious, chosen performativity of gendered sexuality and culturally aware selves (Baudrillard 1983; Butler 1990).

Creative Gothic fantasy and horror inspire a breaking down of boundaries of the imagination, opening up new perspectives, and in this they resemble the enabling critical enterprise of much feminist criticism, and some more realistic historical and culturally engaged fiction. For women of African descent and postcolonial women writers more specifically, the expectation that they will focus perhaps on realistic writing, "a little black pain undressed," has constricted creativity. The literary, especially the postcolonial literary, as David Punter notes, can make connections between lived experience and imaginative alternatives offered as absences and, it could be argued, possibilities: "the peculiar condition of the literary will always be to effect a link between the actuality, the presence of such conditions, however powerful and terrifying, and the imaginary, universality ... in its proper position, in absence" (189). Through their use of Gothic fantasy and horror, postcolonial and postfeminist writers and women writers of African descent represent a vital contemporary force, engaging imaginatively, directly and critically with issues of material gender and culturally inflected human experience, and exploring, constructing and expressing alternative ways of being in the world that enable equality in terms of culture and gendered experience.

"A Habit of Waste"

In terms of losses and gains, waste is a motif that runs throughout "A Habit of Waste," engaging with the internalized self-damage, the negative self-image that paralyses action and is a direct result of racist, sexist denial, destruction and demoralization, forces attacking ontological security and sense of self-worth. The cultural contexts in which racial and gendered hierarchies and norms have historically operated are based on a post-Enlightenment binarism that casts as secondary anyone who is not white and not male. The tale uses the strategies of the postcolonial postfeminist Gothic – images of fantasy and horror, a reversal of postcolonial abjection – and enables a rereading, reclamation of history and of versions of self and identity. Hopkinson's female protagonist regains and re-establishes self-worth and body image in the face of that which would deny her. In this sense, the tale enacts a transformation as the protagonist moves beyond cultural and historical constraints. The text offers a radical challenge to gendered and racialized constructions of the abject, using aspects of the literary Gothic in postcolonial contexts to postcolonial ends. Ghosts, vampires, zombies, werewolves, voodoo horror figures and formulae are vehicles to review, indict and revision versions of what it is to be part of black subculture, black and a woman. Hopkinson revises and reinterprets Afro-Caribbean and international folktales, placing them in contemporary Canada and the Caribbean. Her critique leads to the reclamation of ontological security.

For Cynthia in "A Habit of Waste" this reclamation appears as a newly found, comfortable oneness with her own history and her own body, re-writing and refusing the kinds of alienated cultural denigration that has hitherto written her out of the script, a denigration she internalized to her loss. Cynthia internalized a culturally constructed, negative self-image that is dramatized in the fantastic scenario of total rejection of her body, purchase of a new body and denial of her roots (while still going home for Sunday lunch to surprised parents) grown from her internalization of a cultural commodity of the body that devalued the identities of her ethnic origins. Feminist readings of the text highlight the postcolonial elements, the reclamation of representations in terms of body image and self-worth.

Nalo Hopkinson's *Skin Folk* (2001) contains a number of tales concerned with shape-changing or metamorphosis. For example, "Precious" rewrites a female-gendered version of the King Midas story to create a reverse scenario of abuse and disempowerment based on a male-dominated capitalist context. Spitting out precious stones is at first a version of a profitable development, but when it turns into a reason for bullying and abuse, the female protagonist reclaims her own body's ontological security, and the precious stones cease.

"A Habit of Waste" questions the social and cultural constructions of waste, that which is abjected, extra, disposed of, unsuitable and ill-fitting within strict cultural, gendered boundaries. It focuses on the choices of Cynthia, who works to support the old, sick, poor by providing food aid. Cynthia's questioning of the way in which she has internalized rejection of her homeland and her Caribbean, black female body are suddenly forced on her when she experiences a kind of doppelgänger effect – coming face to face on a streetcar with the woman who has been donated her rejected body. So much loathing does she feel for the body she was born with that Cynthia can only retell tales of the disposal of such waste to crash victims. It is like staring into a mirror that replays at her a rejected self. Sold on a white cosmeticized female ideal, replacing her body with a purchased white body was for Cynthia the ultimate achievement. Her sense of social arrival was gained through attaining a slim, white, female body and blonde hair. But, surprisingly, the recipient of Cynthia's cast-offs does not seem to hate the throwaway body. In fact, although the "same full, tarty-looking lips; same fat thighs, rubbing together with every step; same outsize ass; same narrow torso that seemed grafted onto lower body a good three sizes bigger" (183; that is, her body on someone else) disgusts Cynthia as it did when it contained her, the woman in her body seems at home, actually at ease with, indeed revelling in, it. This stuns Cynthia, who considers the natural hair, the nappy look, "Man, I hated that back-to-Africa nostalgia shit" (184). She saved for five years for the body switch, a fantasy only dreamed of by women who loathe their body shape, size, colour. Her *own* body is no more than waste in the economy of the white, acceptable form.

Cynthia's job also concerns socially constructed definitions of waste. She provides meals to the deprived, doling out measured foodstuffs to those marginal to society and, for her, one regular, Old Man Morris, is little more than a friendly receiver of state handouts in the form of food. But he is more than he appears, a performer, playing several games and covering up his Caribbean accent, which interests Cynthia, who tries to discern his exact origins. He also reminds her of the distance she has travelled from her parents and their origins. Persuading him to eat healthily and accept the appropriate food, as defined in this highly constructed society, seems a waste of time indeed. Mr Morris is himself a kind of waste in a society that provides excess and waste, controls and contains food as it would measure and control people. The catalyst for Cynthia's change comes through his agency, however, when, on the eve of a public holiday, Cynthia takes Mr Morris's food ration to his own part of town and finds herself intrigued and somewhat trapped by his lonely hospitality, unable to refuse his offer of supper just to keep him company. The waste of other people's lives and the vegetable and animal life that springs up in the cracks and corners of this regimented and hierarchized city are the wild and cultivated goods Mr Morris takes as his own. He uses ornamental cabbage (kale) when it would be thrown away and kills wild rabbits with slingshots, arguing, "I ain't really stealin' it; I recyclin' it! They does pull it all up and throw it away when the weather turns cold" (194). He berates Cynthia for treating her own body as waste: "You mean to tell me, you change from a black woman body into this one? Lord, the things you young people do so for fashion, eh?" (192).

He explains his position as one of recuperation from death and waste. Following his wife's death, he went into a decline but one day saw some-one who became an example to him, an old lady who owned nothing, feeding stale bread to the pigeons. Though she could be considered marginal and mad and the pigeons she fed could be considered vermin, her care for others provided the turning point that prevented him giving in and dying. He argues, "You have to make use of what you have" (199). His inventive self-sufficiency gained him a new life from the waste of an insensitive city. Correspondingly, this provides another model for Cynthia. On her way out, Cynthia is nearly mugged by a mean street youth and old Mr Morris's wily skills take the youth out with a slingshot. This is the catalyst she needs to review and reevaluate her life.

Shortly after, visiting her parents for Thanksgiving, Cynthia agrees to eat everything on her plate. Her acceptance of the food is a refusal to turn it into waste. Similarly, she at last accepts what she is and, in so doing, undermines the dominant economy of value, which would reject her original body and ignore someone like Morris. Her "You've got to work with what you've got, after all" echoes Old Man Morris, surprising her mother (201). As she finishes the remains of the morning's cocoa in the pot, Cynthia starts to return to her old ways, content with easing herself back into a version of her old body at some point: "You don't want it to go to waste, do you?" (202). In this reacceptance of the value of her own body shape and size (not colour, however), Hopkinson's Cynthia tackles the devastating internalization of postcolonial abjection and simultaneously challenges cosmeticized fetishism. This cosmeticized version of the body would deny her own black self, valuing it as waste in the economic system where high-rise concrete blocks attempt to crush any entrepreneurial elements of those who, incarcerated in the system themselves, are marginal to its central values. Gothic strategies emphasize Cynthia's doubled image, and the deployment of alternatives that dispute the surface of what is seen and valued as "normal" enact positive change, so she breaks out from, undermines, rejects, re-flowers and re-grows from the constraints, celebrating cooking and her reclaimed body image.

Postcolonial postfeminist Gothic

Postcolonial postfeminist Gothic texts problematize, reconceptualize. Wilson Harris identifies the power of such disruptive energies as "the imagination of the folk involved in a crucial inner re-creative response to the violations of slavery ... the possibility exists for us to become involved in perspectives which can bring into play a figurative meaning beyond an apparently real world or prison of history" (27). For Cynthia, the decision is finally taken to be more comfortable with herself, eat her way back into her own body shape and reject the fashionable construction of woman that would have her always thin, androgynous, white. The body inheriting woman's "proud sexiness" is a challenge to Cynthia's own version of her body as cast-off waste (185). In a society that values wealth, youth and versions of whiteness, the old and poor are even more downtrodden and marginalized, seen as waste, surplus to requirements. The text enables the female protagonist to reclaim her body and identity and, in so doing, to establish a model for others.

Nalo Hopkinson's work can be read and illuminated using postcolonial, postfeminist and Gothic horror theories that expose and undercut disempowering myths of the Other, internalized and performed by black women; as Tiffin and Lawson put it: "Colonial discourse analysis and postcolonial theory are thus critiques of the process of production of knowledge about the Other. As such they produce forms of knowledge themselves, but other knowledge, better knowledge it is hoped" (8). Using strategies of the postcolonial, postfeminist Gothic, Hopkinson's "A Habit of Waste" challenges and undermines the cultural marginalization and devaluation of African originated culture, shapes and worldviews that have been perpetuated in everyday speech and voice in literature, performance and representation, and damagingly undermine self-worth. In Hopkinson's story it is figured in the fantasy exploration of the idea of a body-swap, the casting of your own body as a form of waste in a society whose economy grades you as worth little. Cynthia is aware of short-changing herself, colluding in an oppressive society. She re-writes, re-scripts her own life and body shape, becoming a new version of woman, ever changing and in control of her body, development, values and representations of self and culture. "A Habit of Waste" uses the strategies of postfeminist colonial literary Gothic to challenge disempowering representations and internalized versions of self, to enable re-grounding, a new ontological security, expression and performance – in text, self and body.

Works cited

Ashcroft, Bill, G. Griffiths and H. Tiffin, eds. *The Empire Writes Back*. London: Routledge, 1989.

Baudrillard, Jean. *Simulations*. New York: Semiotext(e), 1983.

Butler, Judith. *Gender Trouble*. Oxford: Blackwell, 1990.

C A E. "Postfeminist Forum." 1996. 1 May 2006 <http:www.altx.com/ebr/ebr3/forum/polem.htm>.

Deleuze, Gilles, and Felix Guattari. *A Thousand Plateaus*. Trans. Brian Massumi. London: Athlone Press, 1988.

Donnell, Alison, and Sarah Lawson Welsh, eds. *The Routledge Reader in Caribbean Literature*. London: Routledge, 1996.

Due, Tananarive. Interview. 17 March 2002. 19 September 2002 <http://www.tananarivedue.com/Interviews.htm>.

Faludi, Susan. *Backlash*. 1992. London: Pluto Press, 2001.

Hall, E., and M. Rodriguez. "The Myth of Postfeminism." *Gender & Society* 17.6 (2003): 878–902.

Harris, Wilson. "History, Fable and Myth in the Caribbean and Guianas." *Caribbean Quarterly* 16.2 (1970): 1–32.

Hodge, Merle. *Crick Crack Monkey*. Oxford: Heinemann, 1970.

Hopkinson, Nalo. "A Habit of Waste." *Skin Folk*. New York: Warner Aspect, 2001. 183–202.

Hopkinson, Slade. "The Madwoman of Papine: Two Cartoons with Captions." *Skin Folk*. New York: Warner Aspect, 2001. 183.

Morrison, Toni. *The Bluest Eye*. London: Triad Grafton, 1970.

——. "Rootedness: The Ancestor As Foundation." *Black Women Writers*. Ed. Mari Evans. London: Pluto Press, 1985. 339–345.

——. *Beloved*. London: Chatto and Windus, 1987.

——. Interview with Andrea Stuart. *Spare Rib* 189 (1988): 15.

Punter, David. *Postcolonial Imaginings: Fictions of a New World Order*. Edinburgh: Edinburgh UP, 2000.

Tiffin, Chris, and Alan Lawson. *De-scribing Empire: Post-Colonialism and Textuality*. London: Routledge, 1994.

Vaid, Urvashi, Naomi Wolf, Gloria Steinem, and bell hooks. "Let's Get Real About Feminism: The Backlash, the Myths, the Movement." *Ms.* 5 (1993): 34–43.

Wallis, Claudia. "Onward Women!" *Time* 4 December 1989: 80–9.

Wisker, G. *Key Concepts in Postcolonial Literature*. Basingstoke: Palgrave Macmillan, 2006.

9
George Elliott Clarke's *Beatrice Chancy*: Sublimity, Pain, Possibility

Donna Heiland

Gothic/sublimity/pain

George Elliott Clarke's verse drama *Beatrice Chancy* takes as its subject the seldom-discussed history of slavery in what is now Canada, and tells that story through the often-recounted life of Beatrice Cenci, who was raped by her father, conspired in his murder, and was then hanged for her so-called crime. Working with reference to a range of literary, cultural and historical traditions, including twenty-seven explicitly acknowledged plays, films, operas, even photographs on the subject of Beatrice, Clarke leads one to understand that the tale he tells – of Beatrice, of slavery – is essentially Gothic.[1]

The Gothic as a genre is about many things, but at its heart are always stories of oppression, told in such a way that the oppression is magnificent in its horror – sublime, to use the aesthetically precise term – and so maximally appealing. The ways in which humans have oppressed each other are so many and so ubiquitous that Gothic can seem to be everywhere. Its earliest examples are in eighteenth-century stories of women oppressed by the patriarchal societies in which they live, and over time the genre has also been used to talk about other forms of oppression, including oppression based on race, and slavery.[2]

In writing a Gothic drama about slavery, Clarke makes clear his understanding of the close ties between the literary form and the lived experience, even as he had earlier acknowledged this connection in an essay on Percy Shelley's play *The Cenci*. In the closing paragraphs of "Racing Shelley, or Reading *The Cenci* As a Gothic Slave Narrative," Clarke meditates on the play's strategies for representing the entrapment that characterizes the Gothic. Focusing on its "resolute reliance upon repetition of a limited vocabulary," he argues that

> [t]ropes are doubled and re-doubled by different characters because the essential behaviours – dangerous and duplicitous – never cease. Worse, the limitation of language restricts policy options, so that no one is able to imagine any future beyond torturous cycles of revenge. ... no members of the Cenci clan are able to break through to some truly liberatory, transcendent and transformative action. Beatrice revolts, but she foments no real revolution. (180–1)

Shelley's Beatrice may not foment revolution, but Clarke does see her as a "symbol and a prophecy" who points to "a future of continued, liberationist struggle," and Clarke's own Beatrice embraces that struggle even as she shows us the terrible cost of doing so (181). She shows us that "truly liberatory, transcendent and transformative action" is sublimely powerful as well as painfully destructive, and in so doing clears the ground for the construction of a new reality. It will be up to Clarke to bring it into existence and his tool for re-invention is his art.

Beatrice Chancy is a Gothic text, but it also critiques the Gothic, and it does so primarily through its engagement with the aesthetic of the sublime. Although sublimity is generally understood to be an inexpressible and all but incommunicable experience, Clarke makes it concrete and comprehensible. Cutting across genres, his verse drama is a combination of poetry and prose meant to be both read and performed, and the possibility for performance of his work – for its embodiment on the stage – qualifies our understanding of it as sublime and perhaps even changes (or does away with) our sense of the sublime altogether. Similarly, *Beatrice Chancy* crafts its language from multiple sources, demonstrating an astonishing range of reference, a sometimes jolting originality, a vivid concreteness, and, again, it is through that concreteness that Clarke mounts his critique of sublimity.[3] Exposing the relationship between the sublimity that is the hallmark of Gothic and the pain in which it is grounded, he shows us the Gothic from the inside out.[4] In so doing, he also finds a way to move beyond the Gothic history he describes into a world of possibility and, yes, chance.

My claim for Clarke's work is a large one, grounded in my reading of the sublime as an aesthetic that is above all about the threat of self-loss.[5] In his *Philosophical Enquiry into the ... Sublime and Beautiful*, Edmund Burke had defined the sublime as an experience inspired by "the ideas of pain, ... danger" and "death" (39), an experience that "hurries us on by

LIVERPOOL JOHN MOORES UNIVERSITY
LEARNING SERVICES

an irresistible force" (57), essentially taking us out of ourselves. Sublime experience is terrifying experience that threatens to subsume individuals into something larger than themselves; it is experience in which boundaries blur and differences of all sorts threaten to vanish: the difference between subject and object, between self and other, even between one time or place and another. An individual might finally be overwhelmed by that "something larger," or might avoid self-loss by instead internalizing and so mastering the idea of the infinite.[6] In both cases, the key point is that the difference between the self and that which threatens it disappears. In Gothic narrative the elimination of that difference is often represented in gendered terms, as violence against women and the deaths of women – embodiments or emblems of difference – repeatedly figure as sources of the sublime. Thus if he does not want to perpetuate the very violence that he seeks to expose and critique, Clarke must finally reject the sublime as the aesthetic mode undergirding his Gothic play. To do so, however, he must first show us the sublime in all its glory – we must see how it works, see the pain it involves, in order to understand why we must turn away from it.

Sublimity and pain are related to each other in complex ways, the former arguably resulting from and also mirroring the latter. I noted that Burke identified the "idea" of pain as a cause of sublime experience, and Luke Gibbons has explored that fundamental connection in Burke's thought, arguing that Burke's sublime is founded on one person's sympathy for another's suffering. This is a powerful reading that sees Burke's sublime as grounded in an experience of pain that can be communicated to others, and it is appealing though perhaps optimistic in its understanding of sublimity as respecting rather than erasing difference. Steven Bruhm argues more cautiously that sympathetic responses can create a "community of shared pain," but states that "pain is ultimately a completely individual experience that isolates the sufferer from all others" (27). Behind the work of both of these critics is that of Elaine Scarry, who theorizes that pain "differs ... from every other bodily and psychic event, by not having an object in the external world." Where "desire is desire of x, fear is fear of y ... pain is not 'of' or 'for' anything," but "is itself alone," an "objectless experience" (161–2). As Bruhm glosses Scarry's thinking, pain has no "external referent ... because pain needs no object to give it meaning. ... Pain eradicates the external world and proclaims the primacy and irreducibility of hurting" (35). In other words, pain is an individual, overwhelming and all but incommunicable experience, like the sublime as I have presented it.

If sublimity and pain are alike in being overwhelming and inarticulable, how is any writer ever to represent them? The short answer is that one cannot. The best one can do is represent the effects of such experiences, or perhaps the process that inspires them, in the hope that the reader of a novel or audience of a play will experience something like what the character is said to have experienced. A further answer is that one might focus not on representing those experiences, but rather on building out from them. Whether one has lost oneself in a sublime experience or isolated oneself in pain, new ties to the world can and indeed must emerge if life is to continue. What will they look like? Scarry's reading of pain as an experience that "unmakes" or dismantles the world goes on to suggest that this experience makes way for the imaginative activity "that eventually brings forth the dense sea of artifacts and symbols that we make and move about in" (162). Indeed, Scarry argues that imagination is

> the only state that is wholly its objects. There is in imagining no activity, no "state," no experienceable condition or felt-occurrence separate from the objects: the only evidence that one is "imagining" is that imaginary objects appear in the mind. Thus, while pain is like seeing or desiring but not like seeing x or desiring y, the opposite but equally extraordinary characteristic belongs to imagining. (162)

For Scarry, pain and imagination are finally "the 'framing events' within whose boundaries all other perceptual, somatic, and emotional events occur; thus, between the two extremes can be mapped the whole terrain of the human psyche" (165).

Clarke sees this as well. Representing slavery as an institution that is not about abstract ideas of pain, danger, death and the sublime thrills they can inspire, but about a reality defined by pain and its attendants, he clears a space for the imagining of alternatives to that reality. His own writing is the first step in that process, eventually turning us to beauty as he has defined it.

Beatrice/Clarke

Clarke's Beatrice is a remarkable figure who exposes sublime experience as grounded in pain, but also as generative and even redemptive. She is the biological daughter of Mafa, a slave whom Chancy raped, and has been raised by Lustra, the woman he married. The two mother figures mirror each other insofar as both are Chancy's property, and Beatrice in turn resembles them both: like Lustra, she is subject to Chancy in his role as patriarchal head of the family, and, like Mafa, she is Chancy's slave and victim of his lust. All three of these women suffer under Chancy's yoke, and Beatrice's great accomplishment is to rise up against the pain that is her heritage. She insists on her desire to marry the slave Lead in spite of her father's prohibition against it, and when her continued pursuit of Lead results in Chancy raping her and beating Lead, she responds to this violence with violence of her own. She collaborates with Lustra and Lead to kill her father. In so doing, she rebels against the slave society in which she lives and the literary tradition out of which she was also born, as the relatively passive virtue of a traditional Gothic heroine (think of Antonia in Lewis's *The Monk*) becomes the fiercely active virtue that fights for itself (think of Lewis's Matilda fighting for God rather than Satan). And, like her predecessors in both life and literature, she pays for that change with her life.

Beatrice's rebellion speaks to a number of histories. Most important is the history of slavery in the black Atlantic generally and what is now Canada specifically, as it has been recovered by writers and scholars, including like Clarke himself.[7] Clarke puts front and centre the imagined voices of slaves whose lives in Nova Scotia are still barely acknowledged, ventriloquizes the voices of the slave owners with damning clarity and undercuts the framework of official history with admirable dispatch (for example, portraying Governor John Wentworth as an ineffectual figure who is said to have freed the slaves only after they have freed themselves – BC 138, 144). Almost as important is the story of the Acadians: French settlers expelled from Nova Scotia by the British in the middle of the eighteenth century, some later returned – their community lastingly disempowered by the displacement – and their narrative is key to Clarke's sense of Beatrice's culture and his own. He and she are both – in his language – Africadians.[8] Not surprisingly, the French Revolution is a further touchstone for Clarke: the play closes with a reference to Floréale, spring-time (April / May) in the short-lived Republican calendar, and expresses general sympathy with revolution in the face of injustice, figuring Beatrice as Charlotte Corday, who killed Marat to aid the Republican cause and was executed for her crime.[9] Finally, Judaeo-Christian history is crucially important to the play. An opening reference to the Jews in exile helps frame the story, as Clarke dates his statement "On Slavery in Nova Scotia" as having been written in "Nisan MCMXCIX" (Nisan is the first month of the biblical Jewish calendar, April/May in the Roman calendar) (BC 8).[10] The play itself is set on a plantation in Nova Scotia's Annapolis Valley that is repeatedly called "Paradise," where "[a]pple trees blaze with blossoms" (BC 12), while Beatrice – as Wilson has also discussed – becomes both a "martyr" to her cause (like her mother before her [*BC* 34]) and a Christ figure who points the way from oppression to salvation.[11]

The play's engagement with Judaeo-Christian history perhaps emerges most clearly in its linking of Beatrice with Christ, but that linking points beyond itself to an interest in that tradition's logocentrism. Let me take this step by step. Beatrice's identification as a Christ figure becomes apparent as soon as her father introduces her as "my daughter, in whom I'm well pleased" (*BC* 52), echoing biblical descriptions of Christ as "my beloved son, in whom I am well pleased" (Matthew 3.17; Mark 1.11). Having returned to her father's plantation on a Good Friday after years at a convent school, she is raped on Easter Sunday, and the next day reflects grimly: "I've died here in just four days, / But won't be resurrected" (*BC* 97). Yet she is, in a sense, coming back to life as what Wilson describes as a seeming "phallic avenger" whose murder of her father leads to her own killing at the hands of the law (268). Beatrice's murder of her father – an act that rises above the personal to slice through the patriarchal structure of the family, the church and the state – asks to be read not simply as vengeance, however, but as a kind of ironic justice. Reflecting on her father's murder, Beatrice tells her inquisitors: "White men, you took away my freedom / And gave me religion. / So be it: I became a devout killer" (*BC* 140; Moynagh also comments on this line [115]). Like Caliban telling his colonizers, "You taught me language and my profit on't / Is, I know how to curse" (*The Tempest* I.ii.363–4), she announces her appropriation of the master's tools and her intent to use them against him. Her killing is an act as raw and ritualistic as Caliban's cursing, and the link between religion and language is no accident. For Judaeo-Christian history is grounded in the idea of language as that which constitutes reality – God's word created the world – and Clarke takes seriously this understanding of language as a creative force. As one willing to speak as well as act against her father, Beatrice weakens the power of patriarchy and slave society, but she escapes that power only in death, a dubious escape at best,[12] and if her story dies with her, then she has not escaped at all, but succumbed to it. Clarke ensures that this does not happen.

Overriding the multiple, determining frames of the play's action is Clarke's knowledge that language is at least part of what brings them into being. Patriarchy, religion, slavery all gain force through the stories that legitimate them, and when he builds his entire play around a family called "Chancy" – a word that meant "lucky" before taking on its current meaning of risky, accidental, haphazard – he opens up a space of contingency and so possibility. While Clarke understands very well the economic, political and psychological dynamics that sustained slavery, he understands even better that the history of slavery was not inevitable. Thus he plays with the language of history and of chance, of good fortune and bad, punning on chance and *méchanceté* – the term he uses to describe Beatrice's hanging, literally translatable as "meanness" or "viciousness," but a term in which a reader will also hear echoes of her name. Into the mix he throws Dice, the black over-seer of slaves on Chancy's land, and a man who may – or may not – be Chancy's son. Other characters are a dreamer (Lead, the "oneiric slave" [*BC* 10]), a visionary (Dumas, the "seer," whose name also connects him to the writers Dumas *père* and *fils*, themselves the mixed-race descendants of a female slave [*BC* 10]), a liberator (Beatrice herself) and a writer (the man who hangs Beatrice says he is a hang-man but also a "poet" [*BC* 147]). With his wordplay Clarke shows us a world of fixed horrors and open possibilities, in which art is necessary to change.

Clarke and his characters understand the transformative and even generative potential of language, yet they also understand its limits. In the play's opening scene Beatrice's lover, Lead, states, "I'm sick of words! / If prayer could bust iron, we'd be free" (*BC* 13), and is himself rebuked for being all talk and no action when Deal tells him: "You talk good, always mashin up white folk, / But you jus flap your dreamin gums" (*BC* 15). Language that is not performative, that does not make something happen, is worthless. It is also clear, however, that language can be used in different ways and to different ends.

The notion that different people use language differently emerges early on in the play. The slave Moses says that "Old men are philoso-phers; / Young men are ruthless," to which Lead replies, "Young men sharpen their swords on old men's words" (*BC* 16–17). Language can motivate, to be sure, but it can do more than that. When Moses tran-scribed Lead's love letters to Beatrice, they were "Such raw, hurting words and lines, / Etching inkwater into spruce paper" that she "feared their ink was blood" (*BC* 40). Lead's words become material emblems of the thoughts and feelings they communicate, and, painful as they are, they also become a source of strength: they have a nurturing power that mimics that of the "victuals" in which they are smuggled to Beatrice, and appear to her as "second scripture" (*BC* 40). Words do not finally substitute for deeds – Beatrice and Lead really do butcher Chancy – but they do have the power to shape our understanding of those deeds.

Words also shape and in some sense constitute being. The "seer" Dumas sings Beatrice's entry on to the stage as she greets her stepmother:

> *Beatrice is pure song,*
> *So elegantly spoken,*
> *A philosophy shaken*
> *Into a new language,*
> *Demanding new lips*
> *And a new heart,*
> *To speak her for who she is.* (BC 30)

She comes into being through language – the product of a *fiat* not divine but human – and it is crucial that this language be new. That newness comes not from invention *ex nihilo*, however, but from the appropriation and re-invention of the multiple languages that inform her experience. In the moments just before she is hanged, the slave/poet Dumas states "Annihilate her and you nullify / Seven millennia of poetry" (*BC* 146), and Beatrice herself fears "becoming words" as "The globe contracts / to the O of a noose" (*BC* 145). Such complete erasure of her identity is not possible, however, so long as her story has voice.

Crucial to Clarke's voicing of Beatrice's story is his engagement with the aesthetic of the sublime, which essentially aims to trigger experience that is beyond the realm of difference and so beyond the realm of language (which – as structuralism has taught us – is constituted precisely through difference). In Chancy's rape of Beatrice, Beatrice's killing of her father, and Beatrice's own death the play offers up three scenes that force one to a critique of that aesthetic and a sharper – less entertaining, more painful – sense of what Gothic experience really is.

In reading Chancy's rape of his daughter as a scene that invokes only to set aside the notion of sublimity, one might recall that John Dennis – writing just a little earlier than Edmund Burke – characterized sublimity as "an invincible force, which commits a pleasing rape upon the very soul of the reader" (37). "Pleasing rape"? That phrase points to what is so distressing about the aesthetic of the sublime: to anyone who is not a sadist, pleasure and rape must be seen as antithetical concepts, and sublimity as not just undesirable but actively to be resisted. When Chancy rapes his daughter, then, Clarke shows us the terrible blurring of boundaries that defines this crime, but in a way that highlights the bathetic – rather than the sublime – results of his action:

> *Beatrice:* I hurt [*two words garbled*] my throat
> [*Several words whited out*] a knife.
> *When her father seizes her, B. cries like snow. Light slumps in darkness.*
> *When it returns, the chapel appears exactly as before, but deserted.*
> *Emotions linger – as if light were memory, a kind of excrement. Outside,*
> *stars bog down in mud – sorrow ground out of rain. (BC 87)*

The violence of this rape consists first of all in the unwanted physical attack on Beatrice, in the fact that it is also an act of incest and in its racial violence as well. This last point is emphasized by the stage direction telling us that words have been "whited out" of the manuscript, and that "whiting out" serves another purpose as well, turning our attention to the textual – rather than the sexual – aspects of the crime.[13] Eliding key moments in a text is a standard Gothic device for increasing horror – one knows something awful has happened, but one does not know quite what. In this case, however, the silencing itself arguably matters more than anything Beatrice might have said, and the words that we do hear her say – "hurt," "throat," "knife" – emphasize that silencing by suggesting that her throat has been cut.[14] As a muted Beatrice disappears into darkness, other discrete entities slide into each other as well – light/memory/excrement, stars/mud, sorrow/rain – in a scene whose inchoate murkiness suggests the very opposite of sublimity. Beatrice and her world are "unmade," to use Scarry's term, in a scene that conveys pain and loss above all.

One might expect the counterpart of the rape to be the killing of Chancy, and the text initially reinforces this expectation. Planning the murder, Beatrice tells Lead, "Dismantle sick organs, demolish sick eyes" (*BC* 124). Speaking as one who wishes to inflict pain in a literal unmaking of Chancy, she says to Lead, "We'll kiss and kill and kiss again, / Feeling only pleasure" (*BC* 124), and one sees how that shift in perspective – from victim to avenger – changes the experience represented. She has a chance at sublime pleasure, and yet when she actually kills Chancy – offstage, as if to guarantee that the audience does not also begin to see the possibility of pleasure in pain – she experiences no such thing. She and Lead enter the stage "*red-spattered, raked by light – astounded by their capacity for cruelty*" (*BC* 128) and talk of a murder that mimicked sexual assault: "Encunted, the dagger fucked his left eye" (*BC* 129). Brutally violent, this murder nonetheless resonates in a very different way from Beatrice's rape. "*Stars bog[ged] down in mud*" when her father attacked her, whereas – says Beatrice – "[h]is death leaves stars unmoved in space" (*BC* 129). He is a "weird fruit" whose end recalls those of so many slaves (*BC* 135, with a nod to Billie Holliday), and in that reversal one sees again that Beatrice stands less for sublime vengeance than for level justice.

Alongside both of these scenes one can read the hanging of Beatrice, who tells the hangman, "Rapture my throat" (*BC* 147). "Rapture," not "rupture" – the hanging will free her from the "prison-house of breath" (*BC* 143), the "penitentiary of flesh" (*BC* 144) as she again loses herself, but this time to religious salvation that she both experiences and generates. She is hanged on Thanksgiving day, with the "liberateds" singing "before I'd be a slave, / I'd be buried in my grave, / And go home to my Lord and be free," and at the moment of her death "[*t*]*he globe goes dark as crucifixion times*" (*BC* 148). She is again identified as a Christ figure, and all of these verbal cues suggest that her experience has been sublime, as maybe it has. This sublimity is tempered, however, when we read not only that her body is miraculously unmarked by the hanging (in contrast to Lustra's) but that "liquefied diamonds" can "[n]owadays" be found near her remains (*BC* 148). Like an Ovidian heroine, Beatrice does not so much die as metamorphose into something of lasting power, something that perhaps conjures the beautiful rather than the sublime.

Sublimity/beauty/change

If Clarke's play finally turns our attention from sublimity to beauty, why does it do so? Beauty is a concept generally seen as opposed to the sublime: where sublimity is characterized by overwhelming experience that threatens self-loss, beauty is associated with social impulses, the formation of community and the containment of sublime excess. As others have seen, however, that opposition breaks down under critical pressure, and the two concepts come to seem increasingly complementary. For a thinker such as Burke, who sees beauty in all that is "small," "smooth," "delicate" and more (113) – all that is stereotypically feminine, in other words – beauty is appealing insofar as it "submits to us" (113). Such a concept of beauty would seem to be as far from sublimity as one can imagine, and yet Frances Ferguson has demonstrated that Burke had it backward, that it is we who submit to beauty, the seductive power of which enervates us and threatens our well-being as much as the sublime ever could (51). For a thinker such as Clarke, who follows Herbert Marcuse in identifying a

"politics of the beautiful" as that which can "transform socio-
economic horror and political tragedy into their opposites," beauty
again resembles the sublime in its capacity to disturb but also disarm
those who encounter it. Clarke sees in beauty "a quality productive of
tumult and crises and revolution" but also a power that Marcuse says
can "check aggression," and therein lies its appeal ("Embracing
Beatrice Chancy" 23).

The power of beauty is the power to stop us in our tracks, make us see
what is in front of us and respond to it. It shows us people and events in
sharp relief, and in this way it is both transformative and redemptive, as
Clarke states:

> I confess that the impulse that made me take up poetry ... was a
> need to discover *Beauty* for – and within – myself and my commu-
> nity. I wanted to war against all the propaganda asserting that
> African people – especially those native to Nova Scotia – were back-
> wards, criminal, illiterate, and expendable. I knew that this prose
> was a lie, but only *Poetry* could declare it so, for *Poetry* is about
> deliverance to the abode of *Beauty* (as is all art). ("Embracing
> *Beatrice Chancy*" 24)

Clarke is like his Beatrice, working in a language that is distinctly his,
a language fashioned from the multiple literary and cultural traditions
on which he draws, but that also transforms those traditions. Beatrice
Cenci alone may not have been able to foment a revolution, but Beatrice
Chancy did, and Clarke's work ensures that the revolution will
continue. He has re-membered this history, and our task is to recognize
that we live with it all the time. Clarke's book goes on after his play has
ended, and its last page is a colophon with these words:

> *And if the African belief is true, then somewhere here with us, in the very
> air we breathe, all that whipping and chaining and raping and starving and
> branding and maiming and castrating and lynching and murdering – all of
> it – is still going on.* – Bradley (*BC* 158)

Clarke's subject is the Gothic history of slavery in Canada, and his
Beatrice points a way through the horrors to a clear vision and continued
struggle. Sublimity exposed as pain becomes concrete, articulate and a catalyst for change, making space for the changed vision – and transformative
power – of beauty.

Notes

1. *Beatrice Chancy* not only tells a Gothic story, but is the product of a creative process that has a distinctly Gothic cast. This essay is about the verse drama *Beatrice Chancy*, which Clarke has described as the "evil twin" of the opera of the same name for which he wrote the libretto and James Rolfe the score. The play is the opera's double, then, and the opera itself was the result – says Clarke – of a "Frankenstein operation ... to transform a Renaissance Italian noblewoman into a mixed-race, Nova Scotian slavegirl and to turn a historical incident of incestuous rape and parricide into a re-enacted news story about colonial crime, lust and greed" ("Embracing *Beatrice Chancy*" 16). Clarke writes eloquently on the multiple contexts for his work. See especially "Embracing *Beatrice Chancy*," which discusses Dante, Shelley and Pound as inspirations for his Beatrice, and "Racing Shelley." Moynagh also offers a fine discussion of Clarke's "citational practice," and especially of the relationship of *Beatrice Chancy* to slave narratives, historical texts and performance traditions.

2. For a fuller discussion of Gothic as a genre, see my *Gothic and Gender: An Introduction* (2004), and for a fuller discussion of the relationship between Gothic fiction, race and slavery, see especially Chapter 7, which reprints and re-contextualizes an earlier essay: "The Unheimlich and the Making of Home: Matthew Lewis's Journal of a West India Proprietor." My own work on this issue owes much to the scholarship cited in both publications.

3. Clarke has written forcefully about how he "had to quarrel with language. To hurt blank verse into black drama" ("Embracing *Beatrice Chancy*" 18), and his dazzling language draws comment from virtually everyone who writes about his work. Particularly astute is Kevin McNeilly's argument that "Clarke's book lovingly mires itself in the formal pleasures of stylized language," manifesting a "latter-day aestheticism" that at the same time cautions against a mindless privileging of the aesthetic: "Clarke doesn't cast out English poetry, but inhabits the language by pushing it to its lyrical limits, exposing the linkages between literary wonderment and human abuse. 'Wolves yowl in bracken,' Lustra, Chancy's neglected wife, tells Beatrice. 'Don't be poetical.' ... And so we too are reminded to listen carefully for the elision of experience into artful deceit, of meaning into music" (176–7). The "elision of experience into artful deceit, of meaning into music" comes close to describing the aesthetic of the sublime as well, as it renders terror a source of pleasure, one person's pain is another's spectacular entertainment, and I agree with McNeilly's further claim that Clarke's play "voices its politics at the level of style" (177).

4. I first explored the relationship between sublimity and pain in "Sublime Subjectivity: Eighteenth-Century Aesthetics and the Fiction of Peter Ackroyd." My work here builds on that paper, and has since been informed by Gibbons, Bruhm and of course Clarke himself, who has said specifically that his first approach to the story of Beatrice Chancy was "to dream an opera of pain" ("Embracing *Beatrice Chancy*" 16).

5. This reading of the sublime condenses that which I most recently articulated in *Gothic and Gender*, chapter 2.

6. Burke's discussion of sublimity encompasses both of these possibilities. He characterizes sublimity as self-loss when, for example, he states that individuals "are, in a manner, annihilated before" ideas of the Deity (68) and as self-assertion

when he notes that "when without danger we are conversant with terrible objects, the mind always claim[s] to itself some part of the dignity and importance of the things which it contemplates" (50–1). Kant explores still more systematically these two aspects of sublime experience, noting that sublime experience is characterized at once by the impossibility of grasping the "transcendent" – which "is for the imagination like an abyss in which it fears to lose itself" – and the assertion of a "supersensible" power that conceptualizes and so contains the transcendent (97).

7. See his *Odysseys Home: Mapping African Canadian Literature*. See also Moynagh, whose superb reading of *Beatrice Chancy* argues for Clarke's recovery/ rewriting of Canada's national memory as one that must include the history of slavery.
8. Wilson elaborates on Clarke's "association of Beatrice with the Acadians" and especially with the figure of Evangeline, whose story is told in Longfellow's poem of the same name (276–77). Moynagh discusses the term Africadian: "a word coined by Clarke as an alternative to *African-Nova Soctian, Afro-Nova Scotian, black Nova Scotian,* or other possible appellations. A fusion of *Africa* and *Acadia,* this term is evocative of an imagined community" (98).
9. See Schama 729–31 and 735–41.
10. Here and throughout this essay, *BC* indicates *Beatrice Chancy*.
11. Noticing – as I did – that slavery is a "neglected" aspect of Canadian history (267), Wilson argues that the play's "liberation of the slaves .... entail[s] the sacrifice of a woman," though she also notes that Beatrice's martyrdom depends on an apparent – and   temporary – "recasting of her gender." On Beatrice as a Christ figure see especially pages 268 and 272 f.
12. For a fuller discussion of death as a way out of Gothic entrapment, see my *Gothic and Gender*.
13. This emphasis on speech rather than – or at least as much as – sexuality recalls Samuel Richardson's similar emphasis in *Pamela*, as discussed in Nancy Armstrong's *Desire and Domestic Fiction*, 108–34.
14. Moynagh also notes the racial comment implicit in the phrase "whited out," though her reading of this scene differs interestingly from mine when she wonders whether we are not meant to read Beatrice's throat – her voice – as a knife, a weapon with which she fights (115).

Works cited

Armstrong, Nancy. *Desire and Domestic Fiction: A Political History of the Novel.* Oxford: Oxford UP, 1990.
Bruhm, Steven. *Gothic Bodies: The Politics of Pain in Romantic Fiction.* Philadelphia: U of Pennsylvania P, 1994.
Burke, Edmund. *A Philosophical Enquiry into the Origin of Our Ideas of the Sublime and Beautiful.* 1757. Ed. James T. Boulton. Notre Dame, IN: U of Notre Dame P, 1968.
Clarke, George Elliott. *Beatrice Chancy.* Victoria, BC: Polestar Book Publishers, 1999.
——. "Racing Shelley, or Reading *The Cenci* As a Gothic Slave Narrative." *European Romantic Review* 11.2 (Spring 2000).
——. "Embracing *Beatrice Chancy*, or In Defence of Poetry." *The New Quarterly: New Directions in Canadian Writing* 20.3: 15–24.
——. *Odysseys Home: Mapping African-Canadian Literature.* Toronto: U of Toronto P, 2002.

Dennis, John. *The Grounds of Criticism in Poetry*. 1704. *The Sublime: A Reader in British Eighteenth-Century Aesthetic Theory*. Ed. Andrew Ashfield and Peter de Bolla. Cambridge: Cambridge UP, 1996. 35–9.

Ferguson, Frances. *Solitude and the Sublime: Romanticism and the Aesthetics of Individuation*. New York: Routledge, 1992.

Gibbons, Luke. *Edmund Burke and Ireland: Aesthetics, Politics, and the Colonial Sublime*. Cambridge: Cambridge UP, 2003.

Heiland, Donna. *Gothic and Gender: An Introduction*. Oxford: Blackwell Publishers, 2004.

——. "The *Unheimlich* and the Making of Home: Matthew Lewis's *Journal of a West India Proprietor*." *Monstrous Dreams of Reason: Cultural Politics, Enlightenment Ideologies*. Ed. Mita Choudhury and Laura Rosenthal. Bucknell UP, 2001. 170–88.

——. "Sublime Subjectivity: Eighteenth-Century Aesthetics and the Fiction of Peter Ackroyd" (printed program title, changed to "Sublimity and Serial Killing: The Case of Hawksmoor" in presentation). Annual Meeting of the Modern Language Association, New York, NY, December 2002.

Kant, Immanuel. *Critique of Judgement*. 1790. Trans. J. H. Bernard. New York: Hafner Press/Macmillan, 1951.

McNeilly, Kevin. "Word Jazz 2." *Canadian Literature: A Quarterly of Criticism and Review* 165 (2000): 176–81.

Moynagh, Maureen. " 'This History's Only Good for Anger': Gender and Cultural Memory in *Beatrice Chancy*." *Signs* 28.1 (2002): 97–124.

Scarry, Elaine. *The Body in Pain: The Making and Unmaking of the World*. Oxford: Oxford UP, 1985.

Schama, Simon. *Citizens: A Chronicle of the French Revolution*. New York: Alfred A. Knopf, 1989.

Shakespeare, William. *The Tempest*. Ed. Northrop Frye. *William Shakespeare: The Complete Works*. 1969. Ed. Alfred Harbage. New York: The Viking Press, 1977. 1369–95.

Wilson, Ann. "*Beatrice Chancy*: Slavery, Martyrdom and the Female Body." *Siting the Other: Re-Visions of Marginality in Australian and English-Canadian Drama*. Ed. Marc Maufort and Franca Bellarsi. Brussels: P.I.E.-Peter Lang S. A./Presses Interuniversitaires Européennes, 2001. 267–78.

10

Sensibility Gone Mad: Or, Drusilla, Buffy and the (D)evolution of the Heroine of Sensibility

Claire Knowles

One of the things that is most often forgotten in discussions of "post-feminism" is the continuity implied between it and other discourses of what we might broadly term "feminism." Just as the term "postmodernism" implies continuity with, even as it claims to break from, the discourse of "modernism," postfeminism affirms its links to, even as it tries to distance itself from, a wider tradition of feminist thought. In her influential book *Postfeminisms: Feminism, Cultural Theory and Cultural Forms* (1997), Ann Brooks suggests that

> *post*feminism can be understood as critically engaging with patriarchy and *post*modernism as similarly engaged with the principles of modernism. It does not assume that either patriarchal or modernist discourses and frames of reference have been replaced or superseded. (1)

Brooks rightly points out that although the use of the prefix "post" might appear to suggest that the aims of earlier configurations of feminism have been achieved, this use of "post" is "highly problematic" (1). Just as second-wave feminism is itself "a continuation of a movement, that earlier phase of feminism which clamoured for civic equality for women via the vote" (Whelehan 3), postfeminism builds upon a critical framework established, in large part, by the work of second-wave feminist thinkers. It is important to point out, then, that despite a widespread hostility towards the term, postfeminism has transcended neither the concerns of second-wave feminism out of which it emerged nor the particular circumstances that led to its emergence. Rather, it remains deeply embedded in a longer history of the struggle for female empowerment.

Postfeminism's often fraught relationship to second-wave feminism has been explored in some detail in recent criticism (e.g. Brooks; Howie and Tauchert; Siegel). However, postfeminism's continuities with and divergences from discourses of female empowerment that predate the emergence of modern feminism continue to be overlooked – accounts of the origins of what some have termed the "third wave" of feminism seem to date back no earlier than the 1960s. When the work of pioneering seventeenth- and eighteenth-century women such as Mary Wollstonecraft and Mary Astell is mentioned in recent studies, its connections to contemporary developments in feminist thought are seldom the subject of critical examination (Howie and Tauchert). This essay argues that such a view of postfeminism, a view that is largely uninterested in the historical underpinnings of the discourse, has clear limitations, not least because the dialogue between early and recent representations of feminine empowerment continues into the twenty-first century. As Diane Elam points out in *Romancing the Postmodern*, "Postmodernism is not a perspectival view on history; it is the rethinking of history as an ironic coexistence of temporalities" (3). The possibilities opened up by such a view of history are lost if we do not recognize that this "coexistence of temporalities" can also be applied to the discourse of postfeminism.

As a cultural form whose popularity shows no sign of waning, Gothic fiction emerges as a useful vehicle through which to trace some of the connections between late eighteenth- and early twenty-first-century configurations of female empowerment. Gothic fiction has, almost from its inception, been concerned with exploring the sufferings visited upon women by the patriarchal cultures in which they live. This essay, then, examines the way in which the postmodern and postfeminist text of *Buffy the Vampire Slayer* (*BTVS*) enters actively into a dialogue with earlier Gothic fiction. In particular, it argues that *BTVS* can be seen as a continuation of a late eighteenth- and early nineteenth-century tradition of feminine Gothic fiction, perhaps best exemplified in the work of novelist Ann Radcliffe. As we will see, many of the protofeminist concerns of early Gothic fiction are still relevant in the postmodern world of Sunnydale. When we compare Buffy and her vampiric nemesis, Drusilla, to their eighteenth-century counterpart, the Radcliffian heroine of sensibility, we see that the very postfeminist text of *BTVS* owes more to its eighteenth-century Gothic precursors than might, at first, be apparent.

The rise of Gothic fiction – in particular, the so-called feminine Gothic fiction of writers such as Radcliffe[1] – coincided with the emergence of what we now recognize as modern-day feminism. One of the main effects of a nascent consumer culture in Britain during the last decades of the eighteenth century was the growth of an increasingly powerful middle class. An important side-effect of this general rise in affluence was an unprecedented increase in female literacy across class boundaries (Davidoff and Hall; Barker-Benfield). The significance of this increase in female literacy in the latter part of the eighteenth century cannot be underestimated. Literacy allowed large numbers of women to partici-pate more actively in the public sphere than they had been able to at any other time in the past. Moreover, it played an instrumental role in expanding the intellectual horizons of women by contributing to "the growth of personality; one's absorption of knowledge of the self and other, and its transformation into one's own terms and purposes, including art" (Barker-Benfield 162). Women were certainly quick to capitalize on the new possibilities opened up by this increase in literacy and, by the end of the century, numerous female poets and novelists had established their own readership in a competitive literary market-place, while female readers gained increasing access to literary works (Newlyn 7).

This is not, of course, to suggest that there had not been important feminist thinkers and writers in Britain before the final decades of the eighteenth century. But it is surely no coincidence that at the same time as increasing numbers of women began to exploit their new-found power in an increasingly consumer-driven economy, writers such as Mary Wollstonecraft began to clamour for their recognition as subjects, and for their right to participate more broadly in public life. Nor can it be an accident that two of the most influential texts in the history of women's writing, *The Mysteries of Udolpho* and *A Vindication of the Rights of Woman*, were published only two years apart (1794 and 1792, respec-tively). Wollstonecraft aimed her famous feminist treatise squarely at the same predominantly middle-class women who read Radcliffe's fiction. And, although Radcliffe would undoubtedly have been unwilling to have her views on women linked publicly with those of her rather more radical (not to mention less respectable) contemporary, the concerns of her female-centred novels suggest an affinity with the cause adopted by Wollstonecraft.

One of the key elements that connects Radcliffe's and Wollstonecraft's writings is their simultaneous investment in, and yet interrogation of, the discourse of sensibility. Sensibility was a quality that, although not inherently gendered, was linked in the eighteenth century to women. It encompassed a number of characteristics, perhaps the most important of which were "the faculty of feeling, the capacity for extremely refined emotion and a quickness to display compassion for suffering" (Todd 7). Because of its focus on the delineation of physical experience, sensibility was adopted by many women writers as an avenue through which to publicize (and often politicize) their experiences of bodily and emotional suffering. But in both fiction and "real life" this deep susceptibility to emotional stimuli had to be kept under the tightest of controls in order to be effective. Too keen a sensibility could result in, on the one hand, a mental disorder akin to madness and, on the other hand, accusations of licentiousness and sexual transgression. Wollstonecraft, for example, argued that excessive sensibility "inflamed" the senses of women and that with their intellect and rationality neglected, these women "become the prey of their senses, delicately termed sensibility, and are blown about by every momentary gust of feeling" (70).

Sensibility plays a key role in Radcliffe's novels, all of which centre upon the experiences of a woman of marriageable age and deep emotional susceptibility who is left to fend for herself upon the death (or mysterious disappearance) of her parents. Emily, the young heroine of *The Mysteries of Udolpho*, possesses a sensibility that manifests itself in an "uncommon delicacy of mind, warm affections, and ready benevolence" (4). However, Radcliffe is also careful to point out that along with these admirable qualities "was observable a degree of susceptibility too exquisite to admit of lasting peace" (4). Emily's sensibility, then, at once reflects her desirable femininity, her noble character and her "softness" of manner, while also leaving her dangerously prey to powerful feeling.

The weakness inherent in Emily's sensibility is of concern to her father, St Aubert, who worries about the dangers to which this excessive sensibility might expose his daughter. To this end, he attempts in the early part of the novel to educate her in the rational tempering of her sensibility. He endeavours "to strengthen her mind; to enure her to habits of self command; to teach her to reject the first impulse of her feelings, and to look, with cool examination, upon the disappointments he sometimes threw in her way" (4). In other words, St Aubert advises Emily to subject all emotional responses to careful rational consideration before taking any action governed by them. Emily has completed her instruction in rational thought by the time that she is left an orphan by her father's early death, and the importance of this education becomes increasingly clear as the novel progresses.

Throughout *The Mysteries of Udolpho* we see that Emily's sensibility, when tempered by rationality, provides her with a source of a distinctly feminine form of empowerment. Perhaps most important, it allows her to resist passively her attempted subjugation by various male figures of authority. After her father's death, Emily is left under the care of her aunt, the rather unsympathetic Madame Cheron. Soon afterwards, Madame Cheron marries the villain of the novel, Montoni, and takes Emily with her to live in the castle of Udolpho, high in the Italian Alps. When Madame Cheron (now Madame Montoni) dies as a result of neglect and starvation at the hands of her husband, she leaves Emily the sole heir of her estate and of all the lands belonging to it (including, it transpires, Udolpho itself). The greedy Montoni, unwilling to relinquish that which he had indirectly killed for, attempts to force Emily to sign this inheritance over to him. But Emily cannot be persuaded to give up what is hers by right, and she refuses to sign the documents. It is, in this case, Emily's education in rational sensibility that guides her actions. Fear alone, driven by powerful emotion, might have compelled her to sign her lands over to Montoni. However, his power over her is weakened by the fact that "a sacred pride was in her heart, that taught it to swell against the pressure of injustice, and almost to glory in the quiet sufferance of ills" (381). Secure in the knowledge that her actions are morally correct, and dismayed by Montoni's unfeeling treatment of her aunt, Emily suffers stoically the consequences of her actions. Indeed, it is precisely the suffering sanctioned by her deployment of rational sensibility that, as Montoni himself acknowledges, makes her into a heroine: " 'You speak like a heroine,' said Montoni contemptuously; 'we shall see whether you can suffer like one' " (381).

But although Emily's rational sensibility guides her response to Montoni, allows her to endure various indignities and plays an instrumental role in her eventual marriage to the hero of the story, Valancourt, sensibility itself remains a double-edged tool of feminine empowerment throughout *The Mysteries of Udolpho*. Radcliffe's Gothic heroines, possessing an abundance of sensibility and subjected to numerous trials and tribulations, can often walk a thin line between rationality and insanity. In fact, sensibility untempered by rational reflection produces many of the archetypal moments of "terror" for which Radcliffe is famous. Terror, of course, is predicated on a belief that the fear of what one imagines to have taken place is always more frightening than what actually occurs. Uncertainty and obscurity are central to the creation of terror because, as Radcliffe herself acknowledges, "obscurity leaves something for the imagination to exaggerate" ("On the Supernatural" 169). In Radcliffean Gothic that which produces terror is typically deflated at the end of the novel – the heroine's irrational fears of ghosts, skeletons and supposed murders are given a rational explanation. Rational sensibility is privileged over irrational sensibility. But although terror can eventually be overcome by the reasoning of a rational mind, the moments of real terror that Emily suffers throughout *The Mysteries of Udolpho* reflect the fact that the process of subjecting sensibility to rational reflection is by no means a simple one.

Rational sensibility is, therefore, rarely, if ever, an innate characteristic of the Gothic heroine. It must be learned. This is demonstrated earlier in the novel when, in a typical moment of Radcliffean terror, Emily becomes convinced that Montoni has murdered her missing aunt. To her great relief, she later discovers that her aunt is alive (although gravely ill) and imprisoned in a remote corner of the castle. However, Emily's emotions have, in this instance, taken over completely from her rational self, suggesting the possibility of a madness that, despite its eventual dismissal, is never entirely exorcised in the novel. As Markman Ellis points out, "Emily's 'sensibility' ... is the foundation of her beauty and appeal, but it also renders her temperament precariously unstable" (54). Radcliffe illustrates the dangers of excessive feminine sensibility by suggesting that sensibility unaccompanied by an educated rationality is never more than a few steps away from madness.

Radcliffe's repeated emphasis on Emily's struggle to contain and redirect her emotional response to the world around her in *The Mysteries of Udolpho* reinforces her ideological links to the form of female empowerment advocated by Wollstonecraft. Like Radcliffe, Wollstonecraft believes that sensibility can be a marker of gentility and refinement in a young woman only if it is tempered by carefully cultivated rational thought:

> Overstretched sensibility naturally relaxes the other powers of the mind, and prevents intellect from attaining the sovereignty which it ought to attain to render a creature useful to others ... for the exercise of the understanding, as life advances, is the only method pointed out by nature to calm the passions. (69)

As this passage demonstrates, women's capacity to reason becomes a sign of their ability to transcend the constraints imposed upon them by the female body. It allows them to become, in Wollstonecraft's own words, "a creature useful to others." In Emily's case, it allows her to triumph over her patriarchal oppressors, stoically to endure psychological and physical hardship, and to realize her full potential as an eighteenth-century woman when she becomes Valancourt's wife.

Sensibility might, at first, appear to be a peculiarly eighteenth-century concept, a concept that has little relevance to the postmodern world of

BTVS. And, on one level, there are very few women in Joss Whedon's popular series who are unable to fend for themselves in dangerous situations, and even fewer who resemble the professional "victims" of Radcliffe's romances. This is in keeping with Whedon's now-famous assertion that the concept for *BTVS* stemmed from a desire to reverse deliberately the Gothic association of femininity with victimhood, to allow the heroine of sensibility the power to fight back. "I thought it would be funny," he has said, "to have that girl [whom we recognize as the Gothic heroine] go into a dark alley where we knew she would get killed and actually have her trash the monster" (qtd. in Ervin-Gore). But despite her superhuman strength and fighting ability, the character of Buffy still embodies many of the typical elements required of the Radcliffean heroine of sensibility. For a start, she is a woman, as are all vampire Slayers. Moreover, she is, like Emily, beautiful, slim and blonde, and she is also, at least for the first five seasons of the show, guided by her Watcher, Giles. Giles, whose stuffy, bespectacled Britishness is presented as the direct opposite of Buffy's sunny Southern Californian disposition, functions throughout the series like St Aubert. He is a benevolent figure of education and paternal authority who attempts to train Buffy to use her powers to their best effect.

Giles is necessary because, like her heroine of sensibility precursors, Buffy more often than not reacts emotionally to the world around her. Buffy too must learn to control and redirect her sensibility through rational thought because it is, in large part, this emotional response to threat that provides the base of her power. Importantly, Buffy's emotional response to the world (that is, her sensibility, transposed into a twenty-first-century context) allows her to challenge perceived limitations and to become very dangerous when those she loves are threatened. It is, in large part, Buffy's capacity to feel deeply and to channel the great power of her emotions that situates her as a typical Gothic heroine. But more than this, Buffy is also able to endure suffering if it is for the right cause, or to ease the suffering of others. We see this in "Becoming, Part Two" (2022)[2] when she kills her vampire boyfriend Angel in order to save the world. Buffy places the needs of others before her own desire to save Angel. She suffers because in suffering herself (by killing Angel and thus closing the Hellmouth – a porthole into demon dimensions) she is ameliorating the suffering of countless others. Like Emily, Buffy's suffering makes her into a heroine.

Buffy is well aware of the positive aspects of her sensibility. As she puts it herself in "What's My Line, Part One" (2009), "my emotions give me power. They're total assets." When the dangerous elements of Buffy's sensibility are channelled productively, this sensibility becomes her greatest tool. Nonetheless, unlike the traditional heroine of sensibility, Buffy's empathic qualities (and empathy is a key element of sensibility) are necessarily limited by virtue of her status as Slayer. In her line of work, too much empathy is a distinct disadvantage. Buffy also questions authority in a way that goes far beyond a heroine like Emily's essentially passive entreaties and her refusal to sign her land over to Montoni. In fact, Buffy openly challenges established Slayer tradition throughout the series. She cuts herself off from the authority of the Watcher's Council, the bureaucratic body to which Giles belongs and which oversees the training of all Slayers and potential Slayers. She does not fight alone but recognizes and takes advantage of the useful qualities offered by her friends (Willow and Tara's education in magic; Spike and Angel's "demon underworld" connections; Giles's academic interest in the history of the occult) and she develops her own increasingly non-hierarchical means of fighting evil. Buffy is, then, an inherently active character, not only in the sense that she is never a passive victim of the vampires but also in the sense that she is physically strong and that she is able to take a control over her life that is denied to her eighteenth-century counterpart. Nowhere is Buffy's physical agency better embodied than in the inevitable slaying sequence that is played out in most episodes. In fact, this narrative convention, part of the internal logic of a *BTVS* episode, appears to be designed explicitly to reinforce Buffy's difference from the archetypal victimized Gothic heroine.

But despite this key difference from early Gothic heroines, Buffy is still trapped inside her body. Granted, it is a strong, active and beautiful body, but Buffy is nonetheless as trapped physically by her calling as Slayer as Emily ever was in the castle at Udolpho. And whereas Emily can be rescued from her predicament by the hero of the story, in order for Buffy to be rescued in the same way from the bodily entrapment upon which her status as a heroine is grounded, she must die. So although Emily's body constrains her in numerous ways throughout *The Mysteries of Udolpho*, it is also in a strange way her saving grace, for eventually it is through her feminine body that her social function as wife and mother can be realized. However, in order for Buffy to cease being a vampire Slayer she must first transcend the physicality that her calling is predicated upon and she can do this only by dying. In other words, Emily's feminine body allows her to be rescued but, as we see in season six, Buffy can be saved only through the destruction of her body. Death is, indeed, Buffy's gift (see "The Gift" [5022]) not just for Dawn, the sister whom she saves by sacrificing her own body in her stead, or for the world, which escapes being taken over by a demon dimension, but also, it transpires, for Buffy herself. We see in "Once More with Feeling" (6007) that the true significance of this "gift" is that it allows Buffy to transcend finally the suffering upon which her calling is predicated. In fact, one of the most wonderful things about her time in Heaven, Buffy sings in this musical episode, is that "there was no pain."

In one of the more overtly feminist moments of the series, the final episode of *BTVS*, "Chosen" (7022), offers a solution to Buffy's entrapment within her feminine body. At no time in the series has Buffy felt the responsibility inherent in her role as Slayer as strongly as when, in season seven, she takes on the task of training potential Slayers in a large-scale fight against the "First Evil". According to the mythology of the show, the First Evil has no corporeal form and it has always existed within the world. The power of evil is depicted as being as much a part of human existence as goodness. Interestingly, however, throughout the season the First Evil takes on explicitly misogynistic configurations in its attempt to defeat Buffy and, in turn, overcome the powers of good. Its key human disciple, Caleb, is a misogynistic, prophecy-spouting preacher whose hatred of Buffy is matched only by his hatred of women in general. As Patricia Pender notes, "Caleb is a monstrous but familiar representative of patriarchal oppression, propounding a dangerous form of sexism under the cover of pastoral care" (168). Given that the First Evil is, in effect, the power of all that is evil in the world, the fight seems hopeless. The First has an army of über-vamps and all Buffy can muster up are (in the First's own words) – "Some thirty-odd pimply-faced girls, don't know the pointy end of a stake" ("Chosen" [7022]). But, in the final episodes of the series, Buffy, inspired by the members of an ancient matriarchal force that predates the Watchers' Council and looks over the affairs of the Slayer, devises an ingenious plan. She takes the powerful weapon given to her by these women (a large scythe), designed to be used only by the Slayer, and, using Willow's magical skills, diffuses its power among all potential Slayers all over the world. In so doing, she gives all girls with the potential to be vampire Slayers, Slayer superpowers.

This scene seizes on the potential for feminist action implied in Foucault's postmodern understanding of power. For Foucault, of course, the possibility for resistance always resides within discourses of power. Moreover, resistance need not take a singular form as

> points of resistance are present everywhere in the power network. Hence there is no single locus of great Refusal, no soul of revolt,

source of all rebelliousness, or pure law of the revolutionary. Instead there is a plurality of resistances, each of them a special case. (95–6)

What happens at the end of "Chosen" is, then, a recognition of the possibilities opened up by these multiple points of resistance that exist within the discourse of power. If the physical setting of this final battle between Buffy, the potential Slayers and the First is within what we might call the space of power (the Hellmouth), then each of the Slayers offers up individual points of resistance from within its boundaries. It is as a result of these multiple points of resistance that the Hellmouth is destroyed and the First Evil vanquished – at least for the time being.

"Chosen" makes clear, then, that the potential for feminine empowerment has always existed within the heroines of Gothic fiction, much as it has always existed within the previously overwhelmed and frightened band of potential Slayers. But, whereas earlier heroines like Emily are constrained in their actions by the limitations imposed upon them by the patriarchal society in which they live, twenty-first-century women are constrained only by their perception of their own limitations. Buffy solves the dilemma of her own Slayer existence by choosing to share her power among all those with the potential to embody it. Even after the Sunnydale Hellmouth is destroyed, evil will continue to exist (Giles remarks dryly that there is another Hellmouth in Cleveland), but rather than being the sole point of resistance in this ongoing battle with evil, a responsibility that will inevitably destroy her, Buffy chooses to reject the individualistic basis of her calling. In doing so, she breaks free of the bonds that have previously limited her subjectivity and creates a world where Slayer power is no longer the dominion of one, but of many.

Buffy can be seen, then, as the logical evolution of the Radcliffean heroine of sensibility – a modernized version of Emily. Her Watcher, her close-knit group of friends and her own growing self-awareness help her to temper her capacity for purely emotional response. But there is one character in *BTVS* whose resemblance to the traditional heroine of sensibility is, perhaps, even more obvious – Spike's vampiric girlfriend, Drusilla. Spike and Dru are the key villains (the "Big Bads") of season two and, according to the mythology established in the series, were turned into vampires in the nineteenth century. Somewhat paradoxically, their power (not to mention appeal) as villains stems from their engagement with, and fondness for, postmodern life. "Truth is," says Spike memorably in "Becoming, Part Two" (2023), "I like this world. You got dog racing, Manchester United, and you got people. Billions of people walking around like happy meals with legs." But despite the fact that

LIVERPOOL JOHN MOORES UNIVERSITY
LEARNING SERVICES

they have adapted wholeheartedly to the twentieth-century world of nightclubs, subcultures and television (regular viewers will know that Spike's favourite show is the camp soap opera *Passions*), Spike and Dru retain significant traces of their nineteenth-century selves. For example, Spike's viciousness as a vampiric predator is in no small part driven by his desire to leave behind the humiliation meted out to him in his past-life as William, the sappy author of "bloody awful" poetry. Similarly, Drusilla's once entirely virtuous sensibility has been warped by her torture by the evil Angelus and her subsequent transformation into a vampire.

In "Becoming, Part One" (2022), we are afforded a glimpse into Drusilla's origins. What is perhaps most interesting about this episode is that it reveals explicitly that Dru was, before her transformation, a typical Gothic heroine. In a flashback to "London, 1860," the viewer is presented with the pre-vampiric Drusilla. The scene is set in a Catholic church to which she has come to receive confession. She appears to be in her late teens or early twenties in this scene, and her plain and demure cotton dress and veil indicate that she is virtuous and modest. Drusilla is, however, trapped within her body by visions that doom her helplessly to see tragic events before they happen. Unable to escape these visions, and told by her mother that they are the work of the devil, she turns (like so many heroines of sensibility before her) to the patriarchal authority of the Catholic church; to the paternal figure who, like St Aubert, is supposed to have her best interests at heart. Drusilla's belief in this system of authority is indicated by the faith she places in the (supposed) priest to absolve her of her sin of second sight. But her faith in her paternal protector, although absolute, is fatally misguided. The priest to whom she has confessed is actually Angelus, a vampire who has been stalking the young woman for days. Angelus, it emerges, is particularly drawn to the virtuous Drusilla, and he soon begins his torture of her – slowly killing off her entire family. Unlike Emily and Buffy, Dru has no "good" father figure to whom to turn for advice, and she is never given the chance to develop her rational sensibility. Consequently, her grasp on sanity becomes more and more tenuous as a result of watching her loved ones picked off one by one. With her family gone and no Valancourt to save her, Drusilla retreats to a convent – away from the world, and into the safety of her feminine body. However, on the day she is to take the veil, she is turned into a vampire by Angelus.

Once Drusilla has been turned into a vampire, the virtues associated with her sensibility are transformed into their transgressive opposites. This transformation is reflected in the exchange of the maidenly dress glimpsed in "Becoming" for outfits of darker, bolder colours and more sensuous fabrics. In fact, the very next scene in the episode lingers over these changes in Drusilla. We watch the twentieth-century Dru wearing an ornate scarlet gown slowly descend the stairs of the mansion she now shares with Spike and Angel (who has recently been turned back into his "bad" alter ego, Angelus, through his first sexual encounter with Buffy). The timid child in the church has become a confident, assertive woman and a keen predator. Perhaps most important, in the process of becoming a vampire, Dru's modesty has become sexuality. In a later episode of Whedon's spin-off series, *Angel*, we see that Dru is driven to sire Spike in large part by her desire for a romantic partner ("Darla" [2007]), and it is the powerful sexual bond between the two that motivates most of their evil actions in season two of *BTVS*. Throughout the season, we see that Dru's disordered emotions often drive her actions, and it soon becomes clear that she is at her most dangerous, and capable of the greatest evil, when these emotions are aroused. But unlike both Buffy and the Radcliffean heroine before her, Drusilla's sensibility cannot be governed by rationality and, as a result, an ongoing side-effect of this sensibility is madness.

Interestingly, then, despite their obvious differences, Buffy and Drusilla are, in many ways, opposite sides of the same coin. In several key respects, they are doubles – both have had romantic relationships with Angel and Spike, both have visionary episodes, both are driven to action by the power of their love. We can see in this doubling of Buffy and Drusilla a contrast between good sensibility and bad emotions (ungoverned sensibility) that is itself a staple of early Gothic fiction – Emily too, it should be pointed out, has a double of dubious sensibility in the figure of her avaricious aunt (the same one who will later be hidden in the castle at Udolpho). However, whereas Buffy is a rational Radcliffean heroine for a postmodern era who, with the help of her friends and the guidance of her Watcher, is able to use her education and strength to save the human world from the demonic elements that would destroy it, Drusilla is an (anti-) heroine who possesses sensibility, but none of the rationality that renders it most effective. The key to Drusilla's madness appears to lie in her inability to reconcile her virtuous pre-vampiric self with her post-vampiric existence. Drusilla not only is tortured and defiled by Angelus, but is forced to live with the consequences of her fall from virtue and piety. There is no question that Dru's visions and her various manifestations of sensibility become increasingly disordered after her transformation into a vampire – removed from rationality they become a weakness rather than strength. Unable definitively to escape from her pre-vampiric self, and unable fully to accept the terms under which her vampiric existence was granted, Drusilla becomes the embodiment of sensibility without rationality – a sensibility gone mad.

Rebecca Munford suggests that "third wave feminists' attention to, and engagement with, the popular has been dismissed [by second-wave feminists] as a privileging of style over politics – of individual over collective empowerment" (144). But, as this short history of feminine Gothic fiction indicates, popular culture, from its very inception, has been a key space for the negotiation and exploration of different forms of feminine empowerment. The "stylishness" of Radcliffe's popular fiction and Whedon's popular television series does not lessen their investment in the exploration of female subjectivity, nor weaken their examination of the limitations placed on the feminine body. In fact, in the doubling of particular aspects of Buffy and Drusilla we see a postfeminist critique of sensibility emerge, just as we can discern an eighteenth-century critique of sensibility in Radcliffe's fiction. Moreover, in a move that only underscores the continuities between Gothic and postmodern discourses of female empowerment, the validation of the rational sensibility exhibited by Buffy (particularly when contrasted to the irrational emotion displayed by Drusilla) owes much to the stance taken earlier in Radcliffe's popular novels.

BTVS's overt borrowings from and re-workings of eighteenth-century discourses of female empowerment are, perhaps, indicative of the series' ideological difference from second-wave feminist texts of the twentieth century. However, they also affirm its participation in a history of the struggle for female empowerment. Given the long history of the Gothic, it is important to understand Buffy – a heroine of sensibility for the twenty-first century – in the context of this broader struggle.

Notes

1. Early Gothic fictions are traditionally divided into two streams, "feminine" and "masculine" Gothic. In masculine, or "horror," Gothic fiction, disturbing events are described in great detail. In feminine, or "terror," Gothic, frightening events are left, in large part, to the reader's imagination. Despite the fact that these terms imply a gendered division among writers, it is important to note that both feminine and masculine Gothic could be written by men and women. For a more detailed account see Fay.
2. The episode numbering system indicates season and episode. Thus, 2022 means second season, episode 22.

Works cited

Angel. Dir. Joss Whedon. Twentieth Century Fox. 1999–2004.

Barker-Benfield, G. J. *The Culture of Sensibility: Sex and Society in Eighteenth Century Britain*. Chicago: U of Chicago P, 1992.

Brooks, Ann. *Postfeminisms: Feminism, Cultural Theory, and Cultural Forms*. London: Routledge, 1997.

Buffy the Vampire Slayer. Dir. Joss Whedon. Twentieth Century Fox. 1997–2003.

Davidoff, Lenore, and Catherine Hall. *Family Fortunes: Men and Women of the English Middle Class, 1780–1850*. London: Hutchinson, 1987.

Elam, Diane. *Romancing the Postmodern*. London: Routledge, 1992.

Ellis, Markman. *The History of Gothic Fiction*. Edinburgh: Edinburgh UP, 2000.

Ervin-Gore, Shawna. "Interview with Joss Whedon." *Dark Horse Comics*. 24 October 2005<http://www.darkhorse.com/news/interviews.php?id=669>.

Fay, Elizabeth. "Women and the Gothic: Literature As Home Politics." *A Feminist Introduction to Romanticism*. Oxford: Blackwell, 1998. 107–48.

Foucault, Michel. *The History of Sexuality: Volume One*. London: Penguin, 1990.

Howie, Gillian, and Ashley Tauchert. "Feminist Dissonance: The Logic of Late Feminism." *Third Wave Feminism: A Critical Exploration*. Ed. Stacy Gillis, Gillian Howie and Rebecca Munford. Houndsmills: Palgrave, 2004. 37–48.

Munford, Rebecca. " 'Wake Up and Smell the Lipgloss': Gender, Generation and the (A)politics of Girl Power." *Third Wave Feminism: A Critical Exploration*. Ed. Stacy Gillis, Gillian Howie and Rebecca Munford. Houndsmills: Palgrave, 2004. 142–53.

Newlyn, Lucy. *Reading, Writing and Romanticism: The Anxiety of Reception*. Oxford: Oxford UP, 2000.

Norton, Rictor. *Mistress of Udolpho: The Life of Ann Radcliffe*. London: Leicester UP, 1999.

Pender, Patricia. " 'Kicking Ass Is Comfort Food': Buffy As Third Wave Feminist Icon." *Third Wave Feminism: A Critical Exploration*. Ed. Stacy Gillis, Gillian Howie and Rebecca Munford. Houndsmills: Palgrave, 2004. 164–74.

Radcliffe, Ann. *The Mysteries of Udolpho*. 1794. Oxford: Oxford UP, 1998.

——. "On the Supernatural in Poetry." Rpt. in *Gothic Documents: A Sourcebook, 1700–1820*. Ed. E. J. Clery and Robert Miles. Manchester: Manchester UP, 2000. 163–72.

Siegel, Deborah L. "Reading between the Waves: Feminist Historiography in a 'Postfeminist' Moment." *Third Wave Agenda: Being Feminist, Doing Feminism*. Ed. Leslie Heywood and Jennifer Drake. Minneapolis: U of Minnesota P, 1997.

Todd, Janet. *Sensibility: An Introduction*. London: Methuen, 1986.

Whelehan, Imelda. *Modern Feminist Thought: From the Second Wave to "Post-Feminism."* New York: New York UP, 1995.

Wollstonecraft, Mary. *A Vindication of the Rights of Woman*. 1792. London: J.M. Dent, 1995.

11
She: Gothic Reverberations in *Star Trek: First Contact*

Linda Dryden

In Gothic, fantasy and horror the representation of women tends to focus on female sexuality, the female as object of the male gaze, and the female as victim, usually in a sexual or erotic manner. Hence much of the imagery and iconography of women in science fiction and related genres is highly sexualized, featuring scantily clad female bodies. Even when the female is an alien, her body is frequently the object of male desire. Thus in *Star Trek: First Contact* (1996) the villain is a cyborg female, with a recognizably human body, provocatively dressed, who uses seduction to subjugate men. Perpetuating the stereotype of women in science fiction as objects of the male gaze, this Borg Queen is a sexual threat to the fraternity of male officers who seek her destruction and that of her race. Furthermore, *First Contact* reverts to some of the tropes and conventions of Gothic fiction, demonstrating the close relationship between the two genres and their representations of women.

This essay examines *Star Trek: First Contact* as an example of postfeminism in terms of its deliberate representation of the cyborg female as an unreconstructed Gothic *femme fatale*. Such a reading of the film positions it within the uncertain and sometimes contradictory ideology of post-feminism as a retrograde attempt to re-appropriate the *femme fatale* as a demonized figure who threatens to sever the bonds of male friendship and loyalty. Comparing the film with H. Rider Haggard's imperial Gothic fantasy *She* (1887) reveals the ideological and figurative founda-tions on which this type of Gothic science fiction is predicated. Yet the film also deals with the postmodern concept of the cyborg, and it is also the purpose here to explore how feminist perceptions of the cyborg, such as Donna Haraway's, contribute to our understanding of the Borg in the film. Through this examination of both film and text it will become evident that the science fiction genre perpetuates female stereotypes from the Gothic genre, and thus *First Contact* demonstrates the slippery and uncertain theoretical parameters of postfeminism.

Star Trek and Feminism

The *Star Trek* franchise has been renowned for tackling contemporary issues since its pilot episode in 1964, "The Cage." This was groundbreaking in featuring a female first officer, but the series was shelved, being deemed unsuitable for the target audience.[1] The format was reworked and a male hierarchy of command was adopted for the now cult original series, with Kirk and Spock as captain and first officer, respectively. The programme has had several incarnations and ten movies have been made featuring the casts of the various series.

Despite its reputation for polystyrene props, rubber monsters and poor acting, *Star Trek* has evolved over the decades to become one of the longest running and most cult of series in television history. Various spin-offs, such as merchandise and pulp novels, often featuring homoerotic plots between Kirk and Spock, have extended its life far beyond initial expectations. Gene Roddenberry, the *Star Trek* series' creator, was always anxious to have storylines that were utopian, exhibiting the most progressive of liberal American values.[2] The first heterosexual interracial kiss took place between Kirk and Lieutenant Uhura in an episode entitled "Plato's Stepchildren" in 1968. The incident caused outrage in a society still riven with racial discrimination: some states in Southern America refused to screen the episode. Twenty years after the first series, the programme was re-launched with a new cast and reflecting the change in values over the decades since the original series. Entitled *Star Trek: The Next Generation* (*TNG*), this series went further than before in breaking down taboos by featuring women in more prominent roles and adopting a more liberal attitude to all types of sexuality.[3] Such high ideals, however, failed to permeate the series throughout, and it was not until *Star Trek: Voyager* in 1995 that the series acquired a female captain, Kathryn Janeway.

In effect, *Star Trek* is generally deeply conservative, despite Roddenberry's ideals. Michèle and Duncan Barrett have shown how the hierarchy and chain of command of the various *Star Trek* starships are closely modelled on a naval structure, with admirals, captains, lieutenants, ships, fleets and so on. Within this rigid structure, feminist concerns are hard to discern. Whereas male characters generally take authoritarian roles, female characters are confined to the caring professions: doctor, counsellor, teacher, botanist and junior officers. As *TNG* progressed, female admirals were introduced, but rarely as regular characters. Females as leading politicians on alien planets were a rarity; strong female characters have tended to be either dangerous *femmes fatales* or the love interest of one of the male officers.

By the time of the second movie to feature the *TNG* cast, Roddenberry had died and the trajectory of the plot was in other hands. *First Contact* moved away from its niche family audience and into something altogether darker. This was the era of the action hero and the evil cyborg: *Die Hard* and *Terminator*, for example. Capitalizing on a public taste for such genres, the creators of *First Contact* cast the hitherto calm, rational and emotionally reticent Captain Jean-Luc Picard as the vest-wearing, muscle-bound all-action hero whose arch-enemy is the cyborg dominatrix, the Borg Queen. In a postfeminist world, the Borg Queen is a power-crazed alien with a sexy line in leather and boots. This blend of preternatural being with erotica and sexual desire typifies the science fiction film genre in recent years, but also recalls the genre of Victorian Gothic and another such *femme fatale*, Ayesha, or She-who-must-be-obeyed in Haggard's *She*. The Borg Queen is a postfeminist Gothic creature with a desire for universe domination, echoing her earlier counterpart's thirst for power over the known world. Framing the film within a Gothic context, reinforcing the masculine values of traditional science fiction and casting the main female character as a terrifying alien, the makers of *First Contact* found a winning formula: the film became one of the most successful of all the *Star Trek* movies.

Male officers, male bonding and the female threat

The original series of *Star Trek* is often noted for the strong bond between the male characters: the crew represent a fraternity of male loyalty and (usually) platonic love.[4] It is a given of *Star Trek* that the *Enterprise*'s captain commands the undivided loyalty of his crew. The interests of the Federation of Planets and the safety of the ship and her crew are the captain's paramount concern.[5] Developing on the original series, and adding new complexities to the captain figure, *TNG* featured Jean-Luc Picard as a handsome, bald, middle-aged bachelor with a penchant for Dickens, Shakespeare, theatre and classical music.[6] He is French, an intellectual and commands unusually powerful loyalty because of his flawless judgement and scrupulously just dealings with all issues of transgression. A particular bond develops between Picard and the android-who-would-be-human, Commander Data. This is largely due to Data's role in rescuing Picard from the Borg, an alien species whose mission is to assimilate all humanoid life forms into the Borg Collective until the Borg populate the whole universe. The television series never posits this captain, unlike Kirk, as an action hero: he is even-tempered, calm in battle situations and rarely involved in armed combat.

For *First Contact* Picard is transformed into a vengeance-seeking vigilante with rippling muscles and a single-minded purpose that threatens to destroy his starship and its crew. The object of this obsessive vengeance is the Borg Queen, and her race of cyborgs who implant human bodies, in this case the crew of the *Enterprise*, with mechanical eyepieces, limbs and other prostheses. Human consciousness is lost once "wired up" to the Borg Collective and thus linked telepathically: in effect all Borg are one. Fred Botting describes the Borg succinctly as "body and machine composed of bodies and machines, a meta-cyborganism" (265). In the television series Picard had been abducted and transformed by the Borg into Locutus and was, it is suggested in the movie, the love interest of the Borg Queen. *First Contact* builds on the plot of the television Borg episodes, and develops a "love triangle" whereby the Borg Queen captures Data, endows him with human flesh and ultimately makes him her consort, replacing Picard/Locutus.

The Borg are terrifying: their blend of organic bodies with cybernetic implants makes them Gothic monsters, hybrids and immoral. As Haraway says, a "cyborg is a cybernetic organism": "Contemporary science fiction is full of cyborgs – creatures simultaneously animal and machine, who populate worlds ambiguously natural and crafted" (149). Haraway argues that the cyborg does not "recognize the Garden of Eden" (151). In other words, the cyborg denies human history as told through Christian mythology, because its very existence is predicated on its organic integration of technology. Instead the cyborg "is resolutely committed to partiality, irony, intimacy, and perversity. It is oppositional, utopian, and completely without innocence" (151). The cyborg is thus a contemporary Gothic creature. Like the monsters of earlier Gothic, Hoffmann's Olimpia in *The Sand-man* (1817), Frankenstein's creature, Stevenson's Mr Hyde, Haggard's Ayesha, Count Dracula or H.G. Wells's Invisible Man, the cyborg is recognizably human but weirdly and dangerously "other." Science fiction builds on earlier forms and earlier narratives, just as it builds on contemporary science and technology. As Joanna Russ states: "Science fiction must not offend against what is known" (6). The monster of the gothic is an ideal prototype for science fiction to appropriate: it is known, but it is also infinitely able to mutate into something new and more terrifying, while remaining recognizable as human-and-not-human.

The Gothic monster threatens the social and political structures of the existing world: Ayesha, Dracula and the Invisible Man all seek dominion over Britain, the Empire and potentially the whole planet. Frankenstein destroys the mate he was creating for his creature out of fear that the monstrous couple would breed a race of monsters to challenge human dominance on the planet. Just as Haraway suggests that the cyborg operates outside accepted human beliefs and value systems, so too the Gothic monster is unrestrained by religion or Western morality. The cyborg, like the Gothic monster, seeks to create its own world populated with its own creatures, ultimately, apart perhaps from Frankenstein's monster, convinced of its own superiority to ordinary humankind.

As Haraway implies, however, the cyborg goes further than earlier Gothic monsters. Science and technology have endowed the cyborg with a new type of consciousness that does not depend upon organic wholeness:

> Unlike Frankenstein's monster, the cyborg does not expect its father to save it through a restoration of the garden: that is, through the fabrication of a heterosexual mate, through its completion in a finished whole, a city and cosmos. (151)

Haraway's cyborg is a product of contemporary Western politics, a creature defined by the fast-evolving culture of technological dependence and technological invasion. Ultimately, Haraway sees the cyborg as a means of challenging established gender and racial positions. Her cyborg is a political creature whose "manifesto" is designed to liberate humanity from such dominant ideologies as patriarchy, religion and late capitalism.

The Borg of *Star Trek* are nowhere near as sophisticated or political in their intentions, yet they do exhibit characteristics of Haraway's cyborg. They have evolved from organic humanity to embrace technology not as an invasion of their bodies, but as a progressive development towards perfection: "perfection" being a key word in Borg vocabulary. Perfection for the Borg involves integration of all that is efficient. The Borg assimilate the uniqueness of other species, adding this to their own consciousness. Their purpose is a homogeneity that, rather than diluting individuation, assimilates it – "assimilation" being another Borg watchword. They seek a new type of utopia predicated upon their own cyborg nature, and thus their "Garden of Eden" will exist once the whole universe is Borg. Thus technology coupled with human organicism is, for the Borg, an ideal union.

The Borg disdain organic physical wholeness: the horror of their practices lies in their calculated replacement of human eyes, arms and legs with cumbersome, but effective technological implants and prosthetics designed to maximize their efficiency. They are, in effect, apart from the Queen, without emotion, terrible killing machines with no conscience: conscience, morality, indeed most human values derived from religion are regarded by the Borg as weaknesses. As such they are related to various emotionally deformed Gothic monsters: Mr Hyde, Ayesha, the Invisible Man and Dracula all exhibit a lack of conscience that becomes terrifying when coupled with power. Hoffmann's Olimpia is even more terrifying because as an automaton she lacks any emotion at all: in this respect she prefigures the Borg "drones," whose human emotions have been erased so that they resemble technologically enhanced zombies.

Presiding over this race of cyborg is the Borg Queen. She is the spokesperson and the unifying element of the Borg collective. Only the Queen has an individual self and an independent mind: she speaks with terrifying calmness of the Borg's mission to assimilate. As with Haraway's contemporary cyborgs, the Queen is deeply ironic in her disdain of human weakness for flesh, which she manipulates sadistically: knowing his desire to be human, the Queen grafts human skin onto Data's forearm. Breathing seductively onto the grafted skin, she arouses sexual desire in the android, and sadistically challenges him to tear off this evidence of humanity. Because Data is fully mechanical, the process of assimilation into Borg must be the reverse of that for organic creatures: Data must experience humanity. This, too, is evidence of the perversity and intimacy of the cyborg. There is no controlling moral world for the Borg: their purpose, like Dracula's, is to multiply and colonize.

Body snatchers: Cybernetic implants and Gothic bodies

The Borg's "refinement" of the organic physical body with technology equates to what Katherine Hayles calls the "posthuman." To a list of conditions determining the posthuman Hayles adds:

> Third, the posthuman view thinks of the body as the original prothesis we all learn to manipulate, so that extending or replacing the body with other protheses becomes a continuation of a process that began before we were born. Fourth, and most important, by these and other means, the posthuman view configures human being so it can be seamlessly articulated with intelligent machines. In the posthuman,

there are no essential differences or absolute demarcations between bodily existence and computer simulation, cybernetic mechanism and biological organism, robot technology and human goals. (3)

Hayles's description of the posthuman defines the Borg body and the Borg "collective" mind in rational terms: it is, however, the hybridity of the Borg that is most terrifying. Their prosthetics are an "improvement" on the weak human physical frame; their "wiring up" to the entire collective allows them to function as one through a communications system linked to their brain. Technology enables a group consciousness devoid of individual thought and individual motivation.[7] Intellectually they function as one; physically each Borg "drone" is adapted to a specific role through its prostheses. Borg technology thus controls the mind of the individual drone, just as Hayles notes happens in Bernard Wolfe's novel *Limbo* (1952): "When the body is integrated into a cybernetic circuit, modification of the circuit will necessarily modify consciousness as well. Connected by multiple feedback loops to the objects it designs, the mind is also an object of design" (115).[8] In the same way, Borg minds are governed by technology that eradicates emotion, conscience, desire and even a personal instinct for survival.

In terms of their physicality, the Borg are more than machines and less than human, but they are also in some ways distinct from Haraway's cyborgs because they are Gothic in conception. The Borg's biological selves are as horrifying as their robotic selves. Unlike say, Maria, the robot in Fritz Lang's *Metropolis* (1927), or the wholly organic monster in *Frankenstein*, the Borg are part-human and part-robot. This makes for a chilling hybrid: the technological invasion of the "snatched" human body effects a grotesque metamorphosis of human flesh that speaks of the Gothic. The visible flesh of the Borg transformation turns a slimy grey, and the skin becomes glisteningly hairless and transparent, revealing the vulnerable fleshiness and veins beneath. The Borg is now not a human; it is a thing, and as Kelly Hurley observes of the Gothic novel, "thingness" describes "that which is not human, undescribable" (29). Indeed, nothing "illustrates the Thingness of matter so admirably as slime" (34).

With their pale grey glistening flesh the Borg remind us of those other Gothic dwellers in the dark, H.G. Wells's Morlocks in *The Time Machine* (1895). But added to the Morlocks' wormlike flesh are an insectlike carapace and mechanical antennae that compound the horror of these creatures. The dark metallic covering of the Borg torso and the protruding sensors from eyes and head are reminiscent of insects. The effect is deliberate: the Borg collective is called a hive, implying bees, the Borg mass are called drones, and as humans pass among the Borg they are left alone unless they represent a threat, suggesting the behaviour of bees or wasps. The noise made by the collective is an insectlike whispering hum and clicking, devoid of words, as in a beehive or like the communications of an insect colony. Their collective mentality, lack of individuality and instinct for protecting the hive also derive from insect behaviour. Except for the Queen, they are silent, grim workers on a collective project to colonize the universe.

As Russ notes, it is a commonplace of science fiction that matriarchies are figured as swarming insect colonies (46). The Borg collective is indeed a postfeminist matriarchy where nearly all the drones are recognizably male, subservient to a twisted and evil Queen: her progeny are the drones, conceived through an unnatural fusion of organic body with a grim technology. Although mainly male these Borg are sexless, almost androgynous: they are the subjects and the slaves of a voracious Queen, the only one of them possessed of independent will and a predatory sexuality. Insectlike matriarchies may be a symptom of the world of science fiction, but the *femme fatale* dominating, enslaving and corrupting the male is a Gothic convention. From Hoffmann's Olimpia to Poe's Ligeia to Haggard's Ayesha to Helen Vaughan in Arthur Machen's *The Great God Pan* (1894), male writers of the Gothic have figured the *femme fatale* as a threat to the enthralled male, fatally dangerous because of her "unnatural" ability to subjugate the normally dominant male. Leaping over a hundred years of repositioning of the woman in literature and in reality, *Star Trek: First Contact* reverts to an earlier Gothic type by giving us the unreconstructed *femme fatale* and confirming the uncertain position of postfeminism.

Things, insects, cyborgs, gross human bodies: the Borg are consummate Gothic monsters who, like Dracula, pierce the flesh of the neck and inject a noxious substance that transforms the human into a something that seems to be the "living dead." In the case of the Borg, postmodern Gothic monsters, the injected substance turns parts of the body to metal that bursts through the fragile flesh in metallic stars that grip the skin in gruesome contortions as the transformation commences. Just as the late nineteenth-century Gothic was preoccupied with transformations and unstable identities, the postmodern Gothic of cyborgs deals with crises of identity within the body transformed by technology. Their hybrid bodies are terrifying because they are distantly recognizable as having once been human; but their human identity has been stolen, wiped out and replaced with a grim purpose that denies their previous humanity. They are, as Botting recognizes, indebted to

Boris Karloff's monster: "the deathly pallor of the skin, the ill-matched bodily assemblage and the unwieldy movements suggest something is missing, aesthetically at least, in the operations of technology on biology" (266). But the Borg are not interested in the aesthetics of wholeness: their concern is with the aesthetics of imperial assimilation. They seek to add the "distinctiveness" of other races to their own, and thus completeness is not on the agenda: these are greedy Gothic monsters who seek a surfeit of "distinctiveness," gorging themselves on the uniqueness of every race in the universe, and their Queen drives this mission with a terrible logic. The coldness of her rationale for assimilation is all the more repulsive because it is uttered by a woman, who in traditional patriarchal discourse should be the locus of emotion and attentive care for the weak and the masculine.

Postfeminist Gothic, the cyborg and the caves of Kôr

In the heart of late nineteenth-century Africa, deep in the mythical caves of Kôr, Rider Haggard's Ayesha, a two-thousand year-old woman, awaits the reincarnation of her dead lover, Kallikrates. Ayesha is so irresistibly beautiful that she must cover her body from head to foot because all men who gaze on her become consumed with lust. Holly and Leo, two English imperial adventurers, enter this lair in search of the solution to a mystery revealed to them in an ancient pottery shard. Leo is unaware that he is the reincarnation of Kallikrates, and although both men are transfixed by her, Ayesha desires only Leo. She will kill any rival for his love: the unfortunate Ustane is "blasted" in jealous rage by a bolt of lightening from Ayesha's fingertips. Ayesha's longevity is due to her immersion in a flame of immortality: in trying to persuade Leo/Kallikrates to join her in everlasting life she re-enters the flame and apparently dies as the flame reverses its initial effects.

A feminist critique of *She* reveals a Gothic *femme fatale*: a merciless, libidinous and murderous female monster whose prey is the male. She is a human spider, luring the unwitting male into her inextricable web. Science fiction movies in the twentieth century have utilized this woman in various comic and horror productions: *Attack of the Fifty-Foot Woman*, *Species* and so on. More recent science fiction films have attempted to pursue a feminist agenda with strong women characters as action heroes and role models: Ripley in the *Alien* series or Sarah Connor in the *Terminator* series. But the mainstream film industry, in science fiction terms at any rate, is more interested in box office returns than agendas such as feminism. It could be argued, therefore, that postfeminism is redundant when it comes to discussing science fiction movies.[9] Within the fantasy/horror/science fiction nexus, female sexuality plays a crucial and bankable role: even feisty female characters, such as Trinity in *The Matrix* series, are ultimately the love interest for the male lead. It is not surprising, therefore, that when it comes to the Borg Queen in *First Contact* we are confronted with an unreconstructed *femme fatale* in the mould of Ayesha. Certain tropes of the Gothic exhibited by *She* are clearly drawn upon in devising the plot of *First Contact* and, consciously or otherwise, *She* and its Gothic counterparts may have informed some of the narrative structure and imagery of the film, and particularly the conception of the Gothic female monster.

Both Ayesha and the Borg Queen seek dominion over the available worlds, to reign supreme over subjugated races. Like *She*, *First Contact* features a woman who is physically transformed: Ayesha's longevity is mirrored by the Borg Queen, who, through her transformation from human female to cyborg, has achieved a near-indestructible body. These awe-inspiring, but terrible women seek to remould their men in their own image: Ayesha tries to persuade both Holly and Leo to enter the flame of life and join her in immortality; the Borg Queen has already once remade Picard as a cyborg and threatens to do so again. She seeks to compromise Data's android identity by introducing human flesh into his mechanical being and thus create a hybrid mate as her equal. Remodelling their men is a means of achieving a state of union for both women whereby they are no longer alone in their status as superbeings. Like the mad scientists of traditional Gothic fiction – Frankenstein, Jekyll – these women defy the natural world and its laws, yet because they are women their goals are not scientific exploration, but sensual pleasure.

Ayesha is terrible and beautiful; the Borg Queen has a sensual beauty despite her viscous skin and lack of hair. Hurley's notion of gothic "thingness" is actively present in both women: neither is fully human because both have transgressed the rules of physical being. Ayesha is as dangerous as a venomous snake, "blasting" humans from a power source at her fingertips. The Borg Queen is possessed of a similar psychic power, creating a forcefield around herself to repel others at will. Whereas Ayesha dresses all in gauzy white to emphasize her femininity and sexuality, the Queen is the dark sexual dominatrix. She wears long leather gloves, and sculpted shiny black body armour into which her smiling head and glinting metal spinal column are mechanically lowered until levers snap into place around her shoulder blades. After this bodily/mechanical unification she writhes sensually, luxuriating in her strange physicality, her body restrained by technological implants, but lithe and dangerous as a snake: Ayesha too, in the tradition of the *femme fatale* enjoys "snake-like" movement (*She* 187). There is more than a touch of the sado-masochist about this Borg creature, and she is compelling in her repulsive sensuality.

The sexuality of both women threatens the integrity of the male and his homosocial world. Data, cast as an innocent childlike android, is seemingly seduced by the Queen's gift of flesh and seems willing to betray his captain. Shuddering with the sexual thrill, Data appears to be converted to the Borg cause, tempted by the Queen with the prospect of a perfect union between his mechanical self and his desired human sensibility. When Picard arrives to rescue the android, the Queen reminds him of their previous intimacy when he was Locutus. "I can still hear our song," she croons, while seductively stroking Picard's lips with her fingertips, her mouth close to his in a promise of unholy passion. Against his will, Picard is aroused and horrified, but the Queen is playing with his human masculinity and deliberately reawakening the lingering traces of his previous Borg self. Using her seductive powers to entrap both men, the Queen thus attempts to sever the bonds of loyalty that bind Picard and Data, and, thus separated, they are weakened and vulnerable to her will.

The Borg Queen is, like Ayesha, represented as pure evil, threatening the integrity of male friendship and seeking supremacy in all relationships. Having seen Ayesha's terrible beauty and fallen under her spell, Holly articulates the misogyny at the heart of *She* when he declares:

> Curses on the fatal curiosity that is ever prompting man to draw the veil from woman, and curses on the natural impulse which begets it! It is the cause of half – ay, and more than half – of our misfortunes. Why cannot men rest content to live alone and be happy, and let the woman live alone and be happy? (132)

Woman reveals man's weakness, the sexual impulse, and for that Ayesha is condemned as a sorceress and a modern Circe. The woman threatens the bond between father and son, between male companions and between captain and his subordinate: only her destruction can restore the "natural" order of the patriarchal world. Holly acts as father to the younger Leo, but is aware of his own devotion to the woman who threatens to sever their familial bonds. In this narrative the existence of the *femme fatale* compromises male loyalties and, weakened by her sexual power, the father figure doubts himself and is torn between the need to protect the "son" and his desire for the woman. At one point Holly is so entranced by Ayesha that he forgets to tend to Leo, who is near death. Cursing women for dragging men into evil, Holly admits: "Actually, for the last half-hour I had scarcely thought of Leo – and this, be it remembered, of the man who for twenty years had been my dearest companion, and the chief interest of my existence" (160). Ayesha now stands between "father" and "son," threatening the integrity of Holly's homosocial world. This is a prefeminist Gothic: untainted by the "transgressive" tendencies of feminists to challenge the hegemonies of a male discourse, this narrative assumes that sexually confident women are promiscuous and dangerous, a Gothic stereotype.

First Contact, on the other hand, is conceived in a postfeminist climate of doubt and retrogressive responses to the feminist advances of the twentieth century. In terms of this slippery and contradictory debate, this film deals with retrenchment rather than progression and consolidation. Repeating the narrative formula of *She*, the Borg Queen snatches the "son," Data, from Picard's side, dragging him by the feet under a descending defensive panel into her "lair." She behaves much like Ayesha, even to the point of causing the sexual frisson in both "father" and "son" that places herself in a position of control over both. Risking his own life to rescue Data, Picard finds his "adopted son" has been stolen from him and is seemingly allied now to his arch-enemy. The Queen, once desirous of Picard as Locutus for her mate and equal, has now found a "superior specimen" in Data and maliciously rejects Picard's self-sacrificial offer to take Data's place. Her severing of their male bond seems complete as Data says of Picard: "He will make an excellent drone."

All of this takes place at the heart of the starship *Enterprise*, its power source and now command centre for the Borg Queen. She threatens the well-ordered naval-style patriarchy of the ship's command system, just as Ayesha had declared from the caves of Kôr that she would overthrow the government of England (206–8). Picard offers his crew strong leadership as a father figure and a moral and behavioural exemplar, thus reinforcing traditional prefeminist family values, structures and authority systems. By seizing the ship, the Queen overturns the established order and challenges Picard's paternalistic role with her own desire for power and control. In the safe hands of the father figure, Picard, the ship functions smoothly and retains its structural integrity. The arrival of the Borg inaugurates a Gothic transformation of the very material of the vessel: they work with the actual fabric of the *Enterprise* to reshape it into a dark, sweaty Borg environment of steam-filled pipes, weak, pale lights and dials and industrial-scale activity. This postfeminist *femme fatale* not only seeks to remake the male in her own image but actively refashions his environment and his symbol of male authority, his ship, to resemble her own. Russ notes how in the mythology of "sexist society" and in Joan Bamberger's research into the Amazon area of South America, male symbols of power are "stolen" by the women:

> To summarize: the men's Sacred Objects – the badge of authority and means of dominion over others – are stolen or contaminated by women, who then become dominant over men. ... Women lose because they abuse this power or are immoral (in various ways, e.g. incest), whereupon the men seize or reclaim the Sacred Objects, sometimes with supernatural aid. The purpose of the story is to show that women cannot handle power, ought not to have it, and cannot keep it. This is the natural order of things. (42)

Such is the narrative trajectory of *First Contact*, beginning with the Queen's appropriation of Picard's ship.

Botting says that "[t]he monsters of Gothic and Science Fiction, whether idealized or degraded figures, participate in a process of defending or transgressing corporeal borders, marking out the limits of individual, social and political bodies" (267). As a Gothic monster, Ayesha transgresses her corporeality through immortality and threatens to redefine the physical boundaries of the British Empire; the Borg Queen transgresses human, spatial and temporal boundaries (the action takes place in the context of time travel). She transgresses humanity's natural laws by usurping Picard's position as controller of the spaceship and gradually begins to assimilate his crew into her own monstrous collective.

Conclusion: Resistance is futile

In the Gothic narratives of *First Contact* and *She*, the power seized illicitly by women must be relinquished and the women must be punished for their transgression. The denouement of each tale is enacted with chillingly ugly vengeance. When Ayesha re-enters the immortal flame it reverses its effects and she ages before the eyes of the awe-struck Leo and Holly until she appears barely human: "She raised herself upon her bony hands and blindly gazed around her, swaying her head slowly from side to side as does a tortoise. She could not see, for her whitish eyes were covered with a bony film. Oh, the horrible pathos of the sight" (237).

The Borg Queen meets an equally gruesome end: Data betrays her and unleashes a lethal flesh-destroying gas. Picard climbs upwards pursued by the Queen, but she becomes engulfed. Like the Wicked Witch of the West, she melts before our eyes until all that is left is a fitfully twitching metal skeleton. As the gas disperses, Picard descends, sneering at the cyborg remains. He grabs the writhing metal spinal column and maliciously snaps it in two. Data, the transplanted patches of transgressive flesh on his face now gone, leaving traces of his cybernetic skull revealed, watches with satisfaction. The homosocial bonds and the patriarchal order of the *Enterprise* are restored with the destruction of the predatory woman, just as the demise of Ayesha reinstates the male loyalties of Holly and Leo.

The demise of the Gothic monster, especially the female Gothic monster, is never anything but ugly and prolonged, usually involving reversion to a repulsive, more viscous incarnation or an acceleration into an atrophied or degraded state. In the case of the monstrous *femme fatale*, all trace of her compelling sexual allure is wiped out, leaving a repellent "thing" in its place, a reminder of the transience of beauty and of the "dangerous" nature of female sexual allure that hides a monstrous threat to male loyalties. In the case of *She* and *First Contact*, the men survive and witness the horrific demise of the woman who sought an unnatural position of dominance over them. Vengeance against these transgressive women is complete.

The Borg Queen, the postfeminist female Gothic monster, is, in all but her technology-invaded body, a reincarnation of an earlier female type in Gothic fiction. It is as if Ayesha had been reawakened after another two thousand years and had proceeded to re-enact her previous rapacious career within a new context. No progress seems to have been made, no notice taken of women's urgent demands to be regarded as equals and not sexual subordinates and objects of the male gaze: the makers of *First Contact* have deliberately exploited attitudes to female sexuality from a prefeminist era. The Victorian imperial Gothic narrative and the science fiction narrative of *Star Trek: First Contact* display identical male attitudes to the possibilities of female ascension to power: the woman must be destroyed before she destroys them.

Certainly the Queen is a monster, and had she been a King would have suffered the same fate. Gender reversals in imperial Gothic fantasies such as *She* would be almost inconceivable in Victorian literature: it is the formula of the genre that the adventurers are male (see e.g. Dryden). The point is that in both cases the villain is a seductress and thus all the more dangerous: her destruction instils even greater satisfaction than the destruction of a male monster by the very fact of her femaleness, her "otherness." The Borg are often heard to warn their human prey, "Resistance is futile": the male antagonists of the Gothic *femme fatale* or the Borg Queen could just as easily have uttered those words with similar conviction. In these narratives resistance to male hegemony is indeed futile.

Notes

1. Majel Barrett played the first officer, but she was demoted to Nurse Chapel in the successful original series. She also provided the voice of the computer in the original *Star Trek* and the *Next Generation* series and starred as Lwaxana Troi, mother of Deanna Troi, in *Star Trek: The Next Generation*. Barrett married Gene Roddenberry, the creator of the series.
2. Roddenberry is famously cited as saying that he wanted to create a "Wagon Train" in space.
3. In an episode entitled "The Host," sapphic overtones emerged as the doctor, Beverley Crusher, is invited, is tempted, but declines, to engage in a lesbian romance. In another episode a race of androgynous beings had their sexuality genetically erased: deviancy for this race means exhibiting sexual preference.
4. It is for this reason that some of the spin-off pulp novels have developed homosexual plots involving sexual liaisons between the officers, notably Kirk and Spock.
5. The Federation is a coalition of planets united in the cause of a peaceful galaxy and clearly modelled on the notion of the United Nations, though its values tend to reflect those of a liberal democratic United States.
6. These interests reflect the fact that the part is played by the Shakespearean actor Patrick Stewart.
7. In the later *Star Trek* series, *Voyager*, a Borg female, Seven of Nine, is integrated back into the crew of the starship and she speaks of her feeling of loneliness because she has become disconnected from the collective consciousness of the Borg.
8. Hayles also notes that *Limbo* features humanity modified with prosthetic limbs as weapons, thus prefiguring the alien Borg.
9. This is not necessarily the case with literature, however, since there have been strong feminist narratives from Angela Carter, Marge Piercey, Joanna Russ and Margaret Attwood, among others, and many of these endure.

Works cited

Barrett, Michèle, and Duncan Barrett. *Star Trek: The Human Frontier*. Cambridge: Polity Press, 2001.

Botting, Fred. " 'Resistance is Futile.' " *Anglophonia: French Journal of English Studies* 15 (2004).

Dryden, Linda. *Joseph Conrad and the Imperial Romance*. Basingstoke: Macmillan, 2000.

Haggard, H. Rider. *She*. London: Hodder and Stoughton, 1957.

Haraway, Donna, J. *Simians, Cyborgs and Women: The Reinvention of Nature*. New York: Routledge, 1991.

Hayles, Katherine. *How We Became Posthuman: Virtual Bodies in Cybernetics, Literature and Informatics*. Chicago: U of Chicago P, 1999.

Hurley, Kelly. *The Gothic Body: Sexuality, Materialism, and Degeneration at the Fin de Siècle*. Cambridge: Cambridge UP, 1996.

Russ, Joanna. *To Write Like a Woman: Essays in Feminism and Science Fiction*. Bloomington: Indiana UP, 1995.

12
Flight of the Heroine

Fred Botting

Chiasmosis

Gothic modernity turns on the question of femininity; feminism returns the question of modern Gothic. It is a critical commonplace to note how women in Gothic fictions are represented as objects of pursuit, imprisonment, violation (critical reversals of this victim status, of course, shift the identification of monstrosity from sexualized otherness to tyrannical patriarchal systems). At the same time, and in a context in which a critical establishment feminized the genre and its readership, Gothic fictions allow a greater space for female authorship, for some degree of female agency and adventurousness in fictions and for flights of fantasy among a growing audience. Lines of interpretation become unclear as lines of flight open up: the feminized monster of Gothic fiction rendered various romantic and domestic freedoms imaginable at the same time as they were configured as an imagined threat to familial and social values. In political terms, too, "Gothic" points in contradictory directions, a sign of the continuity of British constitutional liberties and a mark of the despotism of patrilineage and monarchical government. Appearing at a time when scientific reason was promoted above religious superstition, when industrial urbanity was prevailing over nature and agriculture and when democratic revolutions cast feudal monarchs aside, Gothic fictions simultaneously hark back to and caricature barbarous dark ages. It is not so much nostalgia that governs these inventions: characterizing change in Gothic terms, Edmund Burke looked fearfully towards a near future in which the bonds of custom, order and continuity had broken down in the face of a rampant, revolutionary, monstrous commercialism.

The prefix "post" has come to signal a period of uncertainty, crisis and fragmentation, in which the structures of modernity are rendered unstable and suspect. The prefix for posteriority can also be applied to those structures in their nascent state when lines of differentiation are yet ill formed (Lyotard). The rise of Gothic forms and their current cultural persistence function as a curious knot in the formations of modernity, figures of excess, monstrosity and sublimity around which reason, progress and knowledge cohere or collapse. Combine postmodern and Gothic with (post-)feminism, then, and the pattern becomes even more complex: feminism, taking its bearings from Mary Wollstonecraft's extension of Enlightenment precepts to women, contests modernity on its own terms, opening up categories of human progress, equality, rights and reason as a challenge to patriarchal prejudice; Gothic fictions, disclosing the tyrannical, barbaric and irrational obverse of those structures, seem to offer a regressive movement that counters light with darkness and reason with force. Beyond the oppositions, however, a space of disturbance becomes partially visible in the crossing and reversing of terms, an unknown and ungrounded space linked to the sublime and the unpresentable. In Merleau-Ponty's phenomenological account of seeing and visibility, the chiasmus that emerges between subject and object, sight and body, discloses an "abyss" that leads to a fundamental reversal of relations of seeing (136); in Irigaray's reading of this chiasmus, the place of the other is destabilized by the breach between oppositions, causing the reversibility of world and self and disclosing a nocturnal prediscursive site to appear (*An Ethics* 151–4). Paradigmatically, and against all paradigms, the space becomes a woman's, "awoman," that is, woman before signification has fantasmatically fixed her in a symbolic and subaltern place (Irigaray, *This Sex* 108). This space, for Deleuze in his discussion of sense and series, forms an empty place, a *place vide* that is mobile, constitutive and destructive, locus for the establishment and dissolution of signifying relationships (*Logic of Sense* 49).

Although postmodernism and feminism are linked, often problematically, in opposition to a (patriarchal) monolithic modernity as modes of interrogation, play, resistance and liberation, their respective investments in a unified political project are less secure. Prefixing feminism with a "post" compounds tensions: it solidifies a movement into a formation in order to suggest that its project is finished. The move, as a gesture that simultaneously feigns a concession of defeat on the part of conservatism and conceals a dismissive and restorative reaction, constitutes a "backlash" or "misogynistic turn" that testifies to the contrary (Coppock *et al.*; Negra). It does, however, situate feminism amidst a plural and shifting scene of diverse cultural–political engagements in which the appeal of any unified or binary framework fades. A more positive, if less prescriptive, version of postfeminism emerges, "continuously in process, transforming and challenging itself" (Wright 5), or, further, as a challenge to think in innovative and radical terms and engage with questions of time and futurity: rather than be hung up on an outdated idea of political revolution and its now predictable goals, postfeminism might "generate a new" able to negotiate "the more disconcerting idea of *un*predictable transformation, upheavals in directions and arenas which cannot be known in advance and whose results are inherently uncertain" (Grosz 215). There are questions raised by the invocation of newness: the "post" of the "postmodern" poses an irrevocable challenge to modernity's narrative linearity and teleology; the assimilation of innovation, with the new ceding to novelty, by technoscientific and accelerated market imperatives – as creative or entrepreneurial capitalism – threatens the possibility of imagining the future in any other terms (Lyotard; Goux). The monstrous figure of an unpredictable future, as Derrida once outlined, cedes to the banality of a "normal monstrosity" already homogenized in various hybrid forms of prepackaged connection ("Some Statements"; "Passages"). Such monstrosities emanate from the creativity and inventiveness of marketing and sales rather than any radical innovation of modern artistic, philosophical or political revolution (Deleuze and Guattari, *What Is Philosophy?* 10).

"Post," for all the illusions of a progressive movement (beyond the limitations of modernity or feminism) that its dismissive gesture implies, seems to sanction only a disavowal that liberates a shift to an ateleological circulation of banal monstrosities, commodified presentations, consumerist desires evacuated and exhausted by the entrepreneurial creation of hybrid novelties. The demons spewing from the hellmouth of contemporary culture are no more than simulations parading the "hell of the same" (Baudrillard). In her reading of the witch in the *Blair Witch Project*, Linda Badley notes how, in becoming an icon of postfeminism in a contemporary culture full of Buffys and Willows, what was once a disturbing image of sexualized heterogeneity turns into a homogenized and domesticated picture of contemporary femininity. The movement of "posting" thus fails to move forward, despite a rhetoric of seriality and innovation: its Gothic recourse reverts to a consumerist logic of desiring, defined, in Angela Carter's terms, as that of an "inexhaustible plus" (206). Desire means always wanting more, and wanting more, in postmodern capitalism, is the key to creative entrepreneurship (Goux). "More," moreover, is also the cry of woman constructed in the fantasy of modernity's Man: her sexuality lies in excess of masculine or phallic jouissance; it guarantees her otherness and his identity as the limit both to which he is attracted and from which he is repelled (Lacan; Mitchell and Rose). If the relationship between postfeminism and postmodernity takes the form of a chiasmus, then Gothic productions can be situated at the point of their crossing, interdiction and excess.

Innovation and the mores of modernity's fantasized femininity inhere in Gothic fiction from the start: the Radcliffean heroine's "curiosity," a cipher for the readerly pleasures of suspense, takes the form of a desire that pushes at the limits of paternal law, family and gender. She is looking for something more. The genre, too, especially in the device of the "explained supernatural" – which excites, frustrates and ultimately disappoints readerly curiosity – depends on desire: considered appetitive, sensational, indulgent, feminine, the repetitive fictional formulas are designed to stimulate a passive readership, to inflame curiosity and expectation, to sate base passions and then invent more mysteries and shocks to excite anew. With postmodernism shattering the constraints of cultural tradition, these low exceptions, no longer excluded as gothicized negatives of high romantic culture, become, like Derrida's monstrosities, the norm. With postmodernity, terror becomes endemic and transgression is both limitless and exhausted, ceaselessly used up in playful circulations of aesthetic games. The unpresentable is little more than a resource to be capitalized upon, a space to be filled with so many different images, hyperactivating and passifying consumers at the same time as they leave them wanting more: all readers and spectators have, perhaps, become woman in the process. This woman, however, is only the global instantiation of hypercapitalism's subjectile. There may be other modes of becoming, an awomanly space in which unrecognizable, troubling, unpredictable, monstrous forms have yet to appear.

Becoming – (Gothic) – woman

In Deleuze and Guattari's writing, all becomings turn on becoming woman. This is not "woman" in the conventional sense of a discrete identity tied to a bodily form and represented according to cultural types and signifying structures: there is no final or fixed subject position in Deleuze and Guattari (D&G), only composite, multiple points of movement, change, process. D&G's notion of desiring production locates "woman" as a "line of flight" and as a crucial nexus among the proximities and relations, the flows and dis-connections, by which (in)dividuals remain in fragments, multiple and changing, thereby slipping from the mortifying grasp of regimes of state and signification. A matter of shifting individuations, and always in process, "self" occurs between multiplicities, a "threshold." "Lines of flight" connect these becoming-selves to the movements across territories (of signification, social strata, bodies, lands): a line of flight is a deterritorialization, not just an escape from a system (Deleuze and Parnet 36). It involves change, opening up possibilities, not "running away from" but "causing run offs" since "there is no social system that does not leak from all directions, even if it makes its segments increasingly rigid in order to seal the lines of flight" (Deleuze and Guattari, *A Thousand Plateaus* 204). Hence fleeing can be active and "put a system to flight," or produce "a sort of delirium," a going "off the rails" (Deleuze and Parnet 36, 40).

Writing, for D&G, is an instance of the deterritorializations of lines of flight (Deleuze and Guattari, *A Thousand Plateaus* 276): it presents a conjunction involving the "transmutation of fluxes through which life escapes from the resentment of persons, societies and reigns" (Deleuze and Parnet 50). Gothic forms, too, feature in D&G's discussion of the deterritorializing movements of desire: vampires and werewolves offer images of the fluxes of becoming, infectious figures that cut across lines of patrilinear and familial reproduction and, as packs or multiplicities, undermine the ideological reproduction of identity; nomads and warriors, very much the "northern tribes" associated with the Goths, roam the forests and plains, insurgents destabilizing the military machine of (Roman) imperial domination. Gothic art and architecture, in the shape of the "northern line," transform spaces of formal classical representation with disturbing contours, contrasts and zigzagging lines that allow sublime flights of the imagination.

Woman, writing, Gothic: the assemblage, unsurprisingly, emerges in a period of aesthetic, political, economic, social and familial transformations. Romance offers a world of love and adventure beyond the constraints of paternal control. "Wound up," as one critic of the time noted, by repeated stimulation and mystery, readers, as the metaphor of the clockwork mechanism implies, are little more than desiring machines (Coleridge). The Gothic genre itself becomes a contradictory, multiple site of affects and intensities: anti-classical, it undermines rigid Roman (Augustan) forms; anti-Catholic, it dispels religious ignorance and superstition; freedom-loving (like the Goths), it purveys a counter-imperial tendency. At the same time, it reduplicates the tyrannies, prejudices and corruptions of government; or, in rejecting them, presents the terrifying image of rampant, monstrous commercialism, a market, beyond the restraints of church, state or morality, that monstrously encourages selfishness, vice and excess. In Gothic fictions of the eighteenth century women are transformed economically and psychologically, becoming commodities in a marriage market (Clery). Woman writers, in earning a living, cross over to the world of work, and move beyond the "proper" bounds of gender and genre (Poovey). No wonder sex became such a political topic, especially during a period of revolutionary ferment with its various, and "unsexing," libidinal energies and excitements (Matthias).

Radcliffe's heroines are always in flight. Her novels move towards and away from disturbing worlds of danger and immorality. *Romance of the Forest* begins with Adeline fleeing from convent imprisonment. She is also escaping from a cruel and tyrannical familial order, a victim of a malevolent Marquis, a fratricidal uncle who may be her father. Like many fathers in the genre, his and thus her identity is suspect, the paternal name holding social and symbolic desires in place itself impeached. As a result, desire wanders, off course, flying to "wild zones" where femininity encounters the possibility of becoming something other: the ruins and forests that are uncharted places of darkness and danger are also loci free from the restraints of law. Lines of flight are also lines of fright: a rhythm of pulses and re-pulsions subtends narrative, affects and intensities buffeting and traversing the borders of fictional structure. But the deterritorializations that introduce new fictional, imagined and desiring geographies to eighteenth-century romance readers are accompanied by processes of reterriorialization: the authorial voice of the narrator tries to maintain a controlled and moral perspective on the fanciful flights of heroine and reader alike. Lines of flight are arrested; lines of fright turned against themselves: horror, recoil, expulsion of excess. Nightmare gives way to fairy tale. The becomings of woman are redirected towards becoming a model of bourgeois and domestic femininity.

A machine operates outside moral regimes. The mechanisms, the narrative machinery, of the genre that produces intense affects of horror, terror, thrill and excitement continue to pulse beneath the moral and regulative frameworks of high culture, reconfiguring patterns of identification and affection outside the parameters of spiritual elevation, didacticism or aesthetic education and enabling new conjunctions. In *Frankenstein*, for instance, epistolary techniques and trappings of science combine to engender an Enlightenment monster that refuses its subjection to narrow human and bourgeois structures: as a monstrous conjunction of otherness linking mob, woman, nature and writing itself, its uncontrollable monstrosity reflects back on the systems that produced it at the same time as it moves beyond their grasp. In *Dracula*, the breach in modernity is configured from the outside as an unbearable object – a "Thing" – to be identified and expelled in the restoration of modern boundaries. Throughout, and almost as invisible as the vampire initially appears, an ambivalent and inhuman technology signals a different path for modernity: phonographs, typewriters, telegraphs, railways and timetables tap out a different rhythm and new conjunctions of otherness (Kittler). Vamp-machine, womachine, visible in Lang's *Metropolis*, or a "Future Eve," set the pattern for what, in the popular culture of cinematic makes and remakes, will become different lines of fright and identification. In the horror genre, gazes are dis-engendered in prurient overidentifications and violent reactions (Clover); monsters and vampires find themselves connected to technological reconfigurations like the cyborgs or the "replicunts" that manifest a technological supersession of patriarchal modernity (Haraway; Stone; Plant); or, as vampire celebrities such as Lestat, become entwined with romanticizations of postfeminism and consumption (Doane and Hodges). Gothic, its technological subcurrent raised to visible predominance, finds itself bound up with the delivery of the post, that is, a system of writing and communication that was, always-already, a technological formation. As a genre, it traces lines of flight and fright that move beyond modern and human structures (Land).

Aliensame

The *Alien* series of films traverses the chiasmotic postings of Gothic, modernity, gender and technology, drawing out diverse lines of flight along with various lines of fright. *Alien* (Ridley Scott 1979) paints a future in recognizably dark Gothic colours, giving its account of gender and modernity a familiarly re-pulsive dimension: the crepuscular gloom of a windswept, deserted planet and the cavernous spaces of the crashed alien craft sketch a Gothic landscape and architecture; the slimy abjection of the alien young and their monstrous and parasitic emergence channel a blood-curdling pulse of body horror along lines of invasion and explosion; the chilling alien creature, its dripping carapace, acid blood, razor teeth, a monster from the black lagoon of deep space. The heroine, Ripley, is steadily manoeuvred into the position of Gothic heroine: unable, with the crew, to expunge this utterly destructive threat, she is isolated to become a "final girl" pursued through the labyrinthine corridors of the mining vessel. Her status as persecuted female victim, her sexualized vulnerability fully exposed in the final scenes when she is left in only her underwear, signals a regressive stripping of femininity to a bare object of a persecuting look, her professional status as a skilled crew member reduced, by the mechanisms of callous killing machine and prurient narrative, from efficient pilot and leader to quivering figure of abjection. With a sovereignty born from abjection and desperation, she survives, escaping the ship, the alien and their destruction. A feminized humanity barely saves itself in the face of monstrous, all-consuming horror.

The final destruction of the monster leaves the question of identity open even as it appears to return to strictly opposed differences between human and alien. The ambivalence that characterizes the relationship is never fully expunged, to form the crux of various subsequent permutations in the series. The horror that *Alien* presents to humanity is as much internal as external: bodies are penetrated; seemingly assured identities collapse. The security of imaginary and modern symbolic structures is shattered by the violent proximity of destructive, abject and uncontrollable energies. These, the film suggests, in images of dark, repulsive womblike shapes, connote a conventional patriarchal version of dangerous female sexuality and archaic, primal maternal energy (Creed). For all the disturbances engendered, the images remain tied to patriarchy (Penley): horrifying emergence, bodily penetrations and dissolutions, ultimately – at the very point of utter, abject decomposition – form the occasions for an expulsion from and a restoration of limits.

The black hole of formlessness also provides a point where meanings assigned to the film are confounded, collapse and become diversely re-established. The doubleness of the monstrous figure – alien killing-machine and destructive primal mother, an uncontrollable excess simultaneously from the heart and outer reaches of human imaginings – resonates with an irresolvable ambivalence in interpretations of *Alien* as a feminist, antifeminist, postfeminist or humanist document. Subsequent doublings and shifting pairings condense diverse lines of interpretation. In destroying an alien associated with dangerously abject feminine sexuality (and returning to a more patriarchally recognizable figure of woman), the humanism that is restored at the end takes a traditionally male form in the subordination of women even as it recognizes and refuses a disarmingly female power and excess. The phallic mother is aligned with the phallic monster, the profit-hungry "Company," in the form of its all-controlling computer, "Mother." On the other hand, the film is "seemingly feminist" in its content (Newton 84). With the survivor (and champion of humanity) being female, the contours of heroism are altered in a reversal of conventionally gendered expectations and conventions: in the heroine's emotional attachment to the ship's cat, a recovery of "ideological humanism" is glimpsed. In a chi-square that structures identifications and oppositions, human and animal feeling is paired against the callous rationality of the corporate android (Ash) and its murderous alien prize (Kavanagh 79). Further, female associations and the power of the alien display the inadequacy of paternal authority: the connections between alien and android, company and alien displace monstrosity from the destructive creature to the inhumanity of robot and the "moral monstrosity" of the corporation (Greenberg 100).

Even as boundaries seem to be restored and meanings begin to cohere around the figure of monstrosity (opposed by a progressive, feminized humanity), there is something "almost postfeminist" in the setting: women can be equally strong, weak, reasonable and authoritative members of the crew (Kavanagh 77); the social context is one of a technocratic elite of middle-class professionals without much evidence of internal discrimination (Greenberg 97). The postfeminist trajectory of associations overlaps with postmodern and post-human concerns: "post-modern Gothic and post-gender sexualities are haunting the imaginary of post-industrial societies" (Braidotti 58). The postmodern return of the "others" of modernity – woman, nature, ethnicity (all conventionally modern associations of monstrosity) cohere as symptoms of a postmodern anxiety about social identities and symbolic structures (Braidotti 196). Indeed, it is only in terms of a masterful position that otherness is linked in the form of monstrosity: "only in his gaze are their respective differences flattened out in a generalized category of 'difference' whose pejorative status is structural to the establishment of a norm that is inevitably masculine, white, heterosexist and promoting naturalistic and essentialistic beliefs" (Braidotti 197). In horror, the transgression of norms is manifested and, in repulsion, restored. Monstrosity – the knotting together of callous corporate violence, robotic rationality and primal maternal sexuality – displays the excesses of a normative system and allows its return to traditional gendered, human and modern arrangements. It functions doubly: as a point of coherence and dissolution, a site for the restoration of traditional boundaries and the opening up of different possibilities.

But, in simultaneously impeaching the artifice of the construction of modern norms and remaining incredulous to them, monstrosity suggests a line of flight beyond their restrictions, revelling in the unravelling occasioned by the proximity of horror. This is postfeminism's trajectory as it encounters the pulse and repulsion of horror, questioning the stability of all norms. Opening up modern horror's knot of otherness, the movement of the *Alien* series complicates and compounds traditional patterns and gendered assumptions: Sigourney Weaver emerges as a "post-feminist heroine" (Braidotti 196). In *Aliens* (James Cameron 1986), Ripley returns, a beauty awoken from hypersleep to a world of nightmares, the same figure but different: the film's Vietnam-horror pastiche (*The Green Berets* meets *The Thing*) shows her becoming a strategist and warrior and an aggressively protective surrogate mother. The pattern (it is a James Cameron film) approximates the flights of *The Terminator's* heroine fleeing and becoming a killing-machine, moving away from and towards a terrifyingly apocalyptic future. *Aliens* situates Ripley in a variety of traditionally non-complementary roles, to return to previous themes and to reverse gendered expectations: a redundant, or so it seems, civilian advisor in the eyes of the soldiers, Ripley, early in the film, impresses with her abilities as a machine operator. Characterized as "Snow White" by a female marine, Ripley is the one who comes to the fore as a military leader: fairy-tale femininity, indeed, soon comes to the rescue of battle-hardened marines (Constable 185). At the same time as Ripley is depicted as becoming increasingly active and resourceful, the film further develops her maternal associations in caring for the last survivor among the colonists, a girl nicknamed "Newt." Her similarity to the alien is underlined: a "mother" herself, she rescues Newt from the alien nest and torches the offspring of the breeding queen. Mother, worker, warrior, champion, her becomings coalesce at the film's climax as she straps herself into the mechanical loader's exoskeleton to fight a duel with the vengeful queen: hero/heroine, she again saves humanity.

By *Alien 3* (David Fincher 1992), Ripley is again transformed, becoming the thing she most fears: a breeder of monsters carrying the ultimate horror – another queen – inside her. *Alien 3's* progression, in terms of the series, forms a regression from the hi-tech futures of earlier episodes: it is set in the ruins of an industrial, penitentiary colony populated only by male inmates. As Ripley changes, moving into ever closer proximity to the alien that she still plans to destroy, the human environment becomes increasingly shabbier and degraded: the post-human logic of the series, in which Ripley's humanity is shown to diminish in terms of convention, identification and species, steadily jettisons positive representations of human beings. Humans appear as the cast-offs and detritus of another order, one dominated by aliens and the equally strange figures of the "Company" that appear at the end: led by an android, the soldiers and scientists who arrive to capture Ripley and the alien inside her are dressed in identical white protective suits, their faces concealed by breathing apparatus. Ripley, and the series, it seems, reach a dead-end. The film culminates in a messianic sacrifice: becoming the bearer of all she most fears, she must kill herself to end the alien line, a bringer of apocalyptic fire and monstrosity destroying both "mothers" in a saintly fall into the flames. The religiosity of her final gesture – her body, stat-uesque as a tomb sculpture, forming the shape of a cross as she throws herself backwards into the flames – presents closure as transcendence: life, body, materiality must be sacrificed in order that the spirit of humanity live on. However, the jettisoning of human bodies, nature and materiality also conforms to the logic of post-humanism in which reproduction cedes to replication, and virtuality and code are extracted from the anchors of corporeal and natural material (Hayles).

The last of the series plays upon the religious images of its precursor with messianic sacrifice as a prelude to resurrection. Yet transcendence appears deceptive and multiple: birth and rebirth – staged in so many monstrous forms in the movie (visual, clinical, alien) – occur on the very material and immanent plane of digital and genetic man-ipulation. *Alien Resurrection* (Jean-Pierre Jeunet 1997), even more firmly than its predecessors, is located in a post-human context: set on an experimen-tal military spaceship, the opening scenes of cold, scientific sterility, the unfeeling treatment of human bodies, the physical and moral ugliness of the human body-traffickers, and even the sadism towards cloned aliens, imply that humanity, or any transcendent, ideological idealiza-tion of it, has been erased. Inhumanity is foregrounded in the credit sequence showing the result of genetic experimentation in extreme close-ups: part "unnatural history museum" (Stacey 256) and part circus freak show, the monstrously deformed cloned bodies, neither alien nor human, lay out the stages involved in "resurrecting" Ripley in order to extract an alien queen. Extreme close-up shots of curved glass cases exacerbate physical distortion and the distorting effects of the gaze. A new techno-military-scientific order is presented as the last gasp of paternal dominance: nature, bodies, gender, all otherness is finally brought under the control of an all-powerful rationality that eschews morality, law, humanity in the pursuit of its goals, the realization of another new world order or control society (Haraway; Deleuze, *Negotiations*). Significantly, the central computer has been renamed – it is called "Father."

Father's power and control are as illusory as they are monstrous. The cloned aliens escape to colonize the ship. Ripley, with the tattoo "8" on her arm, is no more than a "meat by-product," like 1–7 in the laboratory freak show. What she "is" is no longer clear: a "mother" to the alien queen, a by-product, a monster to be trained like the aliens, her senses, body and mind have adapted into something utterly other. She is not human, though she aligns herself with a ragged band attempting to flee the ship. She is not a machine, though she seems to care for an android sent to kill her. The android (Call), indeed, passes for a young woman who has been programmed to be humane and compassionate. Her and Call's emotional response to the laboratory of failed clones – the still-living number 7 in particular – "distinguishes them from unfeeling humans" (Stacey 262). Although Ripley is not the same as the alien, she shows some compassion for the queen as she witnesses her labour pains (altered genetically in the process of extraction from a cloned Ripley, the queen has received the gift of a human reproductive system). There is pathos, too, in Ripley's response to the unpleasant demise of the alien offspring – her "grandchild" – a male human–alien hybrid.

The two heroines – Ripley and Call – who are left at the end of the film have only their distinctive feminine appearance to recommend them for illusory human identification. Indeed, their own identifications, their feeling for others, their traces of compassion (programmed or not) and their aesthetic sensibility distinguish them: on seeing the Earth for the first time (the Earth, rather than the inhabitants whom they have saved from aliens), they remark on its beauty. No longer human in any traditional or conventional sense, these two hybrid entities, defined by relationality and process, are, respectively "feminalien" and "feminandroid," new and distinct creations. Nonetheless, they are female in appearance, heroic by dint of their looks and identifications if on no other grounds. Once predicated on rescuing humanity from imminent extinction, the narrative closures (with miniscule cracks) of the series now move beyond humanist considerations: a feminandroid and feminalien gaze upon the Earth at the end of *Alien Resurrection*. A beautiful globe, female figures looking and looking good: lines of flight and lines of sight – movements, projections and identifications enabled by code and vision machines shedding all but the semblance of nature, species, gender. The flight of the heroine, her fears, her desires, her fantasies and anxieties, takes off elsewhere: other identificatory possibilities and configurations (post-, trans-, hyper-) generate other prospects and projections.

The logic of a particular version of the "post" – post-human and post feminist – seems fully realized in *Alien Resurrection*: the categories of human and gender appear obsolete, along with all the ideological bases – nature, bodies, feelings, ideals – that support them. From the black hole of horror, gendered identity and subjectivity seem to have achieved escape velocity, flown beyond any material anchor or gravitational force that would pull them back into conventional categorization. The fourth film in the *Alien* series manifests the "breakdown of traditional models of identity," leaving psychoanalysis and horror conventions "defunct" (Constable 173). Instead, identity becomes a matter of reconfigurations, of "intersecting potentialities" (Constable 197). The film puts any idea of the stability of body or identity to flight and follows paths of becoming in which the mingling, couplings and transformation of relations along particular lines of intersection – such as those between Ripley and/as alien – make any identity "processual," mobile and changeable (Rizzo 333, 342). A certain horror remains: the motility of body, subjectivity and identity is "both a source of freedom and anxiety," cause of both excitement and dread (Rizzo 335). For Rizzo, the message is positive, emphasizing the body's potential to change, adapt and survive. Yet the double affects of the film involve the viewer in the disturbing process of transformation: the use of generic horror techniques – the visceral effects of music, suspense, distorted images – crosses boundaries between film and viewer, to open up watching bodies from the inside with sensations that cause corporeal changes (Rizzo 335–6). The parallels between content and apparatus in *Alien IV* are noted by Stacey: "the monstrous potentiality of cell development in an age of genetic engineering and cloning is given a visual equivalence in the continuously mutating flow of images" (254). The flow, punctuated with an "overpresence of the abject," foregrounds generic conventions and reiterations, placing bodies/genes and identities/images on the same flat, digitally rewritable plane: sameness, normativity, narrative are all technologically reconfigured as surface effects and affects. Cell and image duplication lead to an "excessive sameness" that, because abjection is also foregrounded, cannot be fully expelled: it circulates and mutates continuously in the flow of images and simulations (Stacey 274, 270). Not only does the digitally reconfigured conjunction of image and genetic make-up disturb categories of gender and humanity, its post-human and postfeminist line of flight opens up questions of embodiment, identity and difference, to throw them back onto a plane of simulation: otherness finds itself transformed by the becoming-normal of abjection, absorbed, almost, in the excessive sameness of images without depth or anchor.

Horror is transformed. Gothic, too. Although still evoking effects, the repulsive knot of monstrosity no longer functions as the point where identities dissolve, structures collapse and meanings are confounded: it is no longer the point from which one must recoil in order that sense, system and subjectivity are restored. Instead it engenders moments of sensation, points of intersection and transformations, a site from which various lines of flight and potentiality become possible (Deleuze, *Francis Bacon*). Pulse–re-pulse: horror turns on an excess that cannot be expunged but that, in a continual dynamic of attraction and recoil, underlies systems of simulation, sameness, mutation and hybridization, the very excess that gives them energy and intensity. These couplings of excitement and fear, identification and disgust, thus duplicate the process of digital and genetic mutation presented in and by *Alien Resurrection*, rendering the viewing process mobile, affective and unstable, subject only to pulses and (re-)pulsions, oscillations of identification and abjection. Bodily sensation and perception are confounded, fixed identities displaced and discarded in cinematic techniques and digital apparatuses that produce ecstatic flights of identification – Ripley, Call, the Earth, continue to exert an aesthetic attraction – or repulsion: aliens and humans, on the whole, have little appeal. The bond of horror and humanity is superseded: repulsion from objects of the former (from all that is marked as alien, monstrous, abject) no longer ensures a return to the security of human boundaries. Rather, it causes transformations that reconfigure bodies and identities, letting them fly off in different directions. Or, as the endings of the third and fourth *Alien* films (like 1–7, the series has turned into forms of successive if barely related monstrosities) seem to suggest, to fly off, not in some ecstatic ascension, but downwards: Ripley falls back, down into the flames that consume her; the escape craft crash-lands on Earth. The movement away from traditional human conventions, as presented in the combination of genetics, digital images, feminine figure and alien figures, is linked to a throwing down and throwing away, a discarding of human body, norms, structures and expectations associated with a post-human line of flight casting off bodies, materiality and context in the transformations of code, virtuality and simulation. Humans in the *Alien* series are almost exclusively unappealing. Morally if not physically deformed, they are little more than meat by-products, detritus, waste: post-modernism, post-feminism, post-humanism, post-gothic – a line of shite.

Works cited

Badley, Linda C. "Spiritual Warfare: Postfeminism and the Cultural Politics of the *Blair Witch* Craze." *Intensities* 3 (2003). 31 May 2006 <http://www.cult-media.com/issue3/Abad.htm>.

Baudrillard, Jean. *The Transparency of Evil*. Trans. James Benedict. London: Verso, 1993.

Braidotti, Rosi. *Metamorphoses*. Cambridge: Polity, 2002.

Clery, E. J. *The Rise of Supernatural Fiction 1762–1800*. Cambridge: Cambridge UP, 1995.

Clover, Carol. "Her Body, Himself: Gender in the Slasher Film." *Fantasy and Cinema*. Ed. James Donald. London: BFI Publishing, 1989. 191–233.

Coleridge, S. T. "Review of *The Mysteries of Udolpho.*" *Critical Review* 2nd ser. 11 (1794): 361–72.

Constable, Catherine. "Becoming the Monster's Mother: Morphologies of Identity in the *Alien* Series." *Alien Zone II.* Ed. Annette Kuhn. London: Verso, 1999. 173–200.

Coppock, Vicki, Deena Haydon and Ingrid Richter. *The Illusions of "Post-Feminism."* London: Taylor and Francis, 1995.

Creed, Barbara. *The Monstrous-Feminine.* London: Routledge, 1993.

Deleuze, Gilles. *Logic of Sense.* Trans. Mark Lester. London: Athlone, 1990.

——. *Negotiations.* Trans. Martin Joughin. New York: Columbia UP, 1995.

——. *Francis Bacon: The Logic of Sensation.* Trans. Daniel W. Smith. London: Continuum, 2003.

Deleuze, Gilles, and Felix Guattari. *A Thousand Plateaus.* Trans. Brian Massumi. London: Athlone Press, 1988.

——. *What Is Philosophy?* Trans. Graham Burchell and Hugh Tomlinson. London: Verso, 1994.

Deleuze, Gilles, and Claire Parnet. *Dialogues II.* Trans. Hugh Tomlinson and Barbara Habberjam. London: Continuum, 1987.

Derrida, Jacques. "Some Statements and Truisms about Neologisms, Newisms, Postisms, Parasitisms, and Other Small Seismisms." *The States of "Theory."* Ed. David Carroll. Stanford, CA: Stanford UP, 1990. 63–94.

——. "Passages – From Traumatism to Promise." Trans. Peggy Kamuf *et al. Points.* Stanford, CA: Stanford UP, 1992. 372–95.

Doane, Janice, and Devon Hodges. "Undoing Feminism: From the Preoedipal to Postfeminism in Anne Rice's Vampire Chronicles." *American Literary History* 2.3 (1990): 422–42.

Greenberg, Harvey R. "Reimagining the Gargoyle: Psychoanalytic Notes on *Alien.*" *Close Encounters.* Ed. Constance Penley *et al.* Minneapolis: U of Minnesota P, 1991. 83–104.

Goux, Jean-Joseph. "General Economics and Postmodern Polemics." *Yale French Studies* 78 (1990): 206–24.

Grosz, Elizabeth. "Deleuze's Bergson: Duration, the Virtual and a Politics of the Future." *Deleuze and Feminist Theory.* Ed. Ian Buchanan and Claire Colebrook. Edinburgh: Edinburgh UP, 2000. 214–34.

Haraway, Donna J. *Modest_Witness@Second_Millenium.* London: Routledge, 1997.

Hayles, N. Katherine. *How We Became Posthuman.* Chicago: U of Chicago P, 1999.

Irigaray, Luce. *This Sex Which Is Not One.* Trans. Catherine Porter with Carolyn Burke. New York: Columbia UP, 1985.

——. *An Ethics of Sexual Difference.* Trans. Carolyn Burke and Gillian C. Gill. London: Athlone, 1993.

Kavanagh, James H. "Feminism, Humanism and Science in *Alien.*" *Alien Zone.* Ed. Annette Kuhn. London: Verso, 1990. 73–81.

Kittler, Friedrich. *Essays: Literature Media Information Systems.* Ed. John Johnston. The Netherlands: G + B Arts International, 1997.

Lacan, Jacques. *Encore.* Trans. Bruce Fink. New York: Norton, 1998.

Land, Nick. "Cybergothic." *Virtual Futures.* Ed. Joan Broadhurst Dixon and Eric J. Cassidy. New York: Routledge, 1998. 79–87.

Lyotard, Jean-François. *The Postmodern Condition.* Trans. Geoff Bennington and Brian Massumi. Manchester: Manchester UP, 1984.

Matthias, T. J. *The Pursuits of Literature.* 13th edn. London: Thomas Becket, 1805.

Merleau-Ponty, Maurice. *The Visible and the Invisible.* Trans. Alphonso Lingis. Evanston, IL: Northwestern UP, 1968.

Mitchell, Juliet, and Jacqueline Rose, eds. *Feminine Sexuality: Jacques Lacan and the école freudienne.* Basingstoke: Macmillan, 1982.

Negra, Diane. "Quality Postfeminism?" *Genders* 3 (2004). <http://www.genders.org/g39/g39_negra.html>.

Newton, Judith. "Feminism and Anxiety in *Alien.*" *Alien Zone.* Ed. Annette Kuhn. London: Verso, 1990. 82–7.

Penley, Constance. "Time Travel, Primal Scene, and the Critical Dystopia." *Camera Obscura* 15 (1986): 67–84.

Plant, Sadie. "The Future Looms: Weaving Women and Cybernetics." *Cyberspace/Cyberbodies/Cyberpunk: Cultures of Technological Embodiment.* Ed. Mike Featherstone and Rob Burrows. London: Sage, 1995. 45–64.

Poovey, Mary. "Ideology and *The Mysteries of Udolpho.*" *Criticism* 21.4 (1979): 307–30.

Rizzo, Teresa. "The *Alien* Series: A Deleuzian Perspective." *Women: A Cultural Review* 15.3 (2004): 330–44.

Stacey, Jackie. " 'She is not herself': The Deviant Relations of *Alien Resurrection.*" *Screen* 44.3 (2003): 251–76.

Stone, A. R. *The War of Desire and Technology at the Close of the Mechanical Age.* Cambridge, MA: MIT Press, 1995.

Wright, Elizabeth. *Lacan and Postfeminism.* Cambridge: Icon, 2000.

Index